D1092876

DISPOSED OF
BY LIBRARY
HOUSE OF LORDS

© *Crown copyright 1986*
First published 1986

Design by HMSO: Ian Dobson

ISBN 0 11 290426 2

Contents

GER!

Edited by David Fletcher

The Tiger Tank: A British View

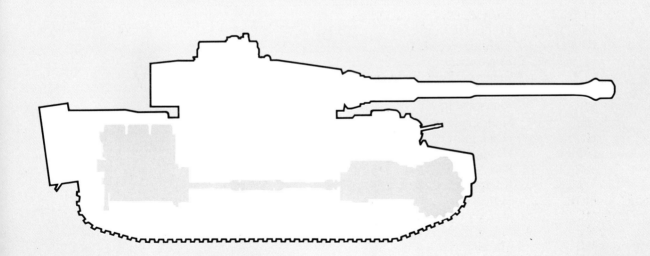

LONDON HER MAJESTY'S STATIONERY OFFICE

Abbreviations

ACIGS	Assistant Chief of the Imperial General Staff	Pz	Panzer (see two following entries)
ADTD	Assistant to Director of Tank Design	PzKpfw PzKw	Panzerkampfwagen ⎫ Panzerkampfwagen ⎬ ⎭ Armoured Fighting Vehicle; 1st & 2nd forms
AFHQ	Armoured Force Headquarters		
AFV	Armoured Fighting Vehicle	QF	Quick Firing
AP	Armour Piercing	RA	Royal Artillery
APCBC	Armour Piercing Capped Ballistic Cap	RAC	Royal Armoured Corps
		RE	Royal Engineers
Armd Div	Armoured Division	Regt	Regiment
A/Tk	Anti-tank	REME	Royal Electrical and Mechanical Engineers
bhp	Brake horsepower		
Bn	Battalion	RM	Royal Marines
Bty	Battery	R/T	Radio Telephone
CO	Commanding Officer	Sitrep	Situation Report
DAFV	Director of Armoured Fighting Vehicles	Sqn	Squadron
		ST Grenade	Sticky Type (anti-tank) Grenade
DDME	Deputy Director of Military Engineering	STT	School of Tank Technology
		SV	Striking Velocity
DG of A	Director General of Artillery	TCV	Troop Carrying Vehicle
DMI	Director of Military Intelligence	WTSFF	Weapons Technical Staff, Field Force
DTD	Director(ate) of Tank Design		
ETO	European Theatre of Operations	ZgKw	Zugkraftwagen (prime-mover)
FOO	Forward Observation Officer		
fs	Feet per second		
FVDD	Fighting Vehicle Design Department		
GOC	General Officer Commanding		
gph	Gallons per hour		
GS	General Staff		
HE	High Explosive		
HQ	Headquarters		
HQRA	Headquarters Royal Artillery		
Kcs	Kilocycles		
KwK	Kampfwagenkanonc (tank gun)		
MAP	Ministry of Air Production		
MCS	Military College of Science		
ME	Middle East		
MG	Machine gun		
MI	Military Intelligence		
mv	Muzzle Velocity		
OC	Officer Commanding		
PAIFORCE	Allied Command in Persia		
Pdr	Pounder		
PIAT	Projector, Infantry Anti Tank		
POW	Prisoner of War		
PW	Prisoner of War		

Introduction

As an object of popular enthusiasm the tank stands in line a long way behind many other evocative machines. Railway engines, aircraft, motor cars and ships have devotees worldwide who are numbered in millions whereas armoured-fighting-vehicle enthusiasts probably do not exceed a few thousand. For all that some famous tanks have impressed themselves on the general public to the extent that they have become household names and, among these, the German heavy tank Tiger is probably best known of all. That its reputation is founded on the same sort of factors that give certain dangerous insects and reptiles an aura of fascination no doubt accounts, to a large extent, for this notoriety but it is probably the best-known tank of all.

Naturally, for this very reason, it has been the subject of much serious study and, in all probability, more books have been devoted specifically to the Tiger than to any other type of tank; the jaded enthusiast might ask what on earth is the justification for yet another.

The answer can only be that there is still something left to tell, and indeed there is. Many of the books devoted to the Tiger are little more than annotated photograph albums while the best are thorough technical and historical appraisals written, naturally enough, by German authors in their own language. It seems, then, that there is room for an English-language version. Yet this is not the end of the language problem. If an author is to produce a worthwhile manuscript he must, as far as possible, rely on original source material and a working knowledge of German is essential to this end. If that author is still struggling to master his native English then, perforce, either he has to resign himself to second-hand sources, thereby running a risk of compounding other people's errors, or he must find a new angle that does not exceed his limitations. Happily such an angle does exist. German pride and interest in this epoch-making tank is only equalled by the respect accorded to it by Allied soldiers. As a consequence Allied intelligence studied it in depth, whenever and wherever it appeared and a sizeable archive of intelligence material, ranging from a single sentence to a fully illustrated report, survives in the library of the Tank Museum, at Bovington Camp, Dorset.

The original plan was to republish the basic report, in much the same way as edited reprints of the Cromwell and Churchill tank handbooks had been, as a joint Tank Museum/HMSO project in 1983. Even so some further research was necessary by way of introduction and this soon revealed that there was far more material available than had at first been appreciated. Gradually the historical significance and the contemporary drama of the originals began to assert itself until the plan changed. As it now appears the book consists almost entirely of verbatim copies of the telegrams and reports as they were issued, interspersed with brief introductory comments that, it is hoped, serve to string them together. Thus the book is a kaleidoscope of styles with a small army of contributors, many of whom, alas, are now unknown.

It has to be admitted that the exercise has been conducted in a liberal fashion. Although, within limits, the original layout and flavour of each entry has been preserved there has been a good deal of arbitrary editing to avoid repetition and to weed out tedious material. There has also been some modification in punctuation and spelling where it seems to be called for, although this has been kept to a minimum and, where it is not included in the original, no attempt has been made to correlate metric and imperial measurements since, it is felt, this can often inhibit or even obliterate the original flow of the text.

For a variety of reasons, space and ignorance not excluded, the temptation to pass retrospective or 'enlightening' comment in the new link-up paragraphs has been resisted as far as possible and the reader is recommended to compare what he reads here with the latest opinions expressed by far more qualified authors, experts in their fields who have written, and will no doubt continue to write, about the Tiger.

The book may be divided roughly into four sections. The first is a brief introduction to the subject that tries to explain some of the mystique surrounding this famous tank. This is followed by a selection of items that show the Allied reaction to the new tank from the time it was first noted by Military Intelligence until, in 1944, a fully operational sample machine arrived in Britain for extensive evaluation. Part three is a true and full copy of the actual report on this captured tank as issued by the School of Tank Technology and the Military College of Science in Britain. Here it must be said that this report was never completed in all its parts. Such was the scale of this evaluation that the war in Europe was over before it was finished and, once the threat was removed, many parts that had not been completed were laid aside. The final section deals with those aspects of the Tiger that came to light while the main report was being compiled. Since it was still vital to keep the troops in the field 'up-to-date' on the latest developments in Italy and France, Military Intelligence continued to circulate whatever came its way, and the sources are as varied as their contents are interesting.

Birth of a legend

If beauty in design, style and finesse had anything to do with it, then the chances of a tank assuming heroic status would be slim indeed. Since the yardstick is more likely to be strength and power then, perhaps, it is not so surprising to discover that, in less than seventy years since the first models were produced, quite a number have earned the right to that hushed awe and grudging respect that is the spring-board of legend. Names like Sherman, Matilda or Centurion may come to mind but, over and above them all there is one name that seems to stand for everything that is best and worst in the lexicon of armour: the Tiger.

One does not have to go far to find the reasons for this. In the first place it was, for nearly three years, the biggest and most powerful armoured fighting vehicle in service anywhere in the world. It fought a galaxy of Allied armies on four major fronts and usually came off best. And what is more it looked the part. Broad shouldered and apparently irresistible, it seemed to crush, or blow to smithereens, everything in its path while, gathered about it, was the sinister, impersonal martial efficiency of the German war machine. The Tiger was the armoured manifestation of the Jackboot.

Distasteful as it is, there is no doubt that some portion, at least, of the Tiger's mystique derives from a lingering fascination with the Nazi ideology. But the Tiger can stand forth quite well on its own account, as anyone who has seen one will testify. One Tiger, the subject of the main report in this book, resides today, quietly, in a corner of the Tank Museum, Bovington. On the inventory it is only one of a growing collection of exhibits that will soon number 160. Yet for all that it holds the visitor spellbound. More enthusiasts pay for the privilege of climbing inside that one impressive tank than all the others put together.

Even the name has something to do with it; quite who or what inspired the Germans, half way through the war, to start naming their tanks after members of the feral cat family is not known. The British stretched credibility to the limit, trying to find new names beginning with the third letter of the alphabet that still retained a martial air, or applying the names of American Civil War generals to lease-lend tanks. Sometimes, in apparent desperation, they chose girl's name, which suited neither category. Homely or colourful they might have been but they lacked that sense of naked aggression that a prowling Tiger conjures up.

Few legends survive close scrutiny unscathed; the image becomes tarnished and the mystery transparent. The legend of Tiger underwent this indignity and survived intact. For one thing by the time all the results of this examination were published the threat, which was a large part of the Tiger's stock in trade, had been removed; for another, try as they may, few of those charged with dismantling the legend could quite get it out of their minds and, indeed, much of what they found only served to impress them the more. With this in mind it is instructive to read the Motion Study Report on the Tiger which appeared in 1947. Justified as his criticisms were in an objective sense this anonymous officer sounds almost mealy mouthed when one appreciates that contemporary Allied tank design (about 1942) was a feeble travesty of the German achievement.

Something else the Tiger had in its favour was the heritage of the Panzers. The very word, coupled with the relentless image of Blitzkrieg, had Wagnerian associations but the threat was as anonymous as the tanks themselves, all of which looked more or less alike in their field grey livery, with their prosaic numerical designations. In Britain the naming of tanks became so complex that people are still trying to sort out their nomenclature: a tank like the Covenanter could also be referred to as the Cruiser Mark V or the Cruiser A13 Mk III. But this inconsistency is a typical and endearing national characteristic. The Germans were supposed to be far more logical yet, for all that, they managed to produce three different types of tank which became known as the Panzer VI, and there were rumours of a fourth. This appeared, on paper, in February 1941 and it is worth recording in the light of later events. Rumours of this, and two other tanks, Panzers V and VII, appeared in A.F.V. Technical Intelligence Summary No. I, the first in a long-running series of military intelligence reports issued by M.I.10, the branch in Whitehall responsible for disseminating technical matters both fact and myth. According to this source, three armoured leviathans were on the stocks and No. 2, the Pz Kw VI was described as being a 45-ton machine with armour to a maximum of 75mm thick, carrying a crew of 18 and armed with one 75 mm gun, two 2 cm guns and four machine guns. It was, so they said, 36 ft long, nearly 10 ft wide and over 6 ft high with a top speed of 25 mph. Somehow the ingenious Germans managed to cram 300 rounds of 75 mm, 800 rounds of 2 cm, and 10,000 rounds of MG ammunition into it and still leave room for the engine!

M.I.10 described their source as trustworthy but not necessarily technically reliable which seems contradictory, and they then went on to cast doubt upon most of the specifications. Referring to the crew they expressed considerable doubt, they would only allow 13 at most and even then they expected some of these to be infantry passengers.

The dimensions, too, were not in keeping with tank design as it was then understood. A tank as long and narrow as that, they opined, would be virtually unmanoeuvrable. They saw nothing improbable in the armament specifications but they refrained from passing any comment on the ammunition stowage and were frankly dubious about the weight when compared against armour thickness and length. They had every right to be. They concluded that either their informant had seen a tank somewhat bigger than usual and made up the rest or, that the German General Staff had released the data deliberately in order to confuse them. If there was even a basis of truth in it then it could only refer to heavy tank projects that pre-dated the Tiger since this design was not initiated until at least May 1941 on Hitler's instructions.

The point, however, was the willingness of British Intelligence to believe that the Germans were well able to produce a tank of a size, as they had once before (the 148 ton K-Wagen of 1918), that was outside the accepted parameters of tank design as understood in 1941. This was all part of the general surrender of technological initiative on AFV development that allowed Germany to outstrip Britain and her allies so decisively for the rest of the war.

Despite the fact that much of the following text is couched in a somewhat inhibiting military style, most of it will be readily understood by the average reader. Technical terms and explanations are unavoidable in a work such as this but most of it was aimed at the layman soldier rather than the scientist so the basic sense can usually be divined if only because the compilers tended to labour rather than gloss over the details. The usual military penchant for abbreviations has dictated the inclusion of a glossary and, beyond that only two or three specific points need to be made.

Quite often, to illustrate a point, the reporter uses the words offside and nearside to indicate a location. It should be remembered that, as a Briton he was thinking in terms of vehicles driving on the left-hand side of the road so these terms should be interpreted as left side (nearside), right side (offside) as one would see them when sitting in the vehicle facing forwards.

Two methods of measuring the qualities of metal plate appear regularly in the text and these should be explained. The Brinnel figure is an indication of hardness arrived at by measuring its resistance to deformation. A steel ball is pressed onto the surface of the plate and the diameter of the impression it makes is compared with known standards.

The Izod test reveals the toughness of a plate; its ability to absorb energy (like a shell strike) without fracturing. It is measured by securing a bar of the subject material in a vice and then breaking by the action of a heavy pendulum. The resulting figure is derived from measuring the energy in foot/lbs. Since hardness and toughness are virtually incompatible qualities the trick is to produce a plate that achieves the best compromise.

An appendix giving brief explanations of other terms relating to armour plate is included at the end of the book.

Tiger in captivity; an officer of the Weapons Technical Staff looks wistfully at the formidable 88mm gun of the first Tiger tank to be captured intact by British forces in Tunisia. This tank, the subject of a report that forms the centrepiece of this book, still survives as one of the most popular exhibits at the Tank Museum, Bovington Camp in Dorset.

Part One

The first intimation the British had of the existence of the Tiger came, in the form of a coded telegram, that was circulated to the heads of selected establishments associated with the development of tanks.

It is clear that nothing very useful could be gained from reading this apart from the intimation that these new heavy tanks could be expected to turn up in the Middle East at some stage. On the other hand a modern reader might pause to ask himself why nothing about this tank had yet come from Moscow; they had been in service on the Russian front since August 1942.

The next document to mention the new tank was again of very limited circulation but altogether more interesting, not least when one ponders the shadowy world that it seems to evoke.

Just who this delicately placed source was may never be known. Most likely a well-disposed member of a neutral embassy in Berlin or, perhaps, a helpful contact in Moscow.

SECRET CIPHER TELEGRAM 1/65667 OF 29 OCTOBER FROM MIDDLE EAST HAS REPORTED THE IDENTIFICATION FROM A CAPTURED GERMAN DOCUMENT? EQUIVALENT TO BRITISH A.C.Is OF THE FOLLOWING AFVs NOT HITHERTO IDENTIFIED.

A NEW TYPE KNOWN AS K.PFW.VI. THIS CONFIRMS THAT AS EXPECTED, A NEW TANK, HEAVIER THAN III OR IV IS BEING BUILT, THE ABSENCE OF ANY REFERENCE TO PZ KPWF V SUGGESTS THAT THIS NOMENCLATURE WAS PROBABLY APPLIED TO THE HEAVY TYPE FIRST REPORTED IN 1937/38, LATER SEEN IN NORWAY AND IN GERMAN PROPAGANDA PAPERS, AND SINCE DISCARDED.

WE HAVE ASKED BOTH MIDDLE EAST AND THE MISSION IN MOSCOW TO TAKE URGENT STEPS TO OBTAIN PRECISE INFORMATION ON THE CHARACTERISTICS OF THE PZ KPFW VI.

M.I.10
3 NOV 1942
EXTN 230

SGD. SHALLARD
MAJOR
FOR LIEUT: COL: G.S.

MOST SECRET

Enemy Weapons
New German Super-Heavy Pz.Kw.VI tank

The following information has been received from a delicately placed, reliable source. It may be communicated, at your discretion, to those whose work is *immediately* affected by it, but it must NOT be generally circulated or reproduced in a summary.

Weight 57 tons
Dimensions
    Length 20 ft 3 in
    Width   11 ft 8 in
Armour   Source does not know but thinks about 100mm.
Armament   8.8 cm Kw.K.
Performance
    Trench crossing
    Step
    Water forded   Source is endeavouring to
    Maximum gradient   obtain details.

No details of the 8.8 cm Kw.K are known. Kw.K is the normal nomenclature given to guns mounted in A.F.V's. as distinct from those on field or self propelled mountings.

The above information has been given to A.C.I.G.S., D.A.F.V ., D.R.A.

Nov.42

for D.M.I.

NEW HEAVY TANK

On 5 December 1942 M.I.10 released two brief references to the new tank to a wider audience within the services, through their Technical Intelligence Summary No. 94.

It is known that a new tank, Pz.Kw. VI., is in existence. No details are yet known, but it seems most probable that the new tank gun 8.8 cm Kw.K.36 is fitted as main armament. This tank should not be expected to bear any resemblance to the Pz.Kw. VI referred to in Summary 49, Appendix A, though it will be heavier than Pz.Kw.III or IV.

(b) *8.8 cm (3.46 in) Kw.K 36 (tank gun)*
The extent to which this differs from the 8.8cm. Flak 36 is not yet known but it is improbable that there is any substantial difference in performance. This gun is probably the main armament of the new Pz.Kw.VI., and in accordance with usual German practice, it will presumably have electric firing mechanism.

To the Germans, of course, the initial period of secrecy was more or less over and the decision to send some tanks out to the North African battlefield was chosen as an opportunity to exploit its propaganda value.

SUBJECT: *Photograph of new German Tank*   *Ref: STT/10/2*

To: Department of Tank Design,
    Long Cross,
    Chobham   *5th January, 1943*

Enclosed herewith is a photograph of the new German Pz.Kw.VI. (see M.I.10 summary No. 94/4). The photograph which was taken from the 'National Zeitung' of 11/12/42, shows the 8.8cm. Gun and part of the suspension which is thought to be based on the same principle as that of the semi-tracked Carriers (Zg.Kw.)

Woodlands,   Sgd.
Egham Hill,   Colonel.
Egham, Surrey   Commandant,
Tel: Egham 858   School of Tank Technology.

This historic photograph, from the German newspaper *National Zeitung* of 11 December 1942, was the first picture of a Tiger ever seen in Britain. It shows a tank of the 501st Heavy Tank Battalion driving through Tunis. At this time the muzzle brake had not been fitted to the 88mm gun and the tank is running on its narrow transport tracks.

M.I.10 examined the photograph thoroughly and, in the light of what they already knew, got a technical illustrator to see what he could make of it.

Assuming that they were not including the gun in their estimate of the overall length, this was a remarkably accurate calculation and, as will be seen, the drawing, such as it was, required very little modification when more information became available.

NEW HEAVY TANK

Reference Summary 94 para. 4, a photograph showing a new type of German tank, said to be passing through Tunis has recently been published in the Continental Press. This photograph forms the basis of the drawing at appendix C.

It is considered that the tank shown is almost certainly the Pz.Kw.VI with 8.8 cm Kw.K.36 mounted in the turret.

Scaling from the photograph, rough estimates for the dimensions are:—

Overall height about:	9 ft 6 in
Overall length about:	21 ft
Overall width about:	10 ft to 10 ft 9 in
Width of track plates:	nearly 2 ft
Diameter of road wheels:	3 ft (approx.)

The suspension is not at all clearly shown in the photograph. Thus, while it is clear that the bogie wheels are of the large armoured disc type, it is not clear whether they are arranged in a straight line or interleaved as in the suspensions of German semi-tracked vehicles. In the drawing, the suspension is provisionally shown as being of the latter type.

Many typical German features will be observed from the drawing. For example:— the conventional German type of gun mounting with armoured sleeve and recoil gear casing; the ball type M.G. mounting on the front of the superstructure; the cupola; and the design of the front of the hull which is not unlike that of the Pz.Kw. IV Model G though the glacis plate is shorter.

It will be noted that the superstructure overhangs the full width of the tracks and in this way no doubt helps to solve the problem of stowage for the 8.8 cm ammunition. This ammunition will possibly be of the Q.F. separate loading type.

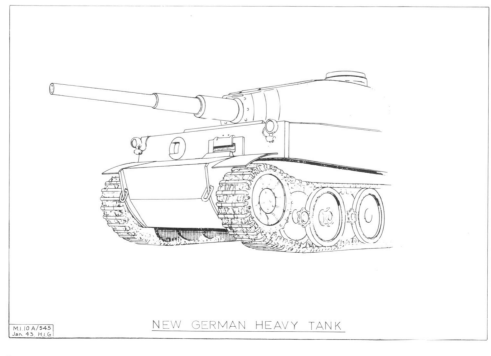

M.I.10 A/545
Jan. 43. H.I.G

NEW GERMAN HEAVY TANK

It was now time for the British public to learn about the tank and the Daily Mail of 30 January 1943, quoting a Reuter's correspondent in Tunisia, announced it under the heading: '62-ton German Tanks Arrive'

62-TON GERMAN TANKS ARRIVE

Germany's new 62-tons monster 'Tiger' tanks, equipped with dual purpose 88mm guns, have now appeared in Tunisia. Their numbers at present however, are small.

The 'land battleships', though not much bigger than the German Mark IV's are about twice the weight — the difference being entirely due to the tremendous armour of the 'Tiger'.

Seven-inch armour plating protects the 'Tiger's' turret, the front of which is additionally strengthened with a further inch of armour.

The sides of the tank are protected by 5in plating.

The tanks are still in an experimental stage, and have apparently been brought here to boost the morale of the Axis troops.

Three 'Tigers' are believed to have had their tracks — their most vulnerable point — blown off last week when they ran over French mines.

Whether Fleet Street exercised its usual penchant for exaggeration by embroidering the Reuter report with a few figures of its own or not they certainly did their best to embellish the legend that Germany was so careful to foster. Further west, in Whitehall, M.I.10 was gradually gathering the hard facts as this Secret Minute of 3 February 1943 shows.

Further to our minute of 3 November 1942 (M.I.10.a./3008) on the subject of new A.F.Vs, and our minute of 4 January on the Pz.Kw.VI., the following particulars of this tank have now been obtained from a document captured in North Africa:—

Weight	56 tons
Length	20 ft 4 in
Length including gun	27 ft 0¾ in
Width	10 ft 11¾ in
Height	9 ft 5½ in

A disabled Pz.Kw.VI, which it was not possible to recover, has been examined, and the particulars will be sent to you as soon as they are received here.

Now they were getting somewhere and, one week later, there was more.

M.I.10   Minute Sheet No.1

The particulars of the new German heavy tank Px.Kw.VI. so far received from A.F.H.Q. are summarized in enclosure 1.a. More information is expected and a full report will be published in due course in our Technical Intelligence Summary.

Certain other points which have so far emerged are the following:—

(i) The drawing issued with our Technical Intelligence Summary No. 97 is substantially correct so far as it goes, but the gun is fitted with the usual German type of muzzle brake.

(ii) The 8.8 cm ammunition is apparently the same as for the 8.8 cm

Flak (Though it may be adapted for electric firing) and therefore A.P. and H.E. performance will no doubt be the same.

(iii) The suspension details are not yet known, but it seems clear that the large disc wheels overlap like those of German semi-tracked vehicles, and it is probable that the wheel discs are armoured.

(iv) No spaced armour is fitted and all plates appear to be of homogeneous quality. The highest Brinell figure reported is 340 on the turret.

(v) Samples of armour plate and tracks are being sent home by air.

(vi) A.F.H.Q. have reported that our 6-pr. A.P. shot has penetrated the turret armour of this tank at 500 yards range. A 6-pr, shot hole has also been found in the superstructure side, the estimated angle of strike in this case being 15 degrees.

(vii) Press reports of armour thickness of 10 inches have proved incorrect. The maximum is, in fact, about 4 inches.

☆ ☆ ☆ ☆ ☆ ☆ ☆ ☆

M.I.10   Minute Sheet IA

Weight: 56 tons.
Armament: Turret-One 8.8 cm. gun and one 7.92 mm. M.G. coaxial.
                  Hull   -One 7.92 mm.M.G. in right front of
                  superstructure.
Dimensions: Length – 20 ft 4 in
                  Length (including gun) 27 ft 0¾ in
                  Width – 10 ft 11¾ in
                  Height – 9 ft 5½ in
                  Track width – 2 ft 4½ in (see note 1)
Armour: All homogeneous quality.

Plate	Thickness	Approx. Angle to vertical
Turret gun mantlet	97mm (See Note 2)	vertical
sides and rear	82mm	vertical
top.	26mm	90
Superstructure. front	102mm	10
sides	82mm	vertical
rear	82mm	20
top	26mm	90
Hull upper nose plate	102mm	20
lower nose plate	62mm	60
glacis plate	62mm	80
sides	62mm	vertical
tail	82mm	20
floor	26mm	90

Note 1. There appear to be two types of track and this is probably the wider of the two types.

Note 2. The thickness of this plate is not yet definite owing to difficulty in measurement.

The disabled tank already referred to was the first to be defeated by British troops but, at an official level, news of this action filtered through slowly. Indeed it seems that the press got hold of the story first and it appeared as a brief notice, on 5 February 1943, in the *Daily Telegraph* and the *Daily Mirror*, both quoting a Reuters report. The Telegraph said ➤

Both were clearly designed to counter the legend that was steadily enveloping the new tank but the low-key approach is noteworthy.

The *Mirror* report was substantially the same but it added ➤

The first official appraisal of the action was prepared some ten days later.

As subsequent reports will show, the two knocked out Tigers did not prove to be the prize they might have been, the ground on which they lay was still in contention and the Germans were soon able to recover the rearmost tank. The other was therefore blown up by

6-POUNDER BEATS NEW NAZI TANK

7-in Armour Pierced

Allied H.Q. N. Africa, Thursday. Examination by tank experts of one of the two Mark VI German tanks captured during the attempted German thrust towards Robaa on Sunday reveals that British six-pounder guns penetrated its armour-plating four times.

The number of Mark VI tanks in Tunisia is believed to be relatively small. The legend of their invulnerability has been completely dissipated by the fact that the six-pounders were able to knock out two of them from a distance of between 400 and 500 yards.

Their exact tonnage has not yet been officially revealed but it is somewhere between 50 and 60 tons. They have 7in armour-plate with an extra 1in-thick shield in front.

The Tiger, technically the Mark VI tank, carries an 88 millimetre gun. It looks like a field gun on caterpillar tracks.

SECRET
RA/O/2/5

H.Q.R.A.,
6th Armd. Div.
15 Feb. 43

Dear

I have sifted all possible information and questioned all witnesses concerning the encounter between 2 Troops A/72 A/Tk Regt R.A. and the German Tank Force on the Robaa Road on 20 Jan. 43.

I have also studied the southern half of the ground.

I am satisfied that the leading tank (a Mark VI) was not engaged at any time at a range less than 500 yards. This tank was hit on the *side* mainly.

The 2nd Mark VI tank was hit and disabled at not less than 800 yards. It was also chiefly engaged by *frontal fire*.

I thought these factors are of sufficient importance to warrant a thorough investigation, as they prove conclusively (to me anyhow) that

the Royal Engineers to prevent it from going the same way. Unfortunately this was done before the tank could be examined by any British tank experts although two, Colonel J.A. Barlow and Lt.-Col. R.D. Neville of the Weapons Technical Staff, Field Force, were on their way. Here is their report:

the 6-pr A/Tank gun can deal most effectively with the Mark VI tank. I hope I may not be proved at a later date to have been wrong.

I believe 16 other tanks were seen following behind — these withdrew. They in turn were followed very closely by the Panzer Regt (Inf) in armoured carriers or TCVs. They were seen to be sitting smartly to attention until engaged by 12 RHA. They then dismounted hurriedly, and delivered a most determined attack on the Buffs.

Yours
(Brig T. Lyon Smith)

REPORT ON GERMAN Pz Kw VI TANK EXAMINED 2/3 FEBRUARY DIARY

1. At First Army HQ. at about 1000 hrs on 1 Feb., a sitrep was seen which stated that two German Pz Kw VI tanks had been knocked out on the ROBAA-PONT DU FAHS road and that one had been recovered by the enemy while the other had been blown up by our sappers.

2. At that time we were without adequate means of transport. Having explained to First Army the necessity for an immediate examination by us of the 'Remains' available, they very kindly produced two cars and we were able to cover 124 miles before dark.

3. Starting early on 2 Feb. we covered a further 132 miles to the Brigade Headquarters concerned. We were told that Staff cars should not go down to the scene of the action; Brigade very kindly lent us a Bantam (Jeep).

4. We arrived at the camp about 1600 hrs. just as GOC, 5 Corps was completing a visit of inspection.
NOTE: In the photographs attached, No: 1 to 4 show the Pz Kw VI tank as it was after being knocked out and before being blown up. These photos were taken by a Canadian RE officer and have been obtained from Intelligence Branch at A.F.H.Q. All that remained of the tank at the time of our arrival on the scene, is shown in photos 5 and 6.

5. An immediate start was made on taking photographs and noting details of armour thickness, etc.

6. At dusk we moved back and camped three miles West of ROBAA.

7. Early on 3 Feb. Brigade Headquarters was again contacted and we asked for the assistance of REME and RE personnel to enable us to take away samples of the various plates for hardness tests.

An oxy-acetylene cutting plant was ordered up by Brigade, and the RE company were instructed by them to help as necessary.

The importance of a technical examination of details of the vehicle with which we were not competent to deal, was stressed.

8. The question of shooting at the front of the tank with 6 pounder was discussed. It was pointed out to Brigade that, provided we obtained samples of the requisite plates, there was no necessity to shoot, although this would be interesting and a rough and ready check on the hardness of the plate. It was explained that if there were any risks to gun or detachment, we certainly would not ask for such a shoot to be carried out — always provided we obtained samples of the plate.

It was decided to lay on a shot from a portee at 1200 hrs. and leave it to the discretion of the gunner officer on the spot, as to whether the shoot was carried out or not.

9. We again borrowed the Brigade Bantam and proceeded to the tank. The gunner officer on the spot told us that the enemy had been shelling the area in which the tank was situated and that therefore the projected shoot was 'off'.

10. The Bantam was left behind the nearest crest and we went forward on foot. Pending arrival of the oxy-acetylene cutting plant, we took further photographs and again checked over the measurements taken the evening before. Using a level obtained from the RE, the angles at which the various plates are set were checked.

11. Two REME officers arrived about 1300 hrs. They reported that the cutting plant was following. Pending its arrival we proceeded to free the muzzle brake from the gun. This entailed some two hours work since the ground round the brake had to be dug away and means devised for shifting the gun (weighing approximately 1½ tons). This was eventually accomplished by the use of a jack from a burnt out Pz Kw III tank nearby.

12. When this was done, and since the cutting plant had not arrived, it was decided to proceed to get the samples of the plates by blowing pieces away.
NOTE: It was subsequently ascertained that the lorry containing the plant had been turned back just outside ROBAA, since it was too conspicuous to come up the road to the tank.

13. At the same time preparations were made for laying Hawkins No. 75 grenade mines under the tracks to ascertain the effect. Since it was unlikely that one grenade would be successful, it was decided to try two grenades, and also a complete box with 3 detonated grenades lying on top (Tank Wrecker).
Unfortunately the RE company were unable to produce GS mines to try as well.

14. As result of the action taken, we were able to obtain samples of the following plates:
    a Drivers front
    b Upper nose
    c Lower side
    d Upper side
    e Turret
In addition the effect of two No 75 grenades, and a box plus three No. 75 grenades was ascertained.

15. An attempt to get a piece of the lower nose plate was unsuccessful. Since it was now nearly dark, work was suspended for the day and we went back and camped with the RE company.
NOTE: Work had necessarily been slow, since there were several occasions on which we had to take cover from enemy planes reconnoitring. It was also considered advisable for not more than 3 or 4 persons to be visible near the tank at any one time.

16. At 0730 hrs next morning Colonel Barlow went to Brigade HQ and explained what had been done, giving the results of the No. 75 grenade tests verbally to the Brigade Major.

▶

These photographs, numbered 1 to 6 in the Barlow report, show a Tiger knocked out on the Robaa road. Alongside the Tiger in two of the pictures can be seen the British Valentine of 6th Armoured Division which ran over a mine at the side of the road. Other views show the same Tiger after it was blown up by the Royal Engineers to prevent the Germans from recapturing it. Visible on the front plate is the stalking tiger symbol of the 501st Heavy Tank Battalion; the parallelogram device is the tactical sign of a Panzer unit.

17. On returning to the RE Company, the importance of carrying out a test with a GS mine was stressed. The company commander, who had only taken over the evening before, in relief of the previous commander wounded during the preliminary attempts to investigate the tank, undertook to see that this was done.

18. Lt. Col. Neville was left to see that the sample from the lower nose plate was obtained and sent back with all speed to A.F.H.Q.
NOTE: A signal has been received to say that this has been done and that the plate is on its way.

Colonel Barlow left for First Army at 0900 hrs. with samples of track, plates as stated in paragraph 14 above, muzzle brake and two smoke generators.

19. Colonel Barlow arrived First Army HQ at 1840 hrs. A call was made at DDME workshops to ascertain whether a hardness testing machine was available. It was found that there was unlikely to be one nearer than ALGIERS.

20. Colonel Barlow reported to SD & T.

In view of the fact that at this time the quality of the plates was not known, and since the present usual practice of the Germans is to use face hardened armour on the front of their tanks, it was thought advisable to stress to SD & T First Army the necessity for siting 6 pounders so that they can normally shoot at the sides of attacking tanks rather than the front.

Full details of the tank were given to GSI First Army and the fact that a complete box plus three No. 75 grenades is an effective stopper for this tank, was explained to SD & T.

A cable to DG of A giving the main particulars of the tank was dispatched at 0200 hrs 5 February. The cable was repeated to WTSFF MIDEAST and PAIFORCE.

21. At 0400 hrs Colonel Barlow left for ALGIERS travelling through the night. He arrived at DME's HQ at 1030 hrs. Brinell hardness testing machine was found and the plates tested. As a check, each plate was drilled by normal means.

22. By 1500 hrs details of the 5 plates had been obtained. They were then loaded again into the staff car and taken to A.F.H.Q., where Colonel Barlow contacted AC/S G–2 and gave him the details obtained to date.

There-after, a further cable was sent to DG of A giving the details of the Brinell figures of the plates.

23. A signal was also dispatched to SD&T First Army giving the same information and stating that in conditions of head-on attacks, the 6 pounder should be able to hole the front armour at three hundred yards and under.

24. On the morning of 6 February, negatives of photographs were handed to Captain Webb for developing and printing, the various exhibits formally handed over to him.

These events exemplify the trials and tribulations of a Technical Staff field officer, but the story did not end there. Lt. Col. Neville was still with the tank and his further adventures were submitted under the title 'Target Point of View'. After reviewing the position so far they continue:

...Lt. Col. Neville was left behind when Colonel Barlow returned to ALGIERS with the five sample plates etc. He obtained the further plate required and also made a thorough and detailed examination of the bits of the tank which had been blown into the wadi on either side of the road.

4. A perforation was found in a large part of the left upper side plate. This was reported back by signal and is included in the report already published. A party of men was obtained and this piece of upper side plate lying in the wadi was turned over. A further search revealed the remaining missing piece of this plate.

5. This further and more leisured examination by Lt.-Col. Neville revealed certain interesting features amongst which was the fact that the tank had been hit ten times in all, of which five had 'holed' it....

6. An account of the action was obtained from the personnel concerned. The angles quoted below are obtained from a survey of the scene of the action and take into consideration the non-effective hits on the upper side plate.

The tank was engaged in left flank by two 6 pdr guns of No 2 Troop (Lt. Heslop R.A.) 'A' Bty 72 A/Tk Regt. Fire was opened by both guns at about 680 yds, the angles of strike from normal being about 45 degrees and 35 degrees respectively due to displacement of the two guns. The range shortened as the tank advanced, to about 630 yds, with angles of strike at about 10 degrees and 15 degrees from normal, where the tank was knocked out. The tank was screened by the side of a cutting during the period when the angle from normal of the side of the tank was about 35 degrees to 30 degrees. The side of the cutting can be seen in photo No. 2 of the report – on the right of the Valentine.

The tanks, of which there were six – two Pz. Kw. VI and four Pz.Kw.III – advanced in the following order:– Pz.Kw.VI, two Pz. Kw. III, Pz. Kw. VI, two Pz. Kw. III.

Two guns of the troop then fired at the leading Pz.Kw. III (680 yds) and set it on fire. The third gun (700 yds) fired some two or three rounds at the second Pz.Kw. III and put it out of action. The same gun then engaged the fifth tank. a Pz.Kw. III (1,000 yds) and put it out of action. The fourth gun engaged the fourth tank, a Pz.Kw. VI at 1,000 yds together with two guns of No. 1 Troop. This tank was put out of action. (N.B. It will be remembered that this second Pz.Kw. VI was recovered by the enemy the same evening.) No 1 Troop also destroyed the sixth tank, another Pz.Kw. III.

NOTE: All guns mentioned were Mk II.

7. Subsequent to the detailed examination of the remains, mentioned in para. 5 above, Lt.-Col. Neville evacuated the remainder of the lower nose plate and carried out a firing trial against it with a 6 pdr Mk II.

The plate was 102mm thick (the Brinell figure has since been ascertained to be 302) was set up at approximately 21 degrees and supported by drums filled with stones both at the back and at the front. The gun was set up 300 yds away. Two hits were obtained with the following results:

Round	Range	Angle	Result
1	300 yds	21 degrees	Shot penetrated 3 inches. Plate cracked vertically. Shot turned and rebounded whole.
2	300 yds	20 degrees	Shot penetrated 3½ inches. Bulge at back. Plate split in two.

The trial was then suspended.

Owing to weather conditions and approaching darkness, photography was not possible. It took six hours to bring the plate some five miles by

Scammell. This was due to wet and muddy roads, the Scammell having to winch itself up every hill.

8. Tests have also been carried out against this Pz.Kw.VI tank with:
   (i) PIAT
   (ii) No. 74 S.T. grenade.

PIAT

(i) Four attempts to hole the lower nose plate 102mm failed. The angles of the explosion to the face of the plate were measured subsequently.

(ii) The 82mm upper side plate was 'holed' at the first attempt.

No 74 S.T. Grenade

Two grenades were tried against the roofing plate, one of which penetrated.

9. *A/Tk Mines and No 75 Grenade Mines.*

We were informed by V Corps that tests had revealed that the tracks of the Pz.Kw.VI could be broken by:

   (i) a GS Mk V mine
   (ii) 4 No 75 grenade mines

A point to note is that the No 75s, if laid parallel to the line of advance, fit into the space between the track plates of the Pz.Kw.VI and conceivably might not function. It is advisable therefore to lay them endways on.

10. *To summarize*

   (i)   In 'comment' 3 of the report it was estimated that the 6 pdr should 'hole' the 102mm front plate at about 300 yards and under. This estimate was based on the machinable quality of the armour. It has not been borne out in the test reported in para. 7 above. The advice tendered in the comment 3 is, however, in no way affected in conditions where head-on attack has to be countered. It is again reiterated, however, that this tank is vulnerable at the sides and should invariably be engaged from the flank except in cases of emergency, i.e. head-on attack on a gun position. In such circumstances several shots at the driver's front plate may cause cracking and collapse of the plate. Similarly hits on the lower nose plate will probably dislodge the spare track and plate behind be collapsed or split in a like manner.
   (ii) The PIAT can be considered to be effective against;
             (a) the side and rear of the turret
             (b) the upper side plate
         It will be of no use against the lower side plates which are protected by the bogey wheels.
             It will not pierce the front armour. PIAT slit trenches should therefore be sited so as to bring enfilade fire to bear on likely lines of approach.
   (iii) The No 74 S T grenade is effective against the 26mm roofing of the turret and fighting compartment.
   (iv) A G S Mk V A/Tk mine is reported to be effective for cutting the track.
   (v)   As distinct from the 'Tank Wrecker' of a box of No 75s plus three previously reported, it has been established that four No 75s will cut the track of this tank.
   (vi) With the 2 pdr the best chance, if one is compelled to take on this tank, is a shot from the flank at the lower side plate (62mm) behind the bogey wheels. For this to be successful, the range

should be less than 400 yds and the angle from normal not more than 20 degrees. There is a very long odds chance of holing at nearly point-blank range at the side of the turret on the upper side plate at normal impact. The chances of these conditions being present are not great.

J. A. Barlow,
Colonel

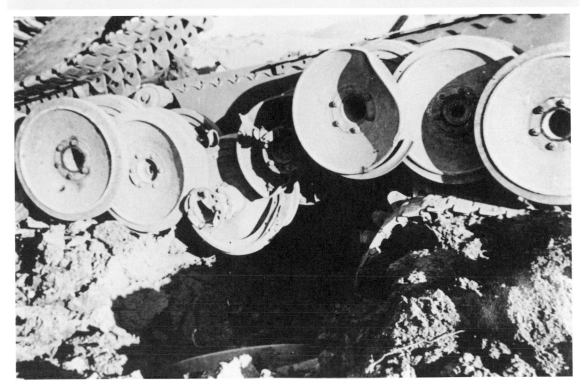

A total of fifteen Hawkins grenade mines were detonated under the tracks of the wrecked tank to discover if they would break the track. This was the result.

Based on the information from North Africa M.I.10 was able, on 20 February 1943, to issue a more detailed report (T.I. Summary No. 99), which included a diagram showing the armour profile. Much of it repeated data already recorded but these extracts are worth noting.

Reference Summary 97, paragraph 6, an amended drawing of the above tank is attached at appendix E together with an armour diagram. These drawings and the information given below are based on advance reports from North Africa.

Armour: All homogeneous quality.

No definite figures have been obtained for the thickness of the gun mantlet, owing to difficulty in measurement.

It may be of interest that the sides of both turret and hull of this tank have been defeated by the 6 pr at about 500 yds range.

A footnote qualifies details of the tank's width.

Two perspective sketches, dated January and March 1943 show, respectively, the narrow and wide tracks with the parallel variations in suspension.

It appears from photographs that there are two types of track, one wider than the other. This may explain the two overall widths reported, and it is thought that the track width quoted, i.e. 2 ft 4½ in., is for the wider type of track.

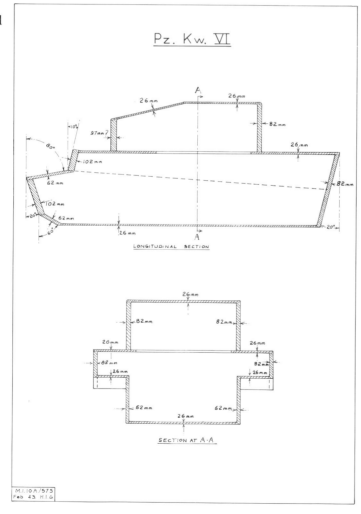

20

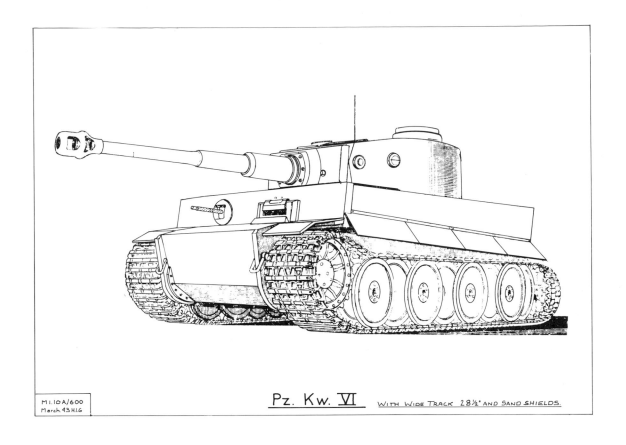

M.I.10 A/600
March. 43 H.I.G

Pz. Kw. VI   WITH WIDE TRACK 28½" AND SAND SHIELDS.

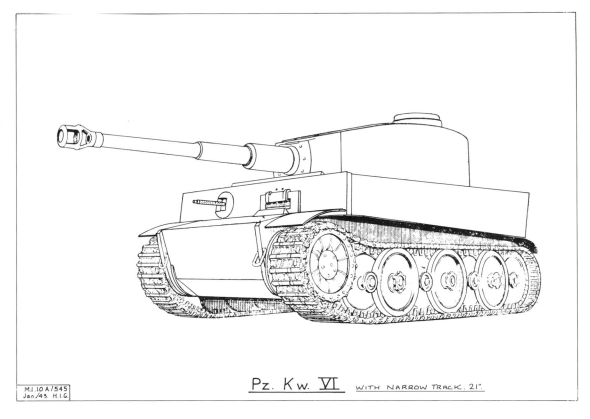

M.I.10 A/545
Jan./43. H.I.G.

Pz. Kw. VI   WITH NARROW TRACK. 21".

On 5 March details of the six pieces of plate, supplied by Messrs Barlow and Neville, were published →

For immediate, practical purposes it was only right that the first priority should be the armour thickness and its quality. The performance of the gun held no great

GERMAN TANK – PZ.KW.VI.
Armour Plate Samples from N. Africa

Position	Thickness	Approx. Dimensions	Brinell Hardness
Driver's Front Plate	102mm/4in	10ft x 1 ft 2in	286
Upper Nose Plate @ 80	62mm/2½in	6ft x 9ft with 2½in dia. hole	293
Lower Nose Plate	102mm/4in	1 ft 4in x 1 ft 1in	302
Upper Side Plate	82mm/3⅛in	12ft x 5in	324
Lower Side Plate	62mm/2½in	9ft x 8in	320
Turret	82mm/3⅛in	10ft x 9in	340

Location of Plates. F.1. Hangar, Farnborough, Hants.

Two pieces of armour plate from the German tank examined at Farnborough. The petalling effect of an armour piercing round is clearly shown.

The mantlet, one of the thickest parts of a Tiger's hide, at first defied accurate measurement in the field.

22

mystery and other technical details, however interesting and vital in the long run, had to take second place. What the men in the field needed to know, as quickly as possible, was how well protected it was and exactly what it would take to defeat it in battle.

When some progress had been made in this direction other matters slowly came to the surface, the first being the suspension. Obviously it was important to know how the Germans had dealt with the problem of weight and its concommitant factor, ground pressure. In addition there was the problem already hinted at, the fact that the heavy tanks appeared, on occasion, with different widths of track and apparent variations in suspension. The first attempt at a detailed examination resulted in the publication of T.I. Summary No. 101 on 20 March 1943, extracts from which, with an accompanying drawing, are shown below.

Reference Summary 99, the general arrangement of the suspension and tracks of the Pz.Kw. VI is illustrated diagrammatically.

There are two alternative types of track, viz. a narrow 21 in. track for transport and travelling on good roads and a wide 28½ in. track for cross-country work. The narrow track is symmetrical and is approximately the same width as the driving sprockets. The wide track is virtually the narrow track with an extension on one side which provides the required increase in width. In the diagram, the outer edge of the narrow track is indicated by a dotted line.

On each side of the tank there are a front sprocket, rear idler and eight load-carrying axles. When the wide track is in use, each axle carries three wheels, two close together forming in effect a double wheel and the third spaced from the other two and single. Axles 1, 3, 5 and 7 have a single wheel on the outside and a double wheel on the inside, this arrangement being reversed on axles 2, 4, 6 and 8. The wheels on adjacent axles overlap as shown in the drawing.

When the narrow track is in use, the outermost wheel is removed from each axle, leaving only two wheels per axle i.e. those inside the dotted line on the drawing.

A sample track link and pin have been examined by D.T.D. who have furnished the following particulars:

Weights

Weight of link	59 lb	Per linkage
Weight of pin	7.375 lb	66.375 lb
Weight of track per foot run	155 lb	

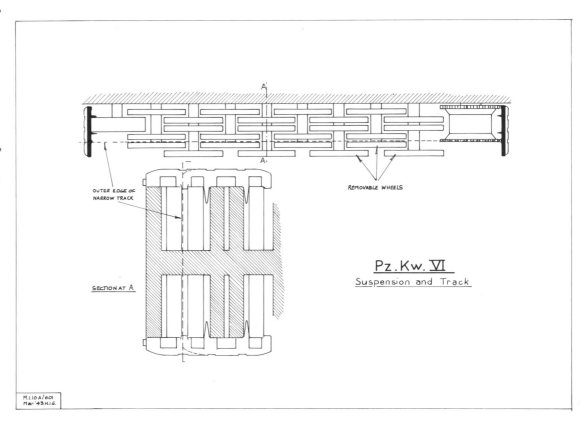

Pz.Kw. VI
Suspension and Track

SECTION AT A

OUTER EDGE OF NARROW TRACK

REMOVABLE WHEELS

M.I.10A/601
Mar '43 H.I.G.

Measurements

Track pitch	5.125 in
Pin hole diameter	1.15 in
Track pin diameter	1.10 in
Pin clearance	.05 in
Mean working pitch	5.175 in

The following additional data has been obtained from photographs:

Number of links per track	92
Length of track on ground	12 ft 6 in

This additional data enables the following to be calculated:

Total weight both tracks (wide type)	5 tons 9 cwt
Track pressure (assuming laden weight 56 tons and no sinkage)	14.7 lbs per sq. in

Since neither the sprocket nor the idler are high off the ground a small sinkage will produce an appreciable reduction in the track pressure.

Detail views comparing the narrow transport tracks with the wider variety used in action.

By the time the British examiners had finished with the first Tiger it was a sorry sight. The final drive assembly and the turret ring are two of the more recognizable items in these views.

Towards the end of March 1943 additional information was forthcoming from North Africa in the form of a Secret Cypher Telegram.

From:– 18 Army Group HQ
To:– The War Office
Recd. 0930, 29 Mar.43
AFVT 9 cipher 28 Mar. Most Secret.
  For Lucas from Rycroft.
Remains of demolished German Mk. VI tank examined. Assume you have seen Barlow's report. Following information additional. All dimensions millimetres. Suspension Torsion Bar. Bar diameter 55 length to A arm 1930 spline length 89. Shock absorbers front and rear units only mounted inside hull. Bogie wheel outside diameter 794. Three tyres per wheel two one side one another arranged alternatively thus if leading bogie has single tyre outside second bogie has single tyre inside. Tyres 70 wide 50 deep to edge of securing ring. Section tyre being flown to you. Centre front and rear bogies 3733. Track pitch 150 pin diameter 27 secured by spring rings in cannelures on pin. Distance between inner and outer sprocket rings measured at tooth centres 489. Engine V12 petrol. Steering apparently not as Mk. III. Details not obtainable. Internal diameter turret ring 1829. Crowded ball race. Total length gun less muzzle brake 4927. Centre trunnions to breech face 1104. Last dimension open to doubt.

Second only to the armour protection, the performance of the Tiger's main armament was of vital importance to those who would have to confront it. Until a complete tank mounted weapon could be tested by the Allies they would have to draw comparisons from the closest known weapon, the 88mm Flak 36. The School of Tank Technology released this interim data ➜

8.8 cm. (3.46 in.) TANK GUN (8.8 cm Kw.K. 36)

1. GENERAL
The new German Pz.Kw.VI is armed with an 8.8 cm gun which is an adaption of the 8.8 cm multi-purpose gun (Flak 36). It is not at present known to what extent this gun has been modified for tank mounting, and the details given below apply to the 8.8 cm Flak 36 in its original form.

  The breech mechanism is semi-automatic and loading is carried out by an automatic rammer operating in conjunction with a loading tray.

2. AMMUNITION
  (i) APCBC shell: Weight of projectile 21.03 lbs.
  (ii) H.E.   shell: Weight of projectile 20.34 lbs.

3. PENETRATION (APCBC Ammunition)

Range	Thickness of homogeneous armour			
Yds.	30		normal	
	mm	ins	mm	ins
1000	105	4.1	120	4.7
1500	93	3.7	106	4.2
2000	80	3.1	93	3.7

4. PARTICULARS OF GUN
Muzzle Velocity	2690 f/s
Rate of fire (practical)	15–20 r.p.m.
Length of piece	56 cals.
Reference:	The 8.8cm Flak 36 is fully described in Notes on Enemy Weapons No. 33.

Technical Intelligence Summary No. 102, dated 9 April 1943, contained most of the information that had been contained in the Secret Cipher Telegram from North Africa of 28 March, it added the fact that the V12 engine was a Maybach and followed it up with a few features that were less certain.

Appendix D to the above report contains what is probably the first attempt by British Intelligence to produce a three-view dimensional drawing of the Tiger which, understandably, suffered most in the plan view.

B. *Additional information which is subject to confirmation*

Crew	5
Ammunition carried	
8.8 cm	86 rounds
7.92 mm	46 belts (number of rounds per belt not stated)

Turret ring protection
No splash strip is fitted for protection of the turret ring.

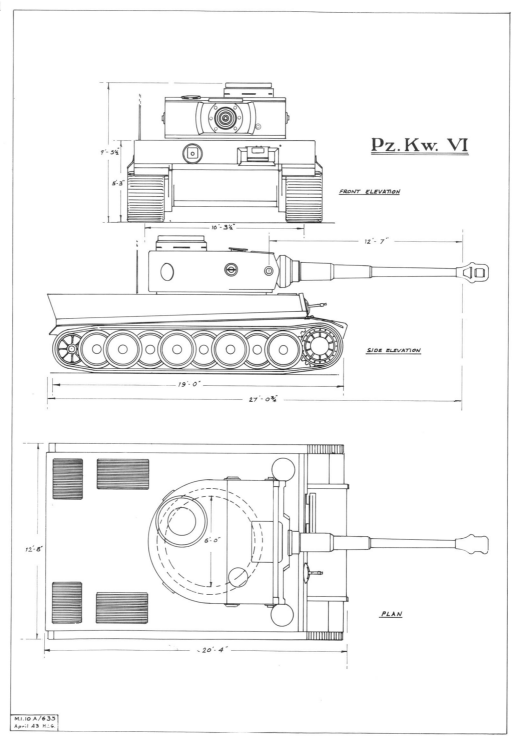

Pz. Kw. VI

FRONT ELEVATION

SIDE ELEVATION

PLAN

M.I.10 A/635
April 43 H.G.

It was still the business of the tracks, and the different widths, that was so baffling.

EXTRACT FROM R.A.C. LIAISON LETTER NO: I
TO NORTH AFRICAN FORCES

10. *GERMAN MARK VI TANK*
The width of the German Mark VI tank is:—
    With 21in   tracks   11 ft 0in
    With 28½in   tracks   12 ft 4in
Although this is wider than the nominal loading gauge of French and German railways it is known that by special loading the Germans do manage to take vehicles of over 11' in width.
2.4.43

An altogether more studied approach to the loading gauge question came from the Enemy Weapons Establishment.

The railway loading gauge on the Continent.

7 May 1943   in R.165
This note on the Continental Railway Loading Gauge points out that whereas the British Loading Gauge for unrestricted travel allows a width of only 8 ft 9in and the absolute maximum width of 9 ft 6in involves considerable restrictions, on the continent the international loading gauge allows a width of 10 ft 4in subject only to reservations that each country may notify the Union of lines on which it can only accept stock to the old width of 10 ft 2in. A list of French so excluded is referred to.

German building instructions are quoted which demand clear spaces of 13 ft 2in, 14 ft 6in and 16 ft 4in wide in various circumstances, indicating that on many lines tanks could be carried of a width considerably exceeding the present British limit of 9 ft 6in.
EWEM/HWR

The Russians, it will be remembered, had been asked back in December 1942 to supply whatever material they could on the Tiger. It is not clear if the material that M.I.10 published was all that was sent or if it was the balance after what we already knew had been edited out. If the former is true then it reveals some odd priorities.

Perhaps this information lost something in the translation.

Information on Pz.Kw. VI from 30 Military Mission, Moscow
30 April, 1943

1. *Submersion*
The Pz.Kw. VI is submersible to a maximum depth of 5 metres (16 ft 5 in) for deep water fording.
(a) All openings are hermetically sealed.
(b) Air for the engine is supplied through an overhead pipe (it is the length of this pipe which limits the fordable depth to 5 metres). There appears to be no additional air supply for the crew when submerged.
(c) Valves are arranged in the exhaust system which close automatically when the engine stops and so prevent water entering.
(d) The fans of the engine cooling system are switched off before submersion.
(e) A water-tight partition between the engine and the radiators enables the latter to be cooled by the external water when the tank is submerged.

2. *Gearbox*
The gearbox, which is similar to that on the Pz.Kw..III, is very well made. It is air cooled by a fan which also cools the exhaust manifold. (NOTE presumably this means it is similar to the Variorex gearbox fitted in the older Pz.Kw.III tanks).

3. *Steering*.
The tank is normally steered by a steering wheel, but supplementary levers are fitted for negotiating especially sharp bends.

4. *Optical instruments*
All of unusually good quality. The tank gunsight is a binocular telescope with a wide field of view. A range scale is fitted on one half only.

5. *8.8 cm gun*
The gun is well-balanced, but details of the means employed for this purpose are not given.

M.I.10
The War Office
4 May 43

NOTES ON TANK TACTICS

Another fruitful source of information, when it can be trusted, is that derived from interrogating prisoners of war. The amount of information a man might impart, over and above the 'name, rank and number' required by the Geneva Convention, would probably owe as much to his personality and state of mind as to the skill and techniques of his interrogators. Prisoners' statements formed part of an interesting set of notes published in the R.A.C. Liaison Letter issued in April 1943.

I. USE OF Pz Kw VI ('TIGER').
(a) Information obtained from PW indicates that the Pz Kw VI was chiefly used in Tunisia to support other armoured units, and mention was made of its employment as mobile artillery. As a support tank it was always used in rear of lighter units. In one reported skirmish however, the lighter Pz Kw IIIs and IVs formed the spearhead of the advance; as soon as our tanks came within range the German 'spearhead' tanks deployed to the flanks, leaving the heavier Pz Kw VI tanks to engage.

(b) A PW who was with RHQ 7 Pz Regiment in Tunisia for some time states that there were some 20 Pz Kw VIs in the regiment. When on the march ten of these moved with the main column, the others moving on the flanks. According to this PW, the tactics in the attack were to seek to engage enemy tanks from hull-down positions at short ranges, even down to 250 yards. On the other hand, this prisoner also reports an engagement in which two Pz Kw VIs brought indirect fire to bear, observation being carried out by an artillery F O O, each tank opening with one round of smoke. In confirmation of this there is another A.F.H.Q. report which speaks of this exploitation by Pz Kw VI gunners of the great range of their 8.8 cm guns.

(c) 30 Military Mission also reports the use of Pz Kw VI in squadron strength on various parts of the Russian Front, especially the South-West.

(d) In conversation with General Martel, Marshal Stalin stated that in Russia, as in the desert, the Pz Kw VI went into battle in rear of a protective screen of lighter tanks.

(e) An A.F.H.Q. training instruction states that the size and weight of the Pz Kw VI present many problems. PW indicated that extensive reconnaissance of terrain, bridges etc., was necessary before operations with this tank could be undertaken. Bridges had to be reinforced in many cases, and it was necessary for the 'going' to be good for the effective employment of the Pz Kw VI.

British Military Intelligence had to rely on the German press for photographs of Tigers in service. This explains the poor quality of these views of two tanks belonging to the 1st Company of the 501st Heavy Tank Battalion.

(f) It would seem that the employment of this tank in a support role is not however invariable, because a German press report of the fighting round Kharkov in March seems to indicate that the Pz Kw VI were used offensively in an independent role.

(g) Another German press report states that during the German withdrawl from Schüsselburg, 'a few' Pz Kw VI formed the most rearward element of the German rearguard, a role in which they were most successful.

(h) An interesting and detailed newspaper article, written towards the end of May, on events on the Leningrad Front, points towards the use of the Tiger as a mobile defensive pillbox. The tanks are described as operating on a defensive front and as having been in action 'for days' (i.e. by inference, that they had been in the same area). These operations were carried out in close co-operation with the infantry manning the defensive positions.

In one particular operation a troop of tanks is described as taking up a defensive position forward of the infantry positions from which (presumably hull-down) advancing Soviet tanks and the following infantry were engaged. All this defensive fire was put down at the halt including the fire from the MGs in the tanks. In order to move to an alternative position because of enemy arty fire it was necessary for the tank commander to obtain permission from the CO Battle Group, under whose command he was operating.

Conclusion: The use of Pz Kw VI tanks in both attack and defence seems, from all available information to hand, to be in a support role.

The use of this type of tank in an independent thrusting role, even when supported by tanks of lighter types, would seem to be discouraged.

II. *USE OF A F Vs IN NORTH AFRICA*

(a) A PW has described how riflemen with MGs were employed for the protection of tanks when in harbour. On the following morning they were withdrawn from this task for rest and in preparation for other duties.

(b) A PW reports that German tanks were always able to intercept Allied RT, on one occasion obtaining in this way an exact location. Pz Kw VI were immediately detailed to engage.

(c) *Voluntary destruction of tanks.*
On 5th December 1942 the following orders were issued by OC 8 Pz Regiment:
'Tanks may be blown up in the following circumstances only:
(i) if the tank cannot be moved
(ii) if the enemy is attacking, and then only,
(iii) if the tank has defended itself to its last round.
The Commander responsible for issuing the order to blow up the tank must make a report to R H Q detailing the circumstances.'

(d) Another report describes as 'typical' a case in which a large concentration of tanks was observed opposite one area on our front, small parties of which were observed 'tapping' along our front, halting to fire from about 2,000 yards.

(e) On another occasion another report describes how an estimated total of 50 German tanks put in a counter-attack in the early evening in two groups, each under smoke cover.

The deliberate destruction of valuable tanks like the Tiger was a desperate measure to prevent them falling into Allied hands. These two machines appear to have become bogged in soft ground and the demolition charges have blown the turrets clear off.

American soldiers examine the turretless hull of a Tiger. The Fiefel supplementary air cleaners, with their associated piping, were fitted to tanks used in the dusty conditions of North Africa. The cooling slits in the exhaust pipe covers identify this as an early model Tiger.

T.I. Summary No. 104 was issued on 16 May 1943. It repeated itself and other sources in many respects but there were new items as well.

Pz Kw VI

The following additional information on the Pz Kw VI has been collated from captured documents and reports from Russia and North Africa:—

(a) The tank can be submerged to a depth of up to 16 ft for fording rivers and other water obstacles. Further information on this development is contained at Appendix C.

(b) An automatic fire extinguisher is provided. Heat-sensitive elements are arranged in suitable positions in the engine compartment. If fire breaks out, one of these elements will cause an electric circuit to operate the extinguisher which will thereupon discharge a fire-extinguishing agent for a period of seven seconds. If the fire is severe, the circuit will remain closed and the process will be repeated one or more times until either the fire is put out or the reservoir of the fire extinguisher is exhausted. The reservoir holds 9 lbs of extinguishing agent.

(c) The gearbox is preselective and is cooled by a fan which also cools the manifold.

(e) Standard German petrol with an octane number of 74 or 78 is used for the engine.

(f) Reference summary 102, appendix D, North Africa now reports that the total amount of 8.8 cm ammunition carried is 92 rounds stowed in racks and bins, 46 rounds each side of the tank.

(g) It is confirmed that the 8.8 cm tank gun is electrically fired.

(h) Oil capacities are as follows:—

Engine	: 28 litres (6.2 galls)
Gearbox and steering units (common sump)	: 32 litres (7 galls)
Final drive units	: 8 litres (14 pints)
Turret traversing gear	: 5 litres (8.75 pts)
Fan drive	: 6 litres (10.5 pts)

British Army examiners erecting the submerged breathing tube on the engine deck of a captured Tiger in Tunisia.

SUBMERSIBLE TANKS

Apparently the author of this review was not aware of the fact that German submerging techniques had been developed as long ago as 1940, for use at sea during the projected invasion of Britain. However, since he obviously appreciated the problem of flotation, he may well have been involved in the contemporary British experiments along the same lines that were tested on a Mark I Cruiser at Christchurch.

The delays and difficulties involved in the transport of tanks across the rivers of Eastern Europe have no doubt forced the Germans to consider very seriously the possible devices for enabling their standard tanks to cross such water obstacles under their own power.

By the summer of 1941, the weight of the Pz. Kw. III had already been increased by the fitting of additional armour and it must have been clear that future developments in armour and armament would necessarily involve still further increases in the weight of this tank. While the trend towards increased weight was in many ways disadvantageous, it was definitely helpful in overcoming one of the major difficulties hitherto encountered in adapting standard tanks for submersion, namely the difficulty of obtaining sufficient adhesion.

It is therefore not surprising that the Germans, in the early stages of their campaign in Russia, were actively experimenting with standard Pz Kw IIIs modified for submersion. These experiments met with a certain degree of success, and under-water river crossings were reported to have been made with these modified tanks under service conditions. The measures employed, according to a report from the Russians, included the sealing of all joints and openings in the tank with indiarubber and the fitting of a flexible air pipe, the free end of which was attached to a float. The supply of air for the crew as well as for the engine was provided for by this flexible pipe. The maximum depth of submersion was five metres (16 ft) and the time taken by a trained crew to prepare the tanks was about 24 hours.

In April 1943 a Pz Kw III, model M examined in North Africa was found to be permanently modified for immersion, if not submersion. There was no mention in the report on this tank of a flexible pipe with float, but this may have been destroyed, since the tank, when examined, had been completely burnt out.

The engine air louvres were provided with cover plates having rubber sealing strips around their edges. These cover plates, which were normally held open by strong springs, could be locked in the closed position before submersion by hooks. After submersion, the springs could be released by Bowden cable from inside the tank. When submerged, both carburettor air and air for the cooling fans were apparently drawn from the fighting compartment. If therefore a flexible pipe were used with this tank no doubt its purpose would be to supply air to the fighting compartment to replace that withdrawn for the carburettor and cooling fans. The two exhaust pipes led to a single silencer mounted high on the tail plate with its outlet at the top. This outlet was fitted with a spring-loaded non-return valve, which during normal running could be secured in the fully open position.

More recently still, documents and reports from Russia have shown that the standard Pz Kw VI (Tiger) is equipped for submersion to depths of up to 5 metres (16ft). In this tank there is provision for hermetically sealing all joints and openings, the doors and covers being provided with suitable rubber seals. The radiators were seperated from the engine by a water-tight partition so that, when the tank is submerged, they can be cooled by water from outside the tank, the cooling fans having been previously switched off. Carburettor air in this case is drawn through a vertical pipe assembled from a number of short sections, but there appears to be no additional supply of air for the crew. A small bilge pump is also fitted to dispose of any water which may leak into the hull through the various seals, packing and stuffing boxes.

It is clear that the Pz. Kw. VI requires only the minimum amount of preparation by the crew before submersion and that its design must be influenced ab initio by the requirement that it should be readily submerged. It is quite possible that the Pz Kw VI could be submerged to greater depths than 5 metres, if it were fitted with a longer air pipe since, although this tank is little larger than the Pz Kw III, it is nearly three times as heavy and track adhesion is unlikely to be a serious problem.

The odd references so far encountered regarding the Tiger's gearbox reveal that this aspect of the design was hardly understood at all up to now. Even when a copy of a Tiger Driver's Handbook was obtained and translated it only explained how to work it; not how it worked. However, a transmission expert at the Department of Tank Design was able to make some astute deductions once he had studied it and, in so doing, to advance a theory that Britain may, unwittingly, have had a hand in the design of the Tiger itself!

A.D.T.D. (G.D.)
Attention Major Stearne

SECRET
Under Cover

Pz Kw VI

I have read with extreme interest the translation of the German Driving Instructions for the Pz Kw VI.

From sections 6 & 7 of these instructions, it is clear that the machine is equipped with the Merritt Controlled Differential Steering system in conjunction with a Maybach preselective change speed mechanism.

The Merritt system is now employed in Churchill, Cromwell and Centaur in conjunction with a David Brown manually operated change speed mechanism; but the original application was to A16E1 in which it was used with Maybach change speed. The original and only experimental Merritt/Maybach box is still available at D.T.D., and is still in A16E1, although the machine is not a runner owing to lack of tracks, sprockets and other spares.

It is clear from the driving instructions that the Pz Kw VI does not materially differ from the original A16 design, which gave 7 forward and three reverse speeds, and two radii of turn in each gear, together with a neutral turn (i.e. the vehicle spins on its axis). The following table gives the radii of turn for comparison on A16 & Cromwell.

Cromwell Z5 Merritt/Brown transmission

Gear	Overall Ratio	Turning Radius ft
N	Inf.	0
1	43	18.3
2	17	33.7
3	10.6	54
4	6.7	86
5	5	115

A16E1 Experimental Tank

Turning Radius Small	Large	Overall Ratio	Gear
0	0	Inf.	N
8.7	26	31	1
12.2	36.7	22.1	2
17.5	52	15.5	3
24.5	73	11.1	4
34	102	7.9	5
48	145	5.54	6
69	207	3.95	7

It should be noted that the A16 design was complicated, as is shown in the schematic layout. The present day Merritt/Brown gearbox is a development from this design, which is much simplified, smaller, lighter, easier to service and requiring many less man-hours to make. The enemy, however, has shown by the Variorex and Aphon type transmissions fitted to the Pz Kw III & IV that he is not afraid of complexity, expenditure of man-hours or the lavish use of ball and roller bearings.

It thus appears that the enemy has put into production (no doubt in a slightly modified form) a design which was originally evolved in the 'M' Section of the Design Department, Royal Arsenal, Woolwich, which is now embodied in D.T.D. It is probable that the means by which the information reached the enemy was the fact that the Change Speed mechanism of the original design was evolved in conjunction with the Design Department by Maybach Gears Ltd. This was a British company, the directors being at that time: General Sir Hubert Gough, A.H. Cranmer, MIAE, C.E.F. Plutte and Ernst Schneider. The last named is a German subject who returned to Germany just before the outbreak of hostilities.

These notes are forwarded for immediate information and in the meantime, a full report on the Merritt/Maybach transmission as we know it is in course of preparation. This will be amplified as soon as we have had an opportunity of examining the gearbox out of an actual Pz Kw VI. We would therefore urge the importance of obtaining in addition to the complete machines which have already been requested, a complete Pz Kw VI transmission for destructive examination.

D.T.D.   (E. McEwen)
Chobham Lane   A.D.T.D. (transmission)
Longcross
19 May 43

The vision of Ernst Schneider, furtively boarding the Boat Train at Victoria with the plans of A16E1 rolled up and tucked under his arm is as engaging as the knowledge that a Government Department, involved in top-secret tank designs, was working hand in hand with a British cadet branch of a major German company is mortifying.

Meanwhile, back in North Africa, a fully operational Tiger had fallen into British hands and a telegram gave brief details of an early examination ➔

SECRET CIPHER TELEGRAM

THIS MESSAGE WILL NOT BE DISTRIBUTED OUTSIDE BRITISH OR U.S. GOVERNMENT DEPARTMENT OF HEADQUARTERS OR RE-TRANSMITTED EVEN IN CIPHER WITHOUT BEING PARAPHRASED.

From: Main Eighth Army   Recd. 2000 23 May 43
To: The War Office

IMMEDIATE
For Lucas from Blagden Rycroft.
One. Examination German Mk.VI Tiger reveals important features. (A) Tank adapted for very deep wading probably over 12 feet with turret completely submerged. (B) Width less than previously reported being 11 feet 9 inches overall with cross country tracks. With road track width should be approx 10 feet 6 inches bringing it within Continental railway loading gauge. (C) Steering by wheels exhibits same characteristics as Merritt Brown but skid brake levers also provided. (D) Engine 63 (or 60) degree Vee twelve cylinder with light alloy block wet liners and cast iron heads. Approx measurements bore 125mm stroke 143mm. Roller main bearings large diameter on circular crankweb.

Two. Hope to ship runner to UK early after rough trials here. Armour trials also in preparation. Full written report follows.

The promise of a fully operational Tiger seems to have put a stop to much of the more speculative reporting but in the meantime some interesting in-depth reports appeared on the subject of armour protection.

The outstanding metallurgical features of the samples examined are the high carbon content of approximately .5 per cent, in association with chromium of 2.5 per cent and molybdenum of .55 per cent, and the low Izod value of 4—11 ft lbs associated with this richly alloyed composition.

The type of steel is new in our experience of the examination of German armour, and the reasons for the use of the high carbon content, together with the high percentage of chromium and molybdenum, are not clear. Properly heat treated, the composition should be capable of giving an Izod of the order of at least 25—30 ft lbs, and the low value observed in the samples would seem to indicate that the full heat treatment had not been employed. It seems probable that the steel was hardened by air cooling after rolling, and the peculiarities of the composition may have been chosen with this end in view. The enemy may also have in mind flame hardening of the steel, and on this assumption the composition chosen also has a bearing.

Recent trials carried out by Col. Blagden in the Middle East with 6-pdr and 75mm ammunition at short range against the side armour of the Pz Kw VI, and the consequent break up of the shot which occurred led Col. Blagden to believe that the plate was face-hardened. While we do not consider that this forms conclusive evidence, we do not discount the possibility, having regard, as above mentioned, to the composition of the steel employed.

Against the 6-pdr attack one at least of the plates which form the subject of the present report behaved well, but, as noted, it is considered that the samples are too few and too small to allow of final conclusions being made as to their real quality.

3.6.43   Assistant Director (Armour)

DEPARTMENT OF TANK DESIGN
ARMOUR BRANCH
SIDE ARMOUR OF PZ. KW. VI
COMMENTS ON FIRING TRIALS CARRIED OUT IN N. AFRICA

The firing trial results obtained are as follows, the target in all cases being the superstructure side (82mm) of the Pz Kw VI.
   (a)   75 mm   M61,   100 yards at 30   plate immune
   (b)   75mm   M61,   100 yards at 18½   shot not through
   (c)   75mm   M61,   100 yards at 16½   shot holed the plate
   (d)   Mk III 6-pdr A.P. failed through shatter *at all angles* at range of 100 yards. The gun was much worn.

75mm M61 versus 82 mm of armour, homogeneous and face hardened
This is an A.P.C.B.C. H.E. projectile of weight 14.4 lbs.

In the tables below are given its expected performances against American homogeneous and face-hardened plates, the figures being taken from curves issued by the American Ordnance Office, Ballistic Section (res. & Eng), 7 March 1942. Estimated performance against British Machinable quality armour of I.I. 80D is also shown. The figures here are obtained by scaling up from the 6-pdr, the projectile being assumed to be a   ▶

solid shot of the same weight and calibre. The usual allowances are made for the presence of the two caps ....

At 100 yards, with a new gun, the striking velocity should be of the order of 2020 f.s. The results of (b) and (c) above give a critical angle, success/failure, of 16½–18½ at S.V. 2020 f.s. These are in good agreement with the tabled estimated performance against face-hardened armour at 20 and S.V. 2075 f.s.

On the other hand it may be that German homogeneous armour of this thickness is sufficiently superior to American armour for the trials results to be in agreement with the tabled estimated performance against homogenous armour at 20 and 1975 f.s. Moreover there is sufficient uncertainty about the correct values of M.V. and S.V. in the M.E. trial to make it impossible on this evidence to reach any definite conclusion about the type of German armour.

6 Pdr versus Pz.Kw. VI

A certain amount of information on one captured Pz. Kw. VI is available, most of it relating to another sample of the plate under discussion.

(a) *Assessment of damage in battle*

    6 pdr (presumed A.P.) versus Pz. Kw. VI.

Perforations, 5 in all;	82mm turret side, range 650 yards, angle of strike about 30°.
	82mm superstructure side, range 650 yards, angle of strike about 15°.
Shot failures (all on superstructure side)	Almost through at 650 yards, angle of strike 25–30°. Scoops from 2in to 2½in deep, range 650 yards, angles of strike 35–45°.

(b) *Mechanical Tests*

Brinell figures for the turret and superstructure side plates of this same tank are as follows:—

Sample of side armour	*Brinell Hardness figures from N. Africa*	*Brinell Hardness figures, examination by Messrs Hadfields*
Turret	340	325–345
Superstructure	324	315–321

These figures confirm the evidence of the trial that these particular samples of 82 mm side armour could not have been face-hardened. Any possible defeat of this thickness of plate at the approximate angles quoted would have been by shatter, while failure would have been by shatter dents, not scoops. Neither success nor failure by shatter gives any indication of the direction of strike.

The shatter of shot and absence of petalling have given rise to the suspicion mentioned in the cables that the Germans are face-hardening this superstructure side. But for the one phrase 'all angles of attack', neither of the two reasons would be considered as conclusive evidence.

Absence of petalling may mean no petalling at all or the shearing off of petals. Without actually seeing it, it is impossible to make any deductions from the surface impression. It is not even clear whether the absence of petalling refers to the 6-pdr attack only or to the 6-pdr and 75mm attacks. If the former, then a shattering shot does not normally leave petals on the surface of any plate. The 75 mm attack was, we presume, purely an angle one, and the plate of this hardness is most unlikely to petal under such conditions.

Shatter is the result of the action and reaction of so many factors that it is not easy to draw safe conclusions from its incidence. The shot used would presumably have passed proof, but whether that proof was the 60mm/30°/1850 f:s. one of pre-August 1942 or the current 70mm/30°/2200 f.s. is unknown. Plates for the latter would be drawn from current production to I.T. 80 D with Brinell figures normally below 300. Success at either proof gives no indication of the quality of the shot when tested against an 82mm plate of Brinell 3204+. This latter is comparable to a standard I.T.80 C plate. Even with a worn-out gun the S.V. at 100 yards is likely to be at least 2400 f.s. Under these conditions and at 20° or possibly even less there is every likelihood of the shot shattering.

It is a little more difficult to account for the shatter at normal attack if this is included in the phrase 'at all angles', except in so far as the shot may have been very unstable. We assume that with a worn gun there is liable to be considerable yaw, and the attack and its results will approximate to those at true angle of attack.

There is no reason to suppose that the face-hardening suspicion may not be confirmed later. All we can say at the moment is that the reasons for the suspicion can be accounted for almost equally well by a variety of other causes- poor quality of shot, good quality hard armour, instability of flight and high velocity. The one specimen of plate that we have received in this country is certainly not face-hardened.

(H. Harris-Jones)
O. i/c Ballistics Section

5.6.43

T.I. Summary No 106, issued on 9 June 1943, shows that news had now reached London regarding another version of the Tiger.

Indeed it was, although there is no suggestion here that M.I.10 realized that the two designs were rivals in the same project or that the Porsche version, the loser, had just entered limited production as the self-propelled gun Ferdinand.

At the same time they published more technical information obtained from the USSR; most of it had been seen before but there was some new data on the engine.

Reference Summary 104 para 8, it is now established from captured documents that there are at least two different types of Pz.Kw. VI (Tiger) tank, namely the Pz. Kw. VI (H) which is the type that has been in action in North Africa and Russia, and the Pz. Kw. VI (P) which is believed to have smaller bogie wheels. The Pz Kw VI (H) is understood to have been developed by Henschel, but it is not known what is the significance of the letter P in the case of the other type, though it has been suggested that it may have some connection with Dr Porsche, the well-known designer.

MAYBACH. Bears label 650 h.p. Has no booster or supercharger
4 carburettors
3 oil cleaners (oil with metal mesh)
Governor fitted
Maximum revs. probably 3000 r.p.m.

Commenting on this
M.I.10 stated →

The bore and stroke of the Pz. Kw. VI(H) engine have recently been reported from N. Africa as 125 mm and 143 mm respectively and the cubic capacity would, therefore appear to be about 21 litres. 650 metric b.h.p. would appear to be an exceptionally high power output for an engine of this class.

A P/W interrogated on this point has stated that the figure on the name plate would be obtained at an engine speed of about 3600. At 3000 revs, running on standard 74 octane petrol, the output would not be above 600 metric b.h.p. Any comments on this explanation would be appreciated.

M.I.10
9 Jun 43

The summer months passed without any further references to the Tiger that were of any value. However T.I. Summary No.111 of 5 September 1943 included drawings and a brief description of the new pattern smoke generator, an example of which had been sent home from Tunisia.

SMOKE GENERATORS ON A.F.Vs

Further details are now available of the new type of smoke generator discharger fitted on the PzKw VI and on the latest models of the PzKw III. An illustration of the individual discharger is given at appendix J.

A normal thermal smoke generator (NbK 39 or NbK S 39) is used. German army orders have also announced the introduction of new smoke generators (NbK Wldg. 1) for these dischargers (Nebelkerzen Wurfgerät), so that presumably the use of the ordinary smoke generators will be discontinued when the new models become available.

The discharger is fired electrically by push button, of which there is a panel of 3 on each side of the commander's seat.

The single pin contact (1) is held by a spring clip (2) on to the discharger base (3) so that current can pass to the brass electric primer (4) which screws into the discharger from the back. The electric primer is similar to those supplied for A.F.V. cartridge cases.

The primer fires a charge of granular black powder contained in a transparent plastic capsule (5) which has a small diameter threaded extension by which it is screwed into the base of the generator (6). This propels the generator from the discharger and at the same time flashes the ignition tube 'N4' (7), fitted into the central channel of the generator. After a short delay smoke is emitted from the generator.

Comment. As with the smoke generator rack normally fitted to the rear of German tanks, there is no means of reloading the dischargers in the heat of battle.

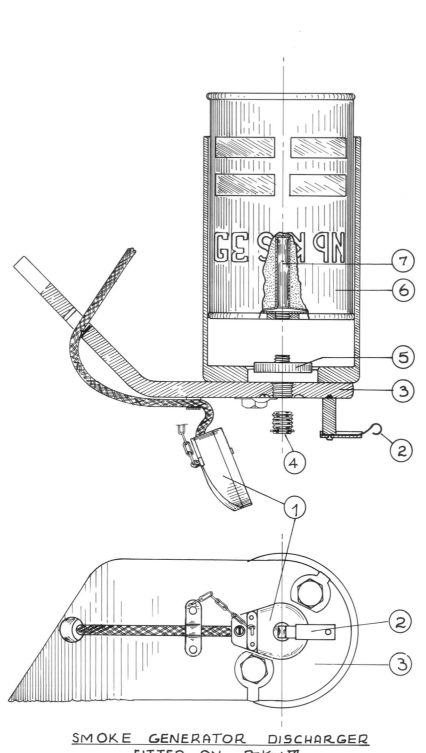

SMOKE GENERATOR DISCHARGER
FITTED ON PzKw VI

Another unusual item to fall into Allied hands was an individual logbook from a Tiger tank. M.I.10 circulated an edited selection of entries in translated form. There is no suggestion that any of the relevations were typical of Tigers in general and it is not at all clear what their value was. Examination of enemy equipment is an exact science, the tape measure or the Brinnell testing machine cannot lie and a well-trained engineer can make all manner of concrete deductions from what he can see and touch. On the other hand any attempt to establish precisely how and why he uses that equipment as he does is much less reliable sincc it calls for a good deal of theorizing. Naturally the art of war is based on many immutable factors so that one professional soldier can make some pretty safe assumptions about his opposite number but, in the last resort, this is bound to involve a fair amount of educated guesswork. When the enemy is obliged to conduct his operations in less than ideal circumstances, for instance when his back is to the wall and his resources diminished, it is that much harder to explain his actions. This is borne out in a review of German tactics in Tunisia,

Mechanical behaviour under service conditions

NOTE ON ENTRIES IN LOG BOOK OF PZ.KW.VI (H)
Chassis No: 250131

1. Entries show that 4917 litres of petrol went into the fuel tanks of this vehicle during a period in which 489 km were covered. In other words, the apparent petrol consumption was over *10 litres per km*. Even if it is assumed that the tanks (total capacity 530 litres) were empty at the start and full at the finish, the consumption would still work out at about *9 litres per km*.

These figures are higher than the petrol consumption quoted in the official German specs, viz:—

Roads. 4.5 litres per km. 1.58 galls per mile.
Cross country. 7.8 litres per km. 2.76 galls per mile.

2. The following additional points have been noted in the log book:—

120 km	Log started.
136 km	Wireless tested.
160 km	Test run by workshops company.
200 km	Wireless tested. Engine oil and air cleaner oil.
343 km	New gearbox fitted.
365 km	Tooth sprocket ring (offside sprocket) changed.
482 km	New engine and new nearside fan drive clutch fitted.
529 km	Engine oil filter cleaned.
609 km	Log closes.

At first his Tigers were very boldly used and, once they were sure that their flanks were secured, they drove straight on. After several of these tanks had been knocked out, however, the crews appeared to be less enterprising and were inclined to use their tanks as mobile pillboxes. The fact remains, however, that in an armoured attack the Tiger tank must be regarded as a very formidable fighting component and, given adequate flank protection, will add very effective weight to the enemy firepower.

In the defensive the Pz Kw VI, usually well sited in a covered and defiladed position, was a particular danger. Despite the comparatively slow traversing rate of its turret, the Pz Kw VI proved an extremely good defensive weapon and could effectively cover a wide area with anti-tank fire. It was often used in good hull-down positions over very difficult ground, which made it hard for the Sherman to deal with it, and no amount of artillery fire could force it out.

Pz Kw IIIs and IVs rarely took up good defensive positions on their own, but were used to watch the flanks of positions occupied by Pz Kw VIs. They were often used in small groups to counter-attack from concealed positions on the flank, from a cactus or olive grove or down a wadi. The terrain forced the enemy to employ rush tactics in close formation, and resulted in these counter-attacks being suitably dealt with.

Tank recovery requires a special note. It was often affected on the spot with speed and courage by attaching tow ropes to the casualties and towing them away by other tanks. Special trips at night were made by

issued by the Director, Royal Armoured Corps, on 4 September 1943. He began with a general assessment of the situation, pointing out that shortages in both material and fuel often cramped the enemy's style. It was also pointed out that the tactics employed at this time were caused mainly by these circumstances and that it should not be taken to indicate a general abandoning of previously held doctrines.

tanks to recover casualties (20 Jan BOU ARADA, and 1 Feb ROBAA). Where the enemy held the battlefield, tractors were brought up and the whole area cleared of recoverable casualties, both theirs and ours, in a very short time. The speed with which the recovery plan was made and carried out made action by our demolition squads very difficult, and where tank casualties were in no-man's-land and unapproachable by day, the enemy would get out to them the moment darkness fell. Sometimes (e.g. ROBAA, BOU ARADA) as much as a company of infantry was used to hold off our patrols or stage a diversion while recovery was in progress.

The enemy used tanks against our Churchills and was quick to take advantage of an unprotected flank.

The Tiger, the embodiment of the might of the Panzers, provided headline material for the German press.

Later in the month M.I.10 released some more information gleaned from prisoners of war. Some of their statements are quite interesting.

'The compression ratio of the 12 litre engine in the Pz Kw III is 12 and that of the 28 litre Pz Kw VI engine is 12½ s.q.

An effort is being made to discover how P/W measures compression ratio. He is very fond of obscure mathematical notations and it is thought that his figures for compression ratios may take into account not only volume, but pressure also.

The gun is balanced by a hydraulic ram.

The Germans do not fire on the move. P/W has tried firing on the move under ideal conditions, (concrete road) with a specially suspended tank, but it was not a success.

Another P/W (lance corporal Tank Regiment) stated that the Panther suspension is good, unlike that of Tiger where the outside front bogie wheel (when the wide tracks are fitted) is badly arranged in relation to the sprocket. Stones would get jammed between them and the track became misplaced in the sprocket. It did not come right off so one had to weld it on (NOTE the word quoted in the report is 'aufschweissen'. Possibly it should have been 'auschweissen' which would mean 'cut if off with a welding torch'). To avoid this trouble the Germans in Sicily ran the Tiger with the outside front bogie wheel removed altogether.

On 30 September 1943 the Armour Branch, Department of Tank Design, issued a detailed report on the armour, and armour arrangement of the Tiger. Considering that this was done before they had even seen a complete tank, it was a very thorough piece of work and extracts are included here since it contains much more information on the subject than ever found its way into the final report.

ARMOUR

The vehicle is constructed of rolled plates, with the exception of the mantlet, which is cast, and possibly of the cupola, which has also been reported to be cast. Thickness and angles are given below according to the latest available information. For diagram showing the arrangement of armour see Attachment (II).

Turret	Gun mantlet (cast)	97–200 mm	Vertical
	Sides & rear	82 mm	Vertical
	Top	26 mm	90
	Cupola (reported cast)	–	–
Superstructure	Front	102 mm	10
	Sides	82 mm	Vertical
	Rear	82 mm	10
	Top	26 mm	90
Hull	Upper nose plate	102 mm	25
	Lower nose plate	62 mm	60
	Glacis plate	62 mm	80
	Sides	62 mm	Vertical
	Tail	82 mm	10
	Floor	26 mm	90

All the armour examined to date has been of machineable quality high carbon 2½% Chromium Molybdenum steel. It will be noted that the Izod values are variable and low. Tests were carried out on the specimen from the turret in oil quenched and tempered, and air cooled and tempered conditions, with the results as shown below:—

Heat treatment	Izod ft. lbs	Brinell
Specimen as received	4.5	345/354
870° Oil, 620° Air	40	337
870° Air, 600° Air	19	333

It will be seen that even the air hardening treatment gives Izod impact values much higher than those obtained from the specimen in its 'as received' condition. It is therefore considered that the original specimen may have been tempered immediately after rolling, or, alternatively, that the turret plate may have been formed at a low temperature with no subsequent heat treatment.

Plates of the high carbon $1\frac{1}{4}$–$1\frac{1}{2}$% chromium molybdenum type for the Pz Kw III have also shown variability of Izod values. The suggestion has been made that these German high carbon chromium molybdenum steels do not receive a normal heat treatment but are air cooled immediately after rolling and then tempered; annealing may be carried out after rolling. On the other hand, a refining bar test carried out on a specimen from the Pz Kw III indicated that in that case the plate had been hardened and tempered. It is however possible that the high carbon $2\frac{1}{2}$% chromium molybdenum composition of the plates from the Pz Kw VI was selected as being suitable for hardening by air cooling after rolling. There must be some good reason for the Germans to use steel of such a high carbon content (0.41–0.52% in the specimen examined) for plates intended for fabrication by welding.

It has also been suggested that the Germans so frequently use a high carbon chromium molybdenum steel because of its suitability for flame-hardening. A number of the $1\frac{1}{4}$–$1\frac{1}{2}$% chromium plates of the Pz Kw III Model J are flame hardened. So far, however, there is no evidence for the use of flame hardened armour on the Pz Kw VI.

The samples from the driver's front plate and the lower nose plate were subjected to firing trials, but the pieces of plate were so small that only one round of 6 pdr A.P. could be put on each. The sample from the nose plate fractured under attack. These specimens had been obtained by blowing them out of the tank, and the piece from the nose plate was damaged when received. The specimen from the driver's front plate was not damaged and did not fracture. It is impossible to say whether or not the fracture was due to the previous damage.

Firing trials have also been carried out in North Africa. A report on the more recent trials will be issued in due course. None of the trials carried out so far has demonstrated the use of other than machineable quality armour for the Pz Kw VI, nor has the examination of battle damage. Much of the armour fired at appeared to be of variable quality and was probably experimental. Though machineable, it was frequently much harder than corresponding British armour, and in many cases it caused shot to shatter, while the plates were liable to crack and flake. The side plates from turret, hull and superstructure etc, have all been found to flake in various cases. The cast mantlet appears to be of good quality, not breaking up or cracking under heavy attack, and no case of a penetration was met. The mantlet covers the entire front of the turret and it was considered that it gives extremely good protection.

METHODS OF CONSTRUCTION

The hull is entirely welded together. The superstructure is bolted to an angle iron frame on the side walls, as is the case with other German vehicles, but in addition the joint is deeply welded. This means that the transmission units in the forward compartment are extremely inaccessible and can only be got at by removing the turret.

A British report highlighted one of the major drawbacks of the Tiger design. Because the turret had to be removed to allow replacement of the final drive unit, a massive portable gantry was an essential item for the maintenance company.

Turret and Hull

The rear and sides of the turret appear to be formed of one large horseshoe-shaped plate with the circular part at the back (photograph 3). Two narrow plates of 100 mm thickness are fitted into slots across the open (front) end of the turret and secured by welding; they form a rectangular frame to receive the mantlet, while the mantlet cheeks are formed by the turret wall. Photograph 4 shows the slot for the top plate, which has in this case been blown away. Photograph 5 shows the ends of the two cross plates, the edges of which are hollowed to fit the cylinder of the mantlet, as is seen in photographs 4 and 6 which also show the cylindrical trunnion bearing and the recess in the mantlet that takes it. The mantlet is cast in one piece, having a flat front plate 92mm thick extending over the full height and breadth of the front of the turret, which is shaped to allow free movement to this front plate when elevating or depressing the gun. The thickness of the mantlet, measured through the gun sight holes is 150 mm; in the central portion, where the front plate is reinforced round the gun, the thickness is approximately 205mm. These thicknesses of over 100 mm are only local and it is thought that the protection afforded by the mantlet as a whole would not be greater than that given by a plate of uniform thickness of 100 mm. A front view of the mantlet is shown in photograph 7.

The cupola is reported to be cast. This is not yet confirmed nor is any information available about its thickness.

45

The turret bearing is of the vertical type with the stationary race inside and the moving race outside. It is a crowded ball bearing with 40 mm balls and no cage. There are elaborate sealing arrangements. The traverse ring is in one piece with a clear diameter of 185 cm. It is comparatively lightly secured, being bolted to the top of the hull by twenty-four bolts of 18 mm diameter, with one large positioning dowel on the near front. The turret seemed to come off very easily, probably as a consequence of the lightness of the fixing. An easily removable turret is probably necessitated by the fact that, as stated above, the transmission units in the forward compartment are only accessible by removing the turret. There is no protection to the turret ring other than that afforded by the driver's vizor plate, the upper edge of which extends about 2 ins above the hull roof, which is not very effective. Another weakness is that the lower edge of the mantlet and turret front appear to deflect projectiles downwards on to the hull roof.

The turret platform is 4 ft 9 in in diameter, connected to the turret by tubular supports and without basket sides. The power traverse hydraulic gear is in the middle and there is a trapdoor at the loader's feet, which, with the turret at 12 o'clock, gives access to an ammunition bin underneath. The floor surrounding the platform is mostly occupied by ammunition bins, but in the two forward corners are cover plates each covering a set of ten grouped lubricating nipples. A total of 92 rounds of 88 mm ammunition is carried, divided between nose fuse H.E. and A.P.C.B.C. H.E.

The Pz Kw VI has a crew of five, of whom the driver and hull gunner cum wireless operator are accommodated in the forward compartment, to the near and offside of the gearbox respectively, while the commander and gunner are on the nearside with the loader and co-axial M.G. on the offside. The 88 mm gun is slightly offset to starboard and its recoil guard extends backwards until it nearly reaches the turret ring, thus dividing the fighting space into two unequal parts. The gunner's seat is well forward and low down on the port side and the commander's immediately behind it and higher up; they occupy the larger of the two portions of the chamber but both are rather cramped. The loader, with the starboard side to himself, has rather more room, but this is needed on account of the size of the ammunition. The co-axial M.G. is readily accessible.

There is no provision for the fitting of spaced armour. Spare track links are carried on the front of the vehicle, in accordance with the normal German practice.

Details of the anti-splash arrangements are not known, but there is a splash protector on the glacis plate in front of the driver's vizor. A splash trap is also fitted behind the gun mantlet in the turret.

Vision devices
There are five horizontal slits in the cupola, placed to give all-round vision. These are without shutters or other means of adjustment and in this differ from those on vehicles previously examined. Two vision ports of this same type are situated in the forward part of the turret. The driver has a vizor with a sliding double shutter in the front superstructure plate. Above the vizor are two holes for the K.F.F. type of episcope binocular but in one case at least these have been found to have been welded up. For vision on the port side he has a fixed periscope in the circular access hatch in the superstructure roof; there is a splash protector fitted on the roof. A similar periscope on the starboard side is in the hull gunner's hatch; he also has an episcopic sight fitted to the ball mounting of his

machine gun. All vision slits and ports are fitted with replaceable laminated glass blocks.

Hatches and revolver ports
A circular hatch about 19 in diameter is provided in the cupola, hinged at about 1.30 o'clock. There is a hatch of the same type in the front left of the superstructure roof, hinged at the outside edge; this is spring loaded for retarded closing and may be fixed in the half open position, and there is a broad, heavy handle on the outside. A similar hatch is fitted on the right front of the superstructure roof. In the right front of the turret roof is a rectangular hatch for the loader, 14 x 20 in, which is hinged at the leading edge; an arm on the cover engages the piston of a compression cylinder, fixed under the turret roof, for slow closing. No splash strips appear to be fitted. The hatch lids fit down over a raised edge and in conjunction with this the rubber sealing rings which are fitted to all

hatches and ports for submersion purposes would give a certain amount of splash protection.

The revolver ports are situated in the rear of the turret wall at 4 & 8 o'clock. These are placed eccentrically in an 8 in disc rotated by a hand lever. On rotation the port coincides with a similar opening on the main plate and an outer protection which is secured to the exterior of the turret by conical-headed bolts. The fact that the rotating disc is not of the full thickness of the turret plate would seem to indicate that this is a weak point in the turret wall. In some vehicles the port by the loader is replaced by a circular escape hatch of the type described above; this is clamped by a sliding bar and two hand-screws and is hinged at the bottom edge. Apart from this there are no doors in the sides of either turret or hull. It may be noted that a similar escape door in the turret of the new German Mark V 'Panther' is hinged at the side instead of the bottom.

There is a large hatch, hinged at the front edge, over the engine compartment, and two heavy grill hatches hinged at the rear, over each of the fan compartments.

Ventilation

There is a circular ventilator in the turret on the right of the cupola and another in the superstructure roof between the driver's and hull gunner's hatches. These are both fitted with electric fans and have mushroom type outlets which have to be fitted with waterproof covers before submersion. There is also a mushroom ventilator in the cover of the engine compartment which can be closed from the outside. This ventilator was probably used to a greater extent in the earlier tanks which were not fitted with pre-cleaners.

Fire Risks

The risk of fire in the Pz Kw VI would appear to be rather high. It is a petrol driven vehicle, the fuel being carried in four large tanks, holding about 125 gallons. One tank is situated in each of the two radiator fan compartments beneath the sloping air inlet, and each of these is connected with the nearer of two further tanks which are arranged one on each side of the engine inside the engine compartment. There is also the question of fire danger from ammunition; 92 rounds of 88 mm ammunition are carried in bins of light-gauge metal. It is not specifically stated but it would appear that these bins are not of armour quality. An automatic fire extinguisher is fitted in the turret.

Conclusions

(i) The Pz Kw VI (H) is a formidable vehicle, the heavy armour of which gives it a very large degree of protection. The front of the tank is immune to 6-pdr except at normal and very short range; the sides at a rather longer range, are immune at angles over 30°. Against the 75 mm Mk V the front is immune; the same conditions for the sides apply as for the 6-pdr. The 17 pdr and the 75mm, 50 calibre gun both have a reasonable chance of knocking out the tank at fighting ranges and angles. Risk of fire from both fuel and ammunition appears to be considerable from the heavier forms of attack capable of defeating the armour.

(ii) The general methods of construction of the hull and superstructure follow those adopted for the Pz Kw III & IV, but the turret is of an entirely new type, eliminating the large number of plates used in previous designs.

Sgnd. J.T. Howard Turner
O i/c Investigations & Trial Records

30.9.43

Until now the Tigers investigated by British Intelligence had all been prepared for operations in a hot dry climate. In these circumstances it seems slightly odd that the Germans should have bothered to take the deep-wading equipment with them but there were other factors that the North African theatre was even less likely to provide. On the Russian front things were very different, especially in winter. Here it was sometimes necessary to operate tanks in conditions well below freezing and this had been accounted for in the Tiger design. This extract from I.T. No. 116 of November 1943 explains.

HEATING APPARATUS USED IN Pz Kw VI(H)

The diagrams at Appendix C illustrate three types of heating apparatus used with the Pz Kw VI(H).

Diagrams 1 and 2 show two methods whereby the radiator water may be pre-heated during cold weather. The first method (Diagram 1) uses the warm water of a tank already running to warm the cooling system of the tank to be started. This is accomplished by means of two lengths of flexible hose, included in the kit of every tank, which are connected between the radiator unions of the two tanks, thus allowing water to circulate between them.

The second method (Diagram 2) makes use of a short length of pipe with water-jacket, a hand-pump keeps the water in circulation, and a blow lamp which warms up the water circulating through the jacket. The suction pipe of the hand-pump is connected to the delivery pipe of the water-cooling system, and the delivery pipe of the hand-pump is connected to the oil cooler. The water circulates as though the engine were running except that the radiator is by-passed; and this is continued until the engine is started up.

No doubt the reason why the Germans use a water cooler for the engine oil of the Pz Kw VI (H) is because, when this pre-heating system is employed, it acts as an oil heater.

Diagram 3 shows a method of warming the fighting compartment. Warm air from the engine cooling system is conveyed to the fighting compartment through a duct, attached over the left radiator, and through a flexible air pipe. The air pipe is stowed away with the duct when not required.

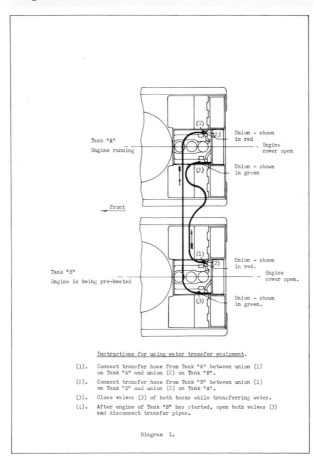

Tank "A"
Engine running

Union – shown in red
Engine cover open
Union – shown in green

front

Tank "B"
Engine is being pre-heated

Union – shown in red
Engine cover open.
Union – shown in green.

Instructions for using water transfer equipment.

(1).   Connect transfer hose from Tank "A" between union (1) on Tank "A" and union (2) on Tank "B".
(2).   Connect transfer hose from Tank "B" between union (1) on Tank "B" and union (2) on Tank "A".
(3).   Close valves (3) of both tanks while transferring water.
(4).   After engine of Tank "B" has started, open both valves (3) and disconnect transfer pipes.

Diagram 1.

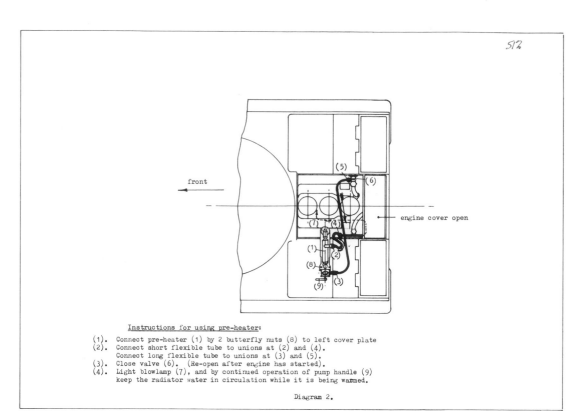

front ⟵

engine cover open

Instructions for using pre-heater:

(1). Connect pre-heater (1) by 2 butterfly nuts (8) to left cover plate
(2). Connect short flexible tube to unions at (2) and (4).
   Connect long flexible tube to unions at (3) and (5).
(3). Close valve (6). (Re-open after engine has started).
(4). Light blowlamp (7), and by continued operation of pump handle (9)
   keep the radiator water in circulation while it is being warmed.

Diagram 2.

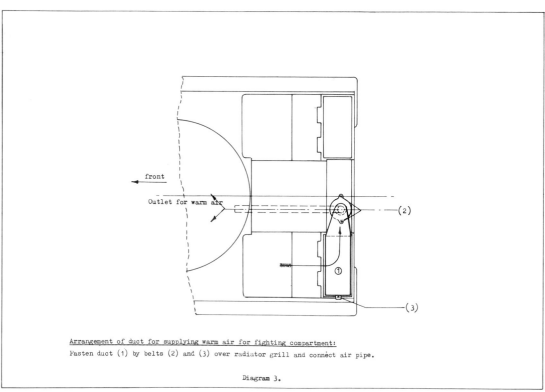

front ⟵

Outlet for warm air

(2)

(3)

Arrangement of duct for supplying warm air for fighting compartment:
Fasten duct (1) by belts (2) and (3) over radiator grill and connect air pipe.

Diagram 3.

As with the armour arrangements, so with the transmission. For some unknown reason this all-important information was not dealt with in any detail by the final report on the Tiger and the best account is to be found in a Military Intelligence Summary dated November 1943.

1. *GEARBOX*

The Maybach-Olvar gearbox provides eight forward speeds and four reverse speeds with pre-selective hydraulic engagement. The gears are arranged on a main shaft, lay shaft and reverse lay shaft, although, in fact, both main shaft and lay shafts consist of four short lengths of shaft each carrying a gear and each able to be engaged or disengaged by a dog clutch. The rearmost dog clutches on both main shaft and lay shafts are controlled by selection forks mounted on a common shaft in such a manner that when one dog is engaged, the other is free. The movement of these selector forks is controlled by a double acting hydraulic cylinder mounted on the top of the gearbox. Likewise the central pair are operated by another cylinder. The remaining dog clutch on the lay shaft is operated by a third cylinder, but has engagement with a different gear at each end of its travel (i.e. no free position). The remaining dog clutch on the main shaft and the dog clutch on the reverse are operated together by a hand lever, so that in the forward position of the hand lever the dog on the main shaft is engaged and that of the reverse shaft free, with the exact opposite for the rear position of the hand lever, whilst in the intermediate position of the hand lever both dogs are free. Thus for forward drive, once the hand lever has been placed in the forward position, all changes of gear are effected through the operation of the hydraulic cylinder. The movement of the gear change lever through its quadrant causes the rotation of a valve which determines the distribution of oil pressure to the appropriate hydraulic cylinder for the ratio required. Side pressure on the gear change lever then admits pressure to that cylinder and effects the gear change. In reverse the procedure is similar but only the four lowest ratios are available. With the exception of the final output gear and the main shaft and reverse shaft meshing with it, all gears are single helical. An extension of the final output shaft carries a spiral bevel for the main drive, whilst an extension of the main shaft carries a small straight bevel for controlling the speed of the steering differentials. At the input end of the main shaft is a multi-disc centrifugal clutch which can, however, be disengaged by the admission of hydraulic pressure to a cylinder, the piston of which operates a withdrawal fork.

The same withdrawal fork is operated by the clutch pedal. A small cone clutch on the input side of the main shaft and the rear end of the lay shaft are geared together and operated by hydraulic pressure giving synchronization of the lay shaft with the engine speed. The input shaft also drives, through two gears, a fore and aft shaft on which are mounted two oil pumps, which provide the pressure necessary for hydraulic operation. Another unit driven from this shaft is the engine rev. counter. Hydraulically operated brake shoes are provided for the slowing of the main clutch and the second gear from the input end on the main shaft, and a hydraulic device adjusts the throttle opening as required. An easily accessible oil filter is provided which serves both gearbox and steering unit which have a common oil level; the level is checked by a dip-stick on the gearbox and replenished through a filler cap. The oil capacity is 32 litres (7 gallons). A metal strip on the gearbox cover bears the following figures:

1 2 3 4 ◇3 5 6 7 8 1 3 5 7 ◇2 2 4 6 8 1 2 5 6 ◇1 3 4 7 8

which can be explained as follows: The figures within the diamonds correspond to the hydraulic cylinder of each selector. The figures before the diamonds in each case representing the number of the gear engaged

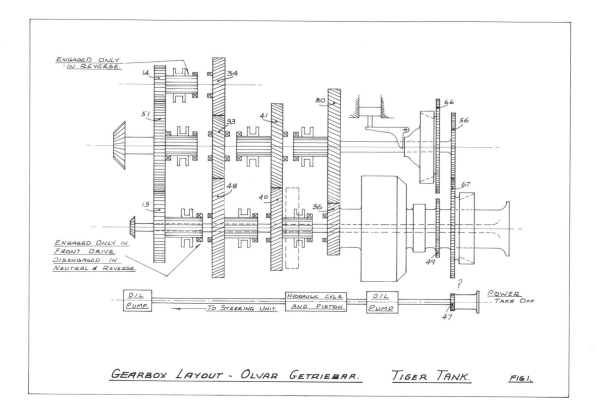

ENGAGED ONLY
IN REVERSE

ENGAGED ONLY IN
FRONT DRIVE.
DISENGAGED IN
NEUTRAL & REVERSE.

OIL PUMP   TO STEERING UNIT.   HYDRAULIC CYLR. AND PISTON   OIL PUMP   POWER TAKE OFF

GEARBOX LAYOUT - OLVAR GETRIEBAR.   TIGER TANK.   FIG 1.

with the selectors in question in the forward position. The figures after the diamonds represent the gear engaged with the selectors in the rear position. The table thus gives the position of each set of selectors for each gear.

The overall ratios from gearbox input flange to steering unit output flanges, including therefore spiral bevel reduction on the gearbox output shaft, are:

8th	.98—1
7th	1.61—1
6th	2.11—1
5th	3.16—1
4th	4.86—1
3rd	7.15—1
2nd	10.2 —1
1st	15.4 —1

The four ratios of reverse correspond to, but are lower than, the four lowest forward gears.

2. STEERING UNIT

Steering is effected by imposing different speeds on to the sun wheel of an epicyclic, whose annulus is positively driven by a bevel meshing with the main gearbox output bevel, and whose planet carrier carries the output flange to the final drive. There is one of these epicyclics at each end of the bevel shaft meshing with the gearbox output bevel.

The direction and speed rotation of the sun wheel and the choice of left or right hand sides are governed by the engagement of two or four hydraulically operated multi-disc clutches. These clutches connect the sun wheels through a lay shaft meshing with the small bevel on the extension of the gearbox input shaft. In this way a choice of two speeds both proportional to engine speed, is imposed at will upon the sun wheel

52

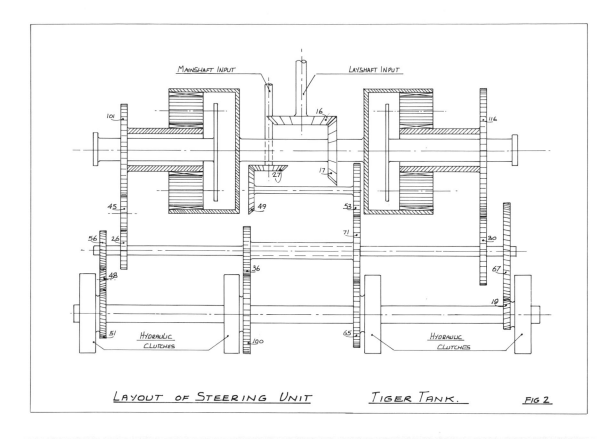

Layout of Steering Unit   Tiger Tank.   Fig 2

of the epicyclic whose annulus is already rotating at a multiple of engine speed according to the gear engaged. In addition, in neutral with no output from the main gearbox bevel, a drive is still obtained from the bevel on the extension of the gearbox input shaft, and this produces with the engagement of the appropriate steering clutch opposing rotations of left and right sun wheels. As the annuli are unable to rotate in opposite directions owing to their being secured to the same shaft this opposite rotation of the sun wheel, of necessity, produces opposite rotation of the output flanges, resulting in a neutral turn. For one full revolution of both output flanges the gearbox input flange performs 117 revs.

Oil pressure from a pump driven by an extension of the fore and aft gearbox shaft is admitted to the required steering clutches through ports in the steering assembly casing, the opening of which is controlled by a piston valve. Movement of piston valve is governed by the driver's steering wheel. In this way two distinct radii of turn are available for each gear engaged, and identical for left and right turns. A mushroom shaped knob on the gearbox casing operates hydraulically a brake on one section of the main shaft, thereby eliminating clutch drag and making the neutral turn more positive.

The tank can also be steered when required by steering levers on each side of the driver which operate the right and left brake assemblies.

3. FINAL DRIVE

The final drive assemblies are bolted directly to the hull from the outside and contain two stages of reduction.

(a) A straight spur reduction, and

(b) An epicyclic.

The steering unit output shafts drive the small pinion of the spur reduction which meshes with the large pinion. The large pinion is

53

mounted on the same shaft as a smaller pinion, which is the sun wheel of the epicyclic reduction of which the planet carrier mounts the driving sprocket, and the annulus is rigidly secured to the final drive casing. The overall ratio is 10.55 to 1. Each final drive casing, which is a steel casting, has its own drain plug and filler plug, and a third plug which gives the correct oil level. Oil capacity 8 litres (14 pints).

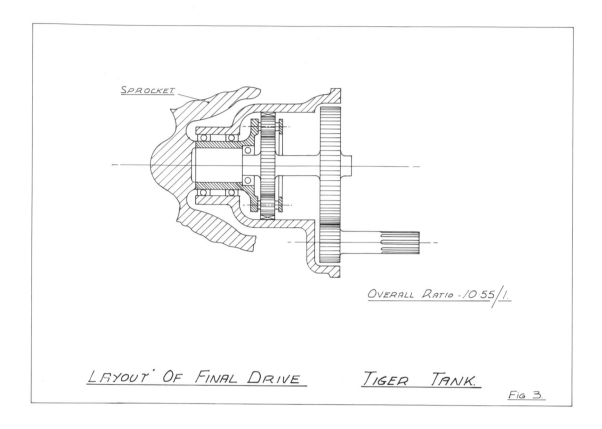

SPROCKET

OVERALL RATIO ·10·55/1.

LAYOUT OF FINAL DRIVE   TIGER TANK.

FIG 3.

A very brief extract from T I Summary No 119, of 22 December 1943, announced a change in designation.

12. *Pz Kw VI (TIGER)*
An official German document indicates that Pz Kw VI (H) Tiger is now officially designated Pz Kw Tiger, Model E.

A further extract from the same summary gave the first details of a new version.

13. *PANTHER AND TIGER COMMANDER'S TANKS*
An official German document contains a reference to commander's versions of both Panther and Tiger tanks.

Whereas the PzKw III commander's tank always had a dummy gun in the turret, there is evidence that at least some of the Tiger commander's tanks retain the normal 88mm Kw K 36. It is not yet known whether the commander's version of the Panther mounts the same gun, 75mm Kw K 43, as the fighting tank, but the indications are that the substitution of a dummy gun will be avoided if possible.

Another branch of Military Intelligence, M.I.14, dealt with the administrative aspects of the German Army rather than the technical side so it appeared less often in the columns of the tank orientated Intelligence Summaries. However the new breed of heavy German tanks caused changes to be made in the establishment of Panzer Regiments and these were recorded in December.

TACTICAL
GERMAN TANK REGIMENTS (Extract M.I.14 paper 21 Dec. 43)
(a) It is believed that tank regiments re-equipped with Pz Kw V and VI tanks are at present intended to have the following organization:
  Two battalions each of three Squadrons of Pz Kw V.
  One heavy battalion of two Squadrons of Pz Kw IV and VI.
  One battalion of assault guns.

(b) Pending re-equipment, the following transistional forms may be encountered in the future;

Tank Regiment of (i) *two* bns each of *one* sqn of Pz Kw III and *two* sqns of Pz Kw IV.
  one assault gun battalion.
  (ii) *two* bns, each of *one* sqn of Pz Kw III and *three* sqns of Pz Kw IV.
  one assault gun battalion.
  (iii) *three* bns, each of *one* sqn of Pz Kw III and *two* sqns of Pz Kw IV.
  one assault gun battalion.
  (iv) *one* bn of *three* sqns of Pz Kw IV
  one bn of *three* sqns of Pz Kw V.
  one assault gun battalion.

(c) The following organization of squadrons and battalions is thought to be the most probable on present evidence:
  (i) *Pz Kw III Sqn*
  H.Q.: 3 Pz Kw III
  Three troops each of 5 Pz Kw III
  Total tanks in sqn: 18 Pz Kw III
  (ii) *Pz Kw IV Sqn*
  H.Q.: 2 Pz Kw IV.
  Three troops each of 4 Pz Kw IV.
  Total tanks in sqn: 14 Pz Kw IV.
Note: Battalions composed of sqns of Pz Kw III and IV have three Pz Kw V in the Battalion H.Q. Sqn.
  (iii) *Pz Kw V (Panther) Sqn*
  H.Q.: 3 Pz Kw V
  Three troops each of 4 Pz Kw V
  Total tanks in sqn: 15 Pz Kw V
  Pz Kw V (Panther) Bn
  H.Q.: Sqn. 3 Pz Kw V
  Three sqns each of 15 Pz Kw V
  Total tanks in Bn: 48 Pz Kw V
  (iv) *Heavy Squadron (Pz Kw IV and VI)*
  H.Q.: 1 Pz Kw VI, 3 Pz KW IV.
  Four troops each of 2 Pz Kw VI and 2 Pz Kw IV.
  Total tanks in sqn: 9 Pz Kw VI and 11 Pz Kw IV.
  Heavy Battalion (Pz Kw IV and VI)
  H.Q. Sqn: 2 Pz Kw VI, 3 Pz Kw IV.
  Two sqns each of 9 Pz Kw VI and 11 Pz Kw IV.
  Total tanks in bn: 20 Pz Kw VI and 25 Pz Kw IV.

It will be recalled that in May 1943 a cable from North Africa had indicated that a fully operational Tiger would shortly be shipped back to the United Kingdom. This tank fell into British hands on 21 April during fighting on the Djebel Djaffa, when Churchills of 48 Royal Tank Regiment came up against a German armoured force in a classic defensive position. Tribute has already been paid to the effectiveness of these heavy tanks in a defensive battle and tests have proved that, approached head on, their armour is proof against the 6-pdr gun at anything but the shortest range. Yet for all that even machine warfare is more than a matter of statistics, it includes chance and the human factor, both of which combined, in this instance, to bring Goliath to his knees again before David's sling. It took two rounds from a Churchill (one bounced of the mantlet bearing and injured the commander. The other slightly damaged the turret ring) to persuade the crew to bale out and, with them, the crews of some other German tanks in the area. This time there was no hope of the Germans recovering the tank or any need for the British to blow it up; instead it was briefly examined *in situ* and then, in due course, returned to Tunis, where HM King George VI and the Prime Minister, Winston Churchill, both had a chance to examine it. In the meantime it was fully equipped with a full set of spare and ancillary parts, including transport and battle tracks taken from other captured specimens.

The tank arrived in Britain in the October and it was passed to the School of Tank Technology at Chertsey for thorough evaluation. It was on public display on Horse Guards Parade for a while in November, then back to Chertsey for a complete strip examination and, later in 1944, down to Lulworth Camp in Dorset for gunnery trials.

The sporadic and separated nature of the evaluation caused the final report on the tank to be issued piecemeal and, in the event, it was never completed. This explains the various dates applied to different section of the report and the obvious gaps in the numerical sequence. The reason was, of course, that while these ponderous volumes were being compiled on a 1942 model tank, albeit an outstanding one, better and in some cases bigger German tanks were now being encountered in the field which indicated that the Tiger was likely to be virtually obsolete before the report was published.

The ommisions notwithstanding, this report is a classic of its kind, thorough in those sections that are published, well presented, with some remarkable illustrations and as accurate as the most painstaking investigation can make it.

The captured Tiger on the Djebel Djaffa. Curious British soldiers clamber all over it while a Churchill tank and a Daimler scout car move past.

Wired off from the idly curious, the tank stands with its wading pipe erect alongside other captured equipment, including a Kettenkrad half-track.

The abandoned tank in its original location with three of its hatches open after the crew baled out.

A rear view of the tank after an initial examination surrounded by Churchills of 48th RTR.

Back in Britain the tank is displayed on Horse Guards Parade.

The Tiger climbs aboard a Pickfords transporter on Horse Guards Parade. Notice that it is now wearing a First Army shield.

57

Restored to running order, the Tiger is tested for manoeuvrability.

Part Two

REPORT ON

Pz Kw VI
(Tiger)
Model E

PART I.
General Description

Military College of Science
SCHOOL OF TANK TECHNOLOGY
Chobham Lane   Chertsey

January   1944

FOREWORD

An example of the Pz. Kw. VI (Tiger) was brought to this country from North Africa in October 1943 for the purpose of detailed examination. With the tank there is a considerable quantity of spare components and these will greatly facilitate the work of examination and the preparation of the report.

Whilst much of the work is being carried out by the School of Tank Technology, it is clearly desirable that specialist firms and other organizations should in some cases be called in to assist. In ensuing sections of this report, therefore, the source of information is always indicated.

The desirability of consolidating all the available information into one publication is obvious, and the responsibility therefore of progressing reports and final publication has been vested with the Foreign Vehicle Section of S.T.T.

The publication of the completed book will take a considerable time. On the other hand it is obviously essential that all data should be made available to the appropriate Branch Heads of D.T.D. and others, as soon as it becomes available. Consequently it has been decided that the report shall be issued in parts of which this forms the first. Each part will be published and distributed as soon as it becomes available.

All parts will be presented in uniform style, so that they may be collated into a suitable loose leaf binding which is being prepared for the purpose.

Major J.D. Barnes, R.T.R.
Mr. D.M. Pearce, B.A. (Cantab.)

INTRODUCTION

The Pz. Kw. VI was introduced into service by the enemy in the Autumn or Winter of 1942, and appeared in North Africa in January 1943 and later in Sicily and on the Russian front.

The vehicle which has been examined is a Pz. Kw. VI or Sd. Kfz. 182 and is also known as the "TIGER". This model is known to have been developed by Henschel u Söhne G.m.b.H.

The "TIGER" is of course outstanding by reason of its being the heaviest A.F.V. in general service, scaling approximately 56 tons in battle order. Its main armament is an 8.8 cm. gun, whilst its heaviest armour (on the front vertical plate) is 102 mm. Another feature of outstanding tactical interest is its deep wading facilities, and limited under water performance, to a depth of approximately 15 ft.

Its size and weight, however, impose certain tactical disadvantages, the most outstanding being the restriction on transportation due to its width, and its limited radius of action, due to heavy fuel consumption, (stated by the enemy as 2.75 gallons per mile on normal cross-country running).

The workmanship appears to be of a high order, and the design has been executed freely from the drawing board, in general unhampered by the utilisation of existing components. There are exceptions however and certain points of detail design appear unnecessarily elaborate and costly to manufacture.

An interesting development in German A.F.V. construction is the introduction of plate interlocking in addition to the normal stepped jointing. This method has no doubt been made necessary by the use of thicker armour.

The steering unit is in principle similar to the " Merritt-Brown " with the further refinement of a twin radius of turn in each gear. This adoption of a fully regenerative steering system is a distinct departure from the simple clutch/brake system hitherto employed on German tanks. The weight of the " TIGER " no doubt enforced a radical change in the steering design and the adoption of this system is therefore of interest. The gearbox has much in common with other Maybach pre-selective units, and probably the outstanding merit of this design is the provision of a large number of forward ratios (in this case eight) in a relatively compact main casing. This use of a fully automatic change speed operation is in distinct contrast with current Allied practice.

The transmission and steering units are extremely complicated and undoubtedly costly in man/hours to produce. The resultant light control of such a heavy vehicle may be some justification, since those who have driven the tank comment favourably on this feature.

As yet there is no indication that the Germans favour a compression ignition engine and the Pz. Kw. VI is powered by a V-12 Maybach petrol engine. This engine which has undoubtedly been expressly designed for a heavy tank, is a logical development of the Maybach V-12 type 120 TRM used in the Pz. Kw. III and Pz. Kw. IV and is similar in general design. As this engine represents the very latest German practice it merits close study, and it must be conceded that the design has achieved its purpose in a great measure. It is compact, light and very accessible.

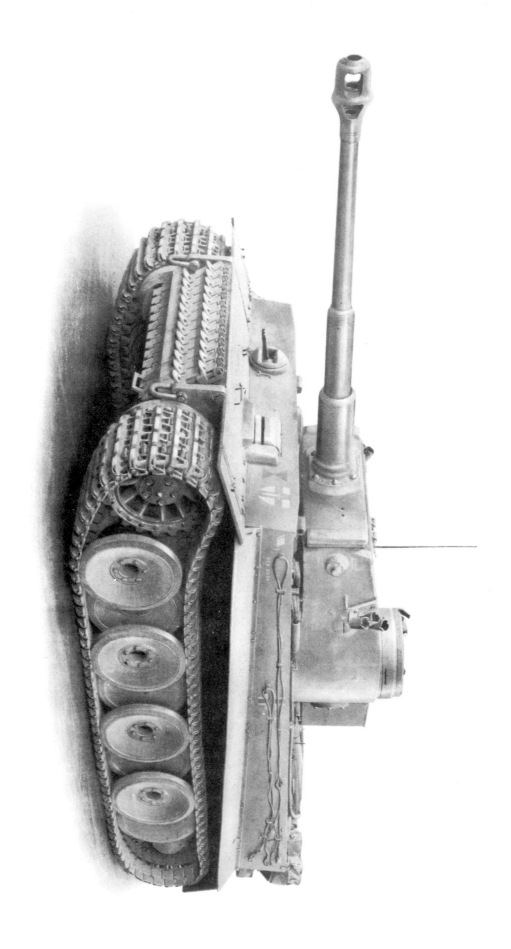

GENERAL DESCRIPTION

As compared with other A.F.V's in service, the "Tiger" is outstandingly well armed and protected. Designed to carry an 8.8 cm. gun and constructed of very heavy armour plate, the vehicle is naturally of exceptional size and weight and it is therefore somewhat surprising to note how it is, to a certain degree, dwarfed by the main armament.

Viewed from the side with the turret at 12 o'clock, the 8.8 cm gun extends beyond the nose of the tank by about a quarter of its length, and the length from the muzzle brake to the mantlet is rather over half the total length of the vehicle.

From the front aspect the great width and extremely wide tracks present a clean formidable appearance, whilst from the rear, the abnormal height of the flat tail plate carrying the large cylindrical silencers and air pre-cleaners, present by contrast an ungainly and untidy appearance.

The use of heavy armour plate has imposed the necessity of employing flat plates wherever possible and the number of plates has been kept to a minimum to facilitate manufacture. This results in a simple box like contour.
Both the superstructure and engine compartments are high and the former overhangs the tracks at each side. This arrangement permits of adequate turret ring diameter to accommodate the 8.8cm. gun. Apart from the tail plate

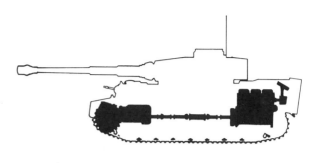

already referred to, the exterior is of generally clean and simple lines.

A notable departure from past German practice is the welding of the superstructure to the main hull; in previous German designs a bolted joint has been used.

The turret also is of simple outline, the vertical sides and rear being formed of a single rolled plate, whilst the mantlet is a steel casting of rectangular section. A conventional German type of cupola is mounted on the nearside of the turret roof.

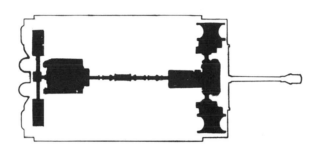

Circular hatches are provided in the superstructure top for the driver and hull gunner. There are three hatches in the turret - a rectangular hatch for the loader in the roof, and two circular hatches, one in the cupola top and one in the turret side.

Massive cast manganese steel tracks of comparatively small pitch are driven by the front sprockets - consistent with normal German practice. Adjustment of the track tension by rear idler is accessible through the tail plate, and the mechanism is all housed within the hull.

The vehicle is sprung on torsion bars. The bogie wheels are arranged to overlap each other thus increasing the number of spring units and resulting in a soft suspension. This arrangement is not altogether unexpected since it has previously been encountered on German tracked vehicles, and its merits are obvious, particularly when dealing with the suspension of an unusually heavy vehicle.

Even distribution of the weight on the tracks is achieved by the use of triple rubber tyred bogie wheels. In order to accommodate the 16 torsion bars on the hull floor, trailing suspension arms are used on one side and leading arms on the other.

The mechanical layout follows orthodox German practice although the elaboration and refinement in design of certain components has been carried to an exceptional degree. The engine is accommodated centrally at the rear and drives forward through a propeller shaft below the turret floor to the gearbox which incorporates the clutch. Bolted to it is the steering unit set transversely in the nose of the tank. A bevel drive is introduced in the steering unit and each track is driven through a final reduction gear in each sprocket. A radiator and twin fan assembly is installed in a separate compartment each side of the engine. Below each compartment two petrol tanks are carried.

Arrangements for wading and total submersion of the tank are necessarily somewhat elaborate, but have evidently not been incorporated as an afterthought. All hatches and doors are rubber sealed, whilst the turret ring is sealed by an inflatable rubber tube. The main air supply for the engine and crew is taken through a demountable telescopic standpipe mounted over the engine compartment. During submersion, the fan drives are disconnected and the radiator compartments flooded.

The excessive width of the vehicle in battle order necessitates special preparation for rail travel. Narrow tracks are substituted and the outer bogie wheels removed as are the track guards and air pre-cleaners.

TANK PREPARED FOR RAIL TRAVEL.

The general layout of the fighting and driving compartments is shown in the perspective drawing. The seating arrangements for the crew follow the normal German practice. In the three man turret the gunner sits on the nearside of the gun with the Commander immediately behind him and the loader sits on the other side of the gun and faces to the rear.
The commander is provided with a cupola in which are five vision slits. In the hull the driver sits in the nearside and the hull gunner, who also operates the wireless, sits opposite in the offside.

Although the turret is unusually spacious, the breech mechanism of the 8.8 cm. gun reaches nearly to the rear wall dividing the compartment in two. The mechanism is of the semi-automatic falling wedge type and is, broadly speaking a scaled up version of the smaller tank guns. It is electrically fired by a control on the elevating handwheel. A 7.92 mm. machine gun is mounted coaxially on the offside and is fired mechanically by a foot pedal.

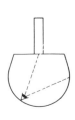

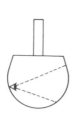

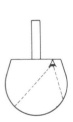

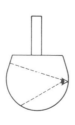

The gunner is provided with a binocular telescope and a turret position dial indicator to his left. The gun is balanced by a large coil spring housed in a cylinder in the offside front of the turret. Elevation and hand traverse are controlled by handwheels to the right and left of the gunner, and an additional handwheel may be used by the commander to give assistance. The hydraulic power traverse is controlled by the gunner by a rocking foot plate.

Around the vertical sides and rear of the turret are various small boxes, brackets and straps for stowing such items as gasmasks, glass blocks, microphones etc., as well as junction and fuse boxes for the turret electrical gear.

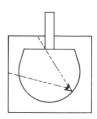

The turret floor rotates with the turret and is suspended on three steel tubes. In the centre is a domed cover for the drive to the hydraulic unit which is bolted to the revolving floor. The drive is taken to the turret rack through shafting and universal joints. Also mounted on the revolving floor is a rack for spare petrol cans and a fire extinguisher. The gunner's seat is carried on a welded tubular extension on the elevating gear, and is situated forward over the hydraulic unit. To the rear on the engine bulkhead are mounted the petrol taps, certain other engine controls and the automatic fire extinguisher unit.

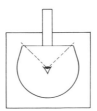

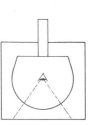

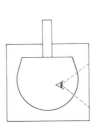

Ammunition for the 3.8 cm. gun is stowed in bins at each side of the fighting compartment. The remainder is stowed under the turret floor and alongside the driver.

The driver is provided with a steering wheel which controls hydraulically the controlled differential steering unit. When the engine is not running this unit is inoperative and orthodox steering levers controlling skid disc brakes may be used. These brakes are also the vehicle brakes and are coupled to a foot pedal and parking brake lever. Other controls are normal. The driver's visor may be closed by a sliding shutter operated by a large handwheel, and a fixed episcope is provided in the escape hatch. A standard German gyro-compass and instrument panel are situated to the right and left respectively.

The 7.92mm. machine gun for the hull gunner is held in a ball mounting in the offside of the front vertical plate. It is fired by a hand trigger and sighted by an orthodox telescope. The wireless sets are carried on a shelf to the right of the hull gunner.

MOUNTING FOR RANGEFINDER (STOWED POSITION)

COMMANDER'S SEAT

SPARE GLASS BLOCKS

TRAVERSE HANDWHEEL (Commander)

PETROL TANK

PETROL PRIMER

FAN DRIVE CLUTCH LEVER

M.G. AMMUNITION

AIR INTAKE VALVE CONTROL

PETROL TAP

MOUNTING FOR SCISSORS TELESCOPE

REVOLVER PORT

8.8 CM. AMMUNITION BINS

TRAVERSE GEARBOX

COMMANDER'S SHIELD

HYDRAULIC TRAVERSE UNIT

GUNNER'S SEAT

VENTILATION CONTROL

WIRELESS AERIAL

TURRET FUZE BOX

EXTRACTOR FAN

ESCAPE HATCH

HYDRAULIC TRAVERSE FOOT CONTROL

TORSION BAR SUSPENSION

M.G. FIRING PEDAL

BINOCULAR TELESCOPE

TURRET HANDWHEEL (Gunner)

ELEVATING HANDWHEEL (Gunner)

HANDWHEEL (Gunner)

FIRE EXTINGUISHER

8.8 CM. AMMUNITION BINS

PETROL TANK

BALANCE SPRING CYLINDER

HOLDER FOR BOX CONTAINING P.L.G. GROUND MOUNTING

FOR WATER BOTTLE

SHOCK ABSORBER

8.8 CM. AMMN. BINS

8.8 CM. GUN FIRING LEVER

GEARBOX

HAND BRAKE

SMOKE GENERATOR DISCHARGERS

M.G. ACCESSORIES

STEERING WHEEL

REAR DIRECTION SELECTOR CONTROL LEVER

FORWARD DIRECTION SELECTOR CONTROL LEVER

STEERING LEVELS

MOUNTING FOR WIRELESS SET

DISC BRAKE DRUM

STEERING UNIT

SHOCK ABSORBER

ACCELERATOR

FOOT BRAKE

CLUTCH

72

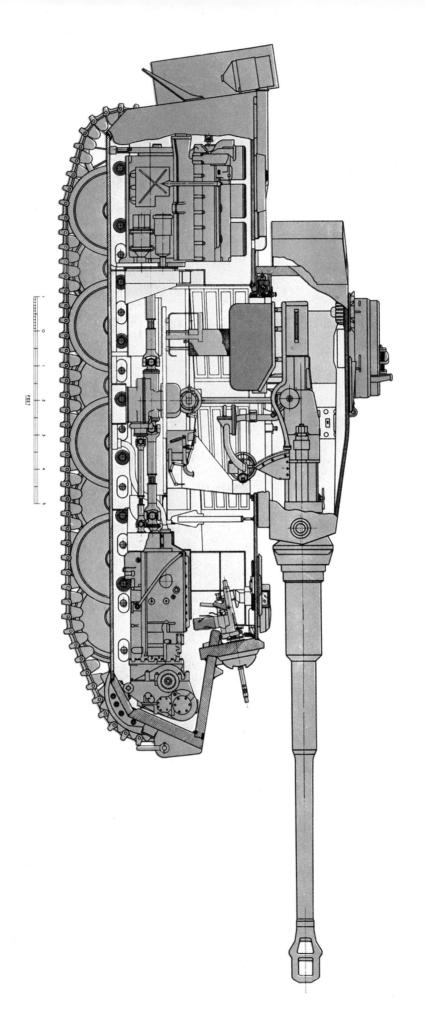

SIDE ELEVATION
WIDE TRACKS

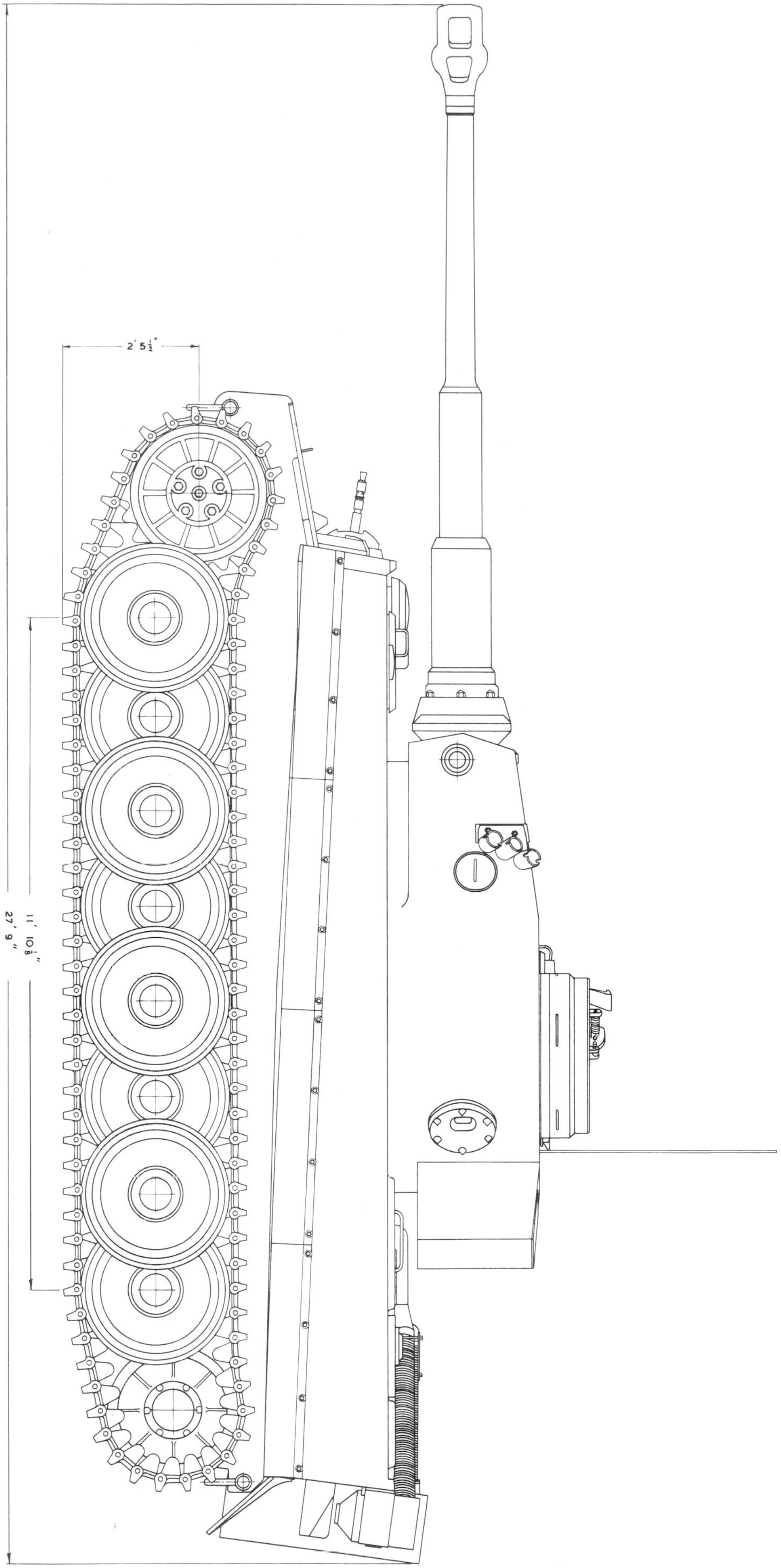

2' 5½"

11' 10⅛"

27' 9"

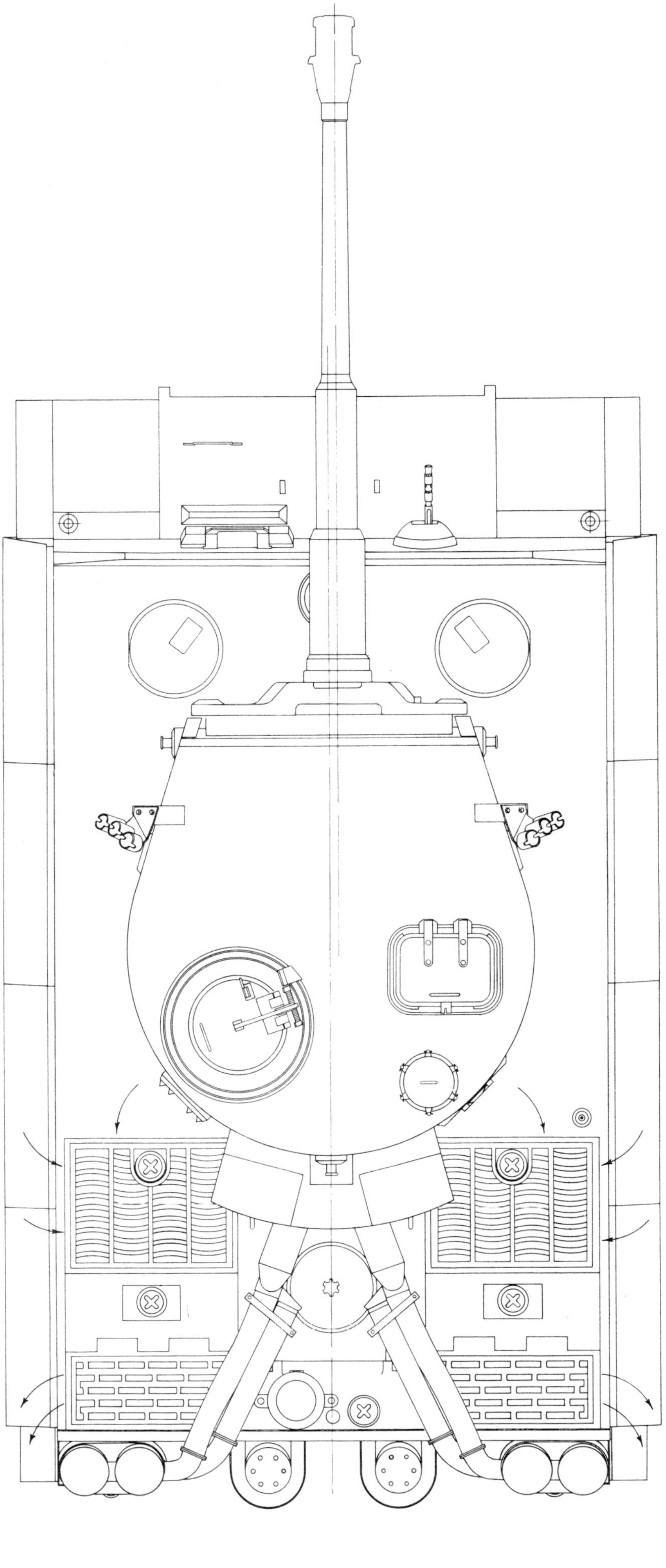

PLAN
WIDE TRACKS

75

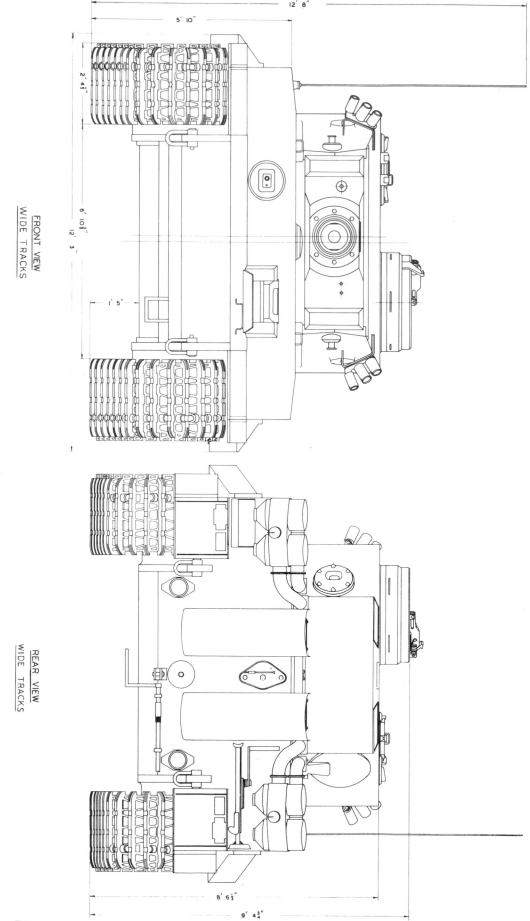

FRONT VIEW
WIDE TRACKS

REAR VIEW
WIDE TRACKS

76

GENERAL SPECIFICATON

TYPE   Panzerkampfwagen (Pz. Kw.) VI.   Model "H" Sd.Kfz. 182

DIMENSIONS   WIDE TRACKS FITTED

Weight (in battle order)   56 tons
Length (excluding gun)   20' 8½"
    "   (including gun at 12 o'clock)   27' 9"
Width (overall)   12' 3"
Height   9' 4¾"
Ground Contact   12' 6"
Track Centres   9' 3½"
Ground clearance   1' 5"

                                NARROW TRACKS FITTED

Weight (partially stowed, less crew)   50 tons 5 cwt.
Width (overall)   10' 4"
Other dimensions as for wide tracks.

ARMAMENT

One 8.8 cm. tank gun KwK 36 electrically fired and one 7.92
M.G. 34 co-axial in turret.
One M.G. 34 in front vertical plate.
One 9mm. machine carbine stowed.
Six Nb. K. Wg. 90 mm. smoke generators - three each side of
turret.
Three minethrowers - unknown calibre mounted on superstructure
roof.

TURRET TRAVERSE

All round hand and power traverse. Power traverse hydraulic
unit driven by take-off from main gearbox through auxiliary
gearbox. Hydraulic unit consists of variable delivery vane
pump supplying a vane motor, both housed in single casting on
turret floor. Pump delivery varied by altering eccentricity
for speed and direction. Additional control giving two positions of eccentricity on motor - in effect a two-speed gear.

SIGHTING

Turret armament - binocular telescope T.Z.F. 9(b)
Hull M.G. - Telescope K.Z.F. 2.

AMMUNITION

8.8cm. - 92 rounds (mixed APCBC, H.E. and A.P.40)
7.92mm. - 34 belts each 150 rounds.

ARMOUR

Vertical and near vertical plate thickness - 60-100 mm.
Horizontal and near horizontal plate "   - 26- 60 mm.

No facehardened armour used and as distinct from previous
German practice, armour is comparable in hardness to British
machineable quality plate.

All welded construction, embodying stepped joints, austenitic
welding and total plate interlocking.

CREW

In Turret
>   Commander
>   Gunner
>   Loader

In Hull
>   Driver
>   Hull Gunner/Wireless Operator

Total   Five

POWER PLANT

Engine

Manufacturer	Maybach
Model	H.L. 210
Type	60° V/12 cylinder - petrol
Rating	650 metric H.P. (642 British B.H.P.)
Bore	125 mm
Stroke	145 mm
Normal capacity	21,400 cc.
Cylinder block and crankcase	Single aluminium casting
Cylinder Heads	Cast Iron
Valves	Overhead - two per cylinder - exhaust sodium cooled.
Valve operation	Single gear driven overhead camshaft to each bank.
Carburettors	4 - Solex type 52 JFF 2
Governor	Centrifugal max speed.
Air Cleaners	2 centrifugal pre-cleaners 3 oil bath cleaners
Lubrication	Dry sump Oil pumps: Gear type - 2 scavenge 1 pressure Oil capacity: 28 litres (6.1 gals)
Ignition	2 Bosch impulse starter magnetos - one to each bank. One Bosch 14mm. plug per cylinder. Fully screened.
Starters	One Bosch 24V axial starter. One Bosch inertia starter.

Engine Cooling System

Radiators	2 gilled tube type mounted one each side at rear of engine compartment.
Fans	2 pairs - axial flow type - gear driven. Two speeds.
Water pump	One - centrifugal type mounted between cylinder heads.
Cooling System Capacity	Approx. 16 gals.

Fuel System

No. of tanks	4 - 2 each side of engine compartment
Total capacity	Approx. 125 gallons
Petrol pumps	4 Solex mechanical type One electric pump for priming One manual pump injects fuel direct to manifold for cold starting.

CLUTCH

Multi-plate incorporated in gearbox. Hydraulic control.

GEARBOX

Type:	Maybach Olvar - preselector
Operation:	Four pairs of gears in constant mesh. Dog clutch engagement. Hydraulic control. Synchronising cone clutches on input and output shafts.
No. of speeds:	8 forward - 4 reverse

Gear Ratios:			
1st	15.4	:	1
2nd	10.2	:	1
3rd	7.15	:	1
4th	4.86	:	1
5th	3.16	:	1
6th	2.11	:	1
7th	1.14	:	1
8th	0.98	:	1

STEERING

Regenerative controlled differential type. An epicyclic train to each sprocket. Annulus driven by gearbox output. Sun wheels driven from gearbox input. Planet carriers form output to final drives. Speed and direction imposed on sun wheels controlled through gearing by hydraulic clutches giving two radii of turn in either direction in each gear. Clutches hydraulically controlled by steering wheel.

Emergency Steering - Orthodox steering levers control disc brakes on each output shaft, enabling the vehicle to be steered when engine is not running.

BRAKES

Emergency steering brakes serve as vehicle brakes operated by foot pedal and hand lever.

FINAL DRIVE

Spur gear reduction to epicyclics housed in sprockets.

SPROCKETS

Steel castings with twin detachable rings.

TRACKS

Wide.

Type:	4/5 lugs
No. of links per track	96
Material:	Cast Manganese steel
Width:	$28\frac{1}{2}$"
Pitch:	5.125"
Pin diameter:	1.1"
Weight of link with one pin:	66.375 lbs.
Pin retention:	Circlips
Track Pressure:	14.7 lbs/sq. in.

Narrow

Width:	$20\frac{1}{2}$"
Weight of link with one pin:	$46\frac{1}{2}$ lbs.
Track Pressure:	20.4 lbs/sq. in.

TRACK ADJUSTMENT

By rear idler mounted on cranked arm. Drawbolt adjustment accessible through tail plate.

SUSPENSION

Triple overlapping wheels independently sprung on torsion bars. Trailing suspension arms on offside - leading arms on nearside. When narrow tracks are fitted for transportation, outer wheels from each unit are removed.

No top rollers fitted, the track being returned on the wheels.

Wheels

Type:	Steel disc type with solid rubber tyres
No.	Eight each side
Diameter:	$31\frac{1}{2}$"

Torsion Bars

No.	16
Diameter	55mm. and 58mm.
Effective Length	1644.6 mm. (5' $4\frac{3}{4}$")

Shock Absorbers

Hydraulic piston type on front and rear wheels only, housed in the hull.

ELECTRICAL EQUIPMENT

Accumulators - Two 12 volt, in parallel for normal supply and in series for starting.

Dynamo - One 12 volt - voltage regulator

Wireless Equipment - W/T, L/T and Intercom. Power supplied through rotary converter.

AUTOMATIC FIRE FIGHTING EQUIPMENT

Bimetal thermostats at points in engine compartment energize a solenoid which opens the delivery valve on a bottle containing C.T.C. under pressure.

From the delivery valve the extinguishing fluid is piped to nozzles at the requisite points.

A clockwork time switch trips the solenoid circuit, limiting the period of operation to seven seconds.

The cycle is repeated until the temperature at the thermostats is sufficiently reduced.

WADING AND SUBMERSION

Full provision for wading and submersion to approx. 15ft. All doors, hatches, etc., have rubber seals. The turret ring is sealed by inflatable rubber ring.

Fan drives disconnected and radiator compartments flooded. Air supply to engine and crew via a telescopic standpipe erected on top of engine compartment. Bilge pump driven by engine through power traverse auxiliary gearbox. Engine exhausts directly into water through non-return flap valves on top of silencers.

RESTRICTED

The information given in this document
is not to be communicated, either directly
or indirectly, to the Press or to any person
not authorized to receive it.

REPORT ON

Pz Kw VI
(Tiger)
Model H

PART II

ARMAMENT, FIGHTING ARRANGEMENTS, STOWAGE

AND POWER TRAVERSE

SECTION I

ARMAMENT

Military College of Science
SCHOOL OF TANK TECHNOLOGY
Chobham Lane   Chertsey

January   1944

PART II

INTRODUCTION

The 8.8 cm. (3.46-in) gun is mounted on a $70\frac{1}{2}$-in. internal diameter ring and has 360° traverse. It is provided with 92 rounds of ammunition. This gun, known as the Kw.K 36, should not be regarded as a development of the Flak 18 and 36 A.A./A.Tk guns, but as a parallel development with the 7.5cm. Kw.K 40 (long) and follows the well known principles of German tank gun design. The only similarity to the Flak 36 lies in the ammunition and ballistics.

The standard Flak 18 and 36 ammunition is fired, except that it is fitted with the C/22 electric primer instead of the C/12 percussion primer.

The combination of a muzzle brake, long recoil (22.8 ins) and a heavy vehicle (approximately 56tons) results in a stable gun platform, thus avoiding one of the difficulties of observation of fire at present being encountered in British tanks.

In addition to the Kw.K 36, the armament of the tank comprises two M.G. 34 7.92 mm Machine guns, one co-axially mounted with the 8.8 cm. gun, and one in a ball mounting on the offside of the front vertical plate.

A curious feature is the provision of a clinometer in conjunction with a simple type azimuth indicator, graduated in clock hours only, as on the Pz.Kw.IV with 7.5 cm. Kw.K (short). On the Pz.Kw.IV with 7.5 cm. Kw.K 40 (long), however, there is an elaborate azimuth indicator graduated in clock hours and mils, with a split pinion drive but no clinometer. Thus, neither of these vehicles has complete equipment for turret down shooting, although this is known to be practised by the Germans.

It is surprising that no attempt has been made to protect the ammunition from splinters, though there is good protection against dust.

The Germans appear to have discarded tail smoke apparatus in favour of turret mounted generator dischargers, obviously as a result of examination of British A.F.V's. As no extra generators are stowed, beyond those in the dischargers, and as the fitting of the primer is not a quick operation, they obviously cannot be reloaded after firing, until coming out of action.

By comparison with those of present British tanks, the turret is fairly roomy and comfortable. It is observed that the standard of workmanship and design in the armament is of a very high order and shows no deterioration when compared with early German designs.

February, 1944   Lieut. P.L.Gudgin, R.T.R.

8 8cm. GUN KW. K 36.

AND MOUNTING

Length of chamber	23.6 ins.
Length of rifling	161.1 "
Length of Bore	184.7 " (53.3 cals)
Depth of breech opening	9.6 "
Length of Piece	194.3 " (56.1 cals)
Additional length of	
Muzzle Brake	15.1 "
Overall Length	209.4 "
Angle of breech block guides	1.5°
Diameter at base of cartridge case	4.06 ins.
Diameter at rim of cartridge case	4.56 "
Bore	3.46 "
Rifling - No. of grooves	32, with uniform right hand twist
Depth of grooves	1.5 mm.
Width of grooves	5 "

References :-

Notes on Enemy Weapons No. 33)

M. I. 10., Summary No. 63/3A)   For Flak 18

M. I. 10., Summary No. 81/2)   and Flak 36

Construction

The weapon has a detachable breech ring provided with two gun lugs, the right hand one being of open type to facilitate removal of the buffer cylinders without removing the gun. (See photo. in Part I.)

Breech Mechanism

The breech mechanism is a scaled-up version of the standard German tank gun pattern, as fitted on the 7.5 cm. Kw. K. 40, 5 cm. Kw. K 39 etc. (See Part I.)

It incorporates the usual falling wedge breech block, (which has two drillings in the lower portion for lightness), electric primer firing, and S.A. operation by means of separate clock springs for opening and closing. The electric firing pencil is of very robust construction, and has external insulating bushes.

Muzzle Brake

This is of double baffle type, secured by means of a locking ring, and a tab washer. The rear baffle has a renewable insert.

Internal diameter
of rear baffle - 95 mm.

Internal diameter
of forward baffle - 105 mm.

Weight, complete
with locking ring - 124 lbs.

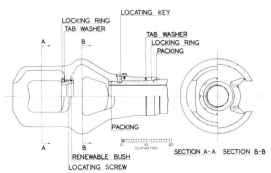

MUZZLE BRAKE

WEIGHT INCLUDING LOCKING RING 124 LBS.

Cradle

The cradle is of standard welded construction and is generally very similar to that on the 7.5 cm. Kw. K 40 (long), but on a larger scale. The left hand gun lug is provided with bronze shoes and runs in an anti-rotation guide inside the left side plate of the cradle. A deflector guard is bolted to the cradle; it is not hinged and effectively divides the fighting chamber into two separate unequal compartments. The deflector guard carries a small capacity (approximately 10 cases) empty cartridge bag on three brackets. The recoil indicator is bolted inside the left side plate.

The gun port water seal is operated by a knob on top of the cradle above the 8.8 cm. gun.

Recoil Gear

The recoil gear is of standard German tank gun pattern; it consists of a hydraulic buffer on the right of the gun, and a hydro-pneumatic recuperator on the left. A spring-loaded hydraulic reservoir with the usual hydraulic safety switch is mounted transversely beneath the gun. The reservoir is much larger than that mounted in previous types of tanks. The stencilled "Braun Ark" on both cylinders indicates that the fluid used therein is an equal mixture of " Bremsflussigkeit braun " (brown buffer fluid) and "Bremsflussigkeit arktisch" (arctic fluid), for use in temperate climates.

The piston rods are nutted to the gun lugs on either side of the breech ring. The right hand gun lug is open and allows the sideways removal of the buffer cylinder. The recoil indicator is graduated from 500 mm. (19.69 inches) to 620 mm. (24.4 inches) with the "Feurerpause" (stop) at 580 mm. (22.8 inches).

The recuperator air pressure was measured and found to be 54 kg/cm^2 or 766.8 lbs/in^2, approximately 54 atmospheres.

The recoil system appears serviceable.

Firing Gear

The Kw. K 36 uses the standard German electric primer type firing system. It is operated by means of a segment shaped trigger bar mounted on the same axis behind the elevating handwheel and parallel with the handwheel rim. (See Part I). It is a 12 volt system supplied from one of the vehicle batteries. The circuit is shown under Electrical Arrangements.

<u>Safety Devices</u>

Standard German electrical safety devices are provided, which prevent firing of the gun if the breech is not closed, the buffer empty, or the gun not fully run out. A mechanical safety switch, of the type fitted in the Pz. Kw. III and IV is mounted near the top right hand side of the breech ring. This switch breaks the firing circuit each time the gun is fired; the gun cannot then be fired until the loader has reset the switch. There is no deflector guard safety switch since the guard does not fold.

<u>Mounting</u>

Maximum elevation	16° 41'	) Limited by stops on
Maximum depression	7° 15'	) the rear face of mantlet.

The mounting is of the external mantlet type. The mantlet is cast in one piece and consists of a large rectangular external shield of approximately the same size as the front of the turret, behind which is a cylindrical portion, roughly hollowed out at the back, working inside the turret. There are two designs of mantlet, apparently in parallel production - one is flush finished on the front face (as on the tank under examination), the other has a raised portion round the telescope openings.

Each turret side wall forms a cheek, carrying a fixed spherical trunnion; these trunnions fit into split spherical bushes in the sides of the cylindrical inner mantlet. The trunnions are continued outwards through the cheeks of the turret walls to form two lifting points for the turret. The front of each cheek is chamfered away above and below the trunnion axis to allow for the elevation and depression of the mantlet. The 8.8 cm. Gun is offset 4 inches to the right. Splash proofing appears to be adequate.

<u>Balance</u>

The piece is mounted very far forward, and the mounting is considerably muzzle heavy. This is counter-acted by means of a large cylinder, containing a strong compression spring (with adjustable compression), horizontally mounted above the right hand side of the turret ring to the right of the loader. The spring is compressed by a piston, the piston rod is connected through a system of levers to a small subsidiary compression cylinder and to the right hand side of the cylindrical inner mantlet. The diagram shows the linkage positions with the mantlet horizontal.

FIXED to GUN MANTLET

<u>Elevating Gear</u>

The elevating gear is of sector and pinion type, the sector having external teeth. It is driven by a handwheel on a transverse axis underneath the gun, and turned by the gunner's right hand. This handwheel is mounted on a tubular swan-necked steel arm which passes under the gun and is welded to the forward offside turret platform support. Drive is transmitted from the handwheel to the elevating pinion by means of a universally jointed shaft inside the hollow arm, a bevel gear, and a worm and worm wheel.

Radius of handwheel	$4\frac{3}{8}$"	
Maximum obtainable elevation	16° 41'	(18 turns)
Maximum obtainable depression	7° 15'	($6\frac{3}{4}$ turns)
Total Arc	23° 56'	($24\frac{3}{4}$ turns)

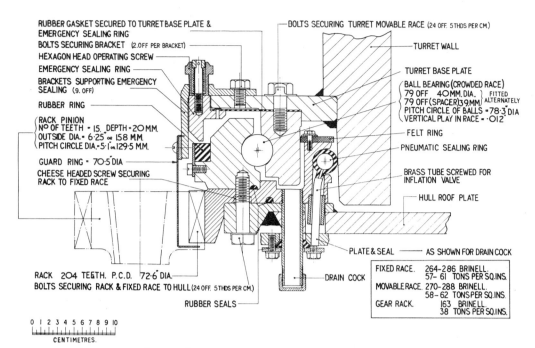

RUBBER GASKET SECURED TO TURRET BASE PLATE & EMERGENCY SEALING RING
BOLTS SECURING BRACKET (2.OFF PER BRACKET)
HEXAGON HEAD OPERATING SCREW
EMERGENCY SEALING RING
BRACKETS SUPPORTING EMERGENCY SEALING (9. OFF)
RUBBER RING
RACK PINION
NO OF TEETH = 15. DEPTH = 20 MM.
OUTSIDE DIA.= 6·25 = 158 MM.
PITCH CIRCLE DIA.= 5·1 = 129·5 MM.
GUARD RING = 70·5 DIA
CHEESE HEADED SCREW SECURING RACK TO FIXED RACE

BOLTS SECURING TURRET MOVABLE RACE (24 OFF. 5 THDS PER CM.)
TURRET WALL
TURRET BASE PLATE
BALL BEARING (CROWDED RACE)
79 OFF 40 MM. DIA. } FITTED
79 OFF (SPACER) 39 MM } ALTERNATELY
PITCH CIRCLE OF BALLS = 78·3″ DIA
VERTICAL PLAY IN RACE = ·012″
FELT RING
PNEUMATIC SEALING RING
BRASS TUBE SCREWED FOR INFLATION VALVE
HULL ROOF PLATE

RACK 204 TEETH. P.C.D. 72·6 DIA.
BOLTS SECURING RACK & FIXED RACE TO HULL (24 OFF. 5 THDS PER CM.)
RUBBER SEALS
PLATE & SEAL — AS SHOWN FOR DRAIN COCK
DRAIN COCK

FIXED RACE.	264-286 BRINELL. 57- 61 TONS PER SQ.INS.
MOVABLE RACE.	270-288 BRINELL. 58-62 TONS PER SQ.INS.
GEAR RACK.	163 BRINELL. 38 TONS PER SQ.INS.

0 1 2 3 4 5 6 7 8 9 10
CENTIMETRES.

Composite section of turret suspension

Ratio - approximately 1°/turn

Maximum workable elevation - 11° (approx)

Maximum workable depression - 4°   "

Total Arc   15°

Clearance between sector and sector pinion .004 ins. At maximum depression, the breech ring fouls the elevation lock, and at maximum elevation the deflector guard fouls the water cans on the floor. When firing, therefore, the maximum workable elevation and depression is considerably smaller than the maximum possible.

The elevation lock consists of two hooks, pivoted from the turret roof which engage studs on either side of the breech ring, and a screw clamp which presses on the top of the breech ring and forces the studs into the hooks. In the locked position, the gun is horizontal. This rather complicated arrangement prevents chatter when travelling.

Turret Suspension

The turret is carried on a vertical bearing, of the crowded ball race type. There are 79 load carrying balls of 40 mm. diameter and 262 grammes weight, and 79 spacer balls of 39 mm. diameter and 241 grammes weight. The stationary race is on the inside and the moving race on the outside.

The turret rack is in one piece and has the following dimensions:-

Root circle diameter	186.4 cm.	(73.4 ins)
Pitch circle diameter	184.4 cm.	(72.6 ins)
Addendum circle diameter	182.4 cm.	(71.8 ins)
No. of teeth	204	
Diameter to centre of balls	198.8 cm.	(78.3 ins)
Vertical play in turret race	.012 of an inch.	

The turret ring is sealed by means of an inflatable rubber tube (of 1.14-ins external diameter deflated) carried in an annular groove on the outside of the stationary race. Above this, is a felt ring clamped to the stationary race. The joints between the various components of the stationary race are sealed by rubber sealing rings.

There is no external protection of the turret ring joint, apart from that afforded by the projection of the front vertical plate above the superstructure roof. Adequate splash protection is provided by the sectional shape of the turret ring.

Traverse Gear

Full traverse of the turret through 360° is provided, both by power and hand.

Hand Traverse - the hand traverse is provided with two wheels, one for use by the gunner and an auxiliary wheel for the commander. They are inter-connected by means of universally jointed shafts, but the commander's handwheel may not be turned without first disengaging the plunger type lock on the gunner's handwheel.

Both wheels are geared with considerable reduction into the turret rack through a gearbox above the gunner's handwheel.

Radius of gunner's handwheel	- $5^{1}/5$"
No. of turns of gunner's handwheel for 360°	- 720 ($\frac{1}{2}$°/turn)
Radius of commander's handwheel	- 4"
No. of turns of Commander's handwheel for 360°	- 595 (.6°/" approx.)

Power Traverse - the turret may be power traversed by the engine through a hydraulic unit consisting of a variable delivery pump and motor. The drive to the unit is taken from a power take-off at the rear of the gear box, through an auxiliary gearbox situated centrally below the revolving turret floor and vertical shaft passing through the floor. The unit itself is bolted to the turret floor. The drive from the unit is taken to the turret rack through bevel gears and shafting. The auxiliary gearbox is provided with a gear lever situated on the hull gunner's side of the gearbox.

The hydraulic unit in the centre of the turntable floor carries two control levers, one of which operates a multiplate clutch on the input shaft and the other a two speed motor control.

The gunner's main traverse control consists of a rocking footplate under his right foot. To traverse right it is rocked forward, to traverse left, backward. Variable speeds forward and reverse are obtained, within the limits of the 2-speed control, according to the angle to which the footplate is rocked. The footplate is in a comfortable position, but the arc of movement (24°) is too large for comfortable operation, especially by the heel.

A full technical report on the power traverse components and performance details will be found in Section V.

It will be noted that, as all the hydraulic mechanism is contained in the turret, the complication of a rotating hydraulic joint is avoided and no disconnection is required when removing the turret. The dog clutch on the vertical drive shaft comes away, leaving the base junction in position on the hull floor.

There is no Broadside Indicating System fitted in spite of the large overhang of the gun barrel (9 ft. 6 ins.) Neither was it present on the Pz.Kw.IV, Model G, with the long 7.5 cm. Kw.K 40, although it appeared on all earlier tanks.

DRAIN TAP   **INFLATOR VALVE**

A plunger type traverse lock is provided under the superstructure roof in the forward near side of the fighting compartment, by means of which the turret may be locked in the 12 o'clock, 6 o'clock and 11 o'clock positions. It consists of a spring loaded plunger, which engages in recesses drilled in the turret skirt and is engaged or disengaged by means of a lever.

CO-AXIAL MACHINE GUN

This is the M.G. 34 and has the new type feed block (used on the infantry M.G. 34 for taking 50-round belt drums). This gives feed from left hand side only. For details of this gun, see M.I.10 Summaries Nos. 110/2/C and 66/4. Also "Notes on Enemy Weapons No. 5.," and "Enemy Weapons, Part I."

Cradle

The cradle is exactly similar to that on the Pz.Kw.IV, incorporating a spring buffer and carrying two belt bags (one full and one for empty cases). It supports the firing linkage and also the belt guide, with check pawl, to prevent the belt " running back ". Vertical and lateral zeroing adjustments are incorporated and provision is made for swinging the M.G. body clear for changing barrels.

<u>Firing Gear</u>

This is of the rod and lever type and is operated by a foot pedal situated above the power traverse control footplate. It is placed for use by the gunner's right foot, thus the M.G. cannot be fired when the turret is being traversed by power.

AUXILIARY MACHINE GUN

The auxiliary M.G. 34 is of the same type as the co-axial, with the new type breech block and is mounted in the offside of the front vertical plate. The mounting is of the standard German ball type, the Kugelblende 100 (the 100 is believed to be the thickness of armour used in the mounting), with a fixed hemispherical external mantlet. It is similar to that on the Pz. Kw. IV, the ball being inserted from the outside. It incorporates a head pan and a compensating tension spring anchored to the superstructure roof to counteract the breech heaviness of the mounting. This gives the same fault as that on the Pz. Kw. IV, Model G, of pulling the gun off, upwards and to the left.

The travelling lock is identical with that on the Pz. Kw. IV and locks the gun pointing slightly downwards and to the left.

Elevation	—	20°
Depression	—	7°
Total Arc	—	27°

Traverse left	—	15°
Traverse right	—	15°
Total Arc	—	30°

SIGHTS

<u>Main Armament</u>

<u>Telescope</u> - Sighting of the turret armament is done by means of an articulated, binocular telescope, type T.Z.F.9 (b), mounted on the left of the 8.8 cm. gun. It is a binocular development of the T.Z.F.5 series with similar optical characteristics, and has adjustable interocular distance ($2\frac{3}{8}$" - $3\frac{3}{8}$") by rotation of the cranked eyepieces. These are geared together by two toothed sectors giving a 1 : 1 ratio. The interocular distance may be locked by means of a knurled knob above the right hand eyepiece. The telescope is of stationary eyepiece type, the eyepieces being slung from the roof on a strengthened support, and locked in it by a pin. The lenses are bloomed, and this fact, taken in conjunction with the " (T) " marking, tends to confirm our previous surmise that the "(T)" indicates bloomed lenses. Contrary to previous reports, the telescope is not a coincidence rangefinder, a separate instrument being carried for this purpose.

War Office T.I. Summary No. 115 gives the following data :-

Magnification	—	x 2.5 (approx)
Field of view	—	23° (approx)
Overall length	—	33 inches (approx)
Overall width	—	$11\frac{3}{8}$ "
Weight	—	49 lbs. 14 ozs.
Exit Pupil dia:	—	6 mm.

The telescope in the vehicle under examination was numbered '171'.

Parts of other telescopes, Nos. 97, 74 and 53 were also received. All had the "T" marking, and bloomed lenses, but none was complete or serviceable. The eyepieces were removed from No. 53 to make No. 171 complete.

No. 171 is the only instrument so far examined with a number greater than 100. There appear to have been minor changes in design after the first 100 models - for example, the aiming marks in the first 100 were of normal type, consisting of complete triangles, whereas on this model the bases of the smaller triangles are not put in.

The caps on the graticule adjusters on this telescope are of a different design from the previous ones.

The graticules in both telescopes are illuminated from the same light source by means of a divided prism inserted in the centre of the graticule box.

The inside of the telescope bodies are smoked to prevent reflection.

There is a graticule with horizontal and vertical adjustment in each telescope. They are of standard pattern except for the omission of the bases of the triangular aiming marks in later models. The later models also have a vertical line below the central aiming mark in the left hand telescope. The purpose of the left hand telescope graticule is not clear, unless it serves as a battle sight, to be set at given ranges before going into action. It may be moved sideways in and out of view by means of a lever on the left rear of the graticule box. A standard type range scale for 8.8 cm. and M.G. is provided in the right hand telescope. It is adjustable to give ranges from 0 - 4000 metres (in hundreds) for the 8.8 cm. gun and from 0 - 1200 metres (also in hundreds) for the M.G. Range is put on by means of a standard type lever vertically mounted under the telescopes. The range scale and aiming mark glasses do not appear to be bloomed. It should be noted that the graticule adjustment controls are most inaccessible, and adjustment is difficult when the telescope is mounted.

An adjustable browpad of standard German type is provided. There is no open sight, contrary to earlier German practice.

Another report on this instrument has been prepared by the Aberdeen Proving Ground, Project No. FMFC-108, which contains photographs, data and a drawing of the original pattern of graticule.

Clinometer - A clinometer on the left side of the cradle is held in position at the top by means of a stud and at the bottom by a spring-loaded plunger. The stud is on an adjustable eccentric, to which is welded a knurled disc with seven drillings. The disc is locked in position by a bolt which may be threaded into one of three drillings in the cradle and through any of the seven drillings in the disc. As received, the bolt was in position in the centre drillings in both disc and cradle. When the disc is turned, alteration of 1 mil is caused in the relative elevation of clinometer and gun. Thus, a total adjustment of 9 mils is possible in the clinometer mounting by using a combination of both sets of drillings.

The clinometer arc is graduated on the left hand side from 0 to 400 mils (25°) of elevation, in black figures, and from 0 to 100 mils (5.6°) depression, in red figures. On the right of the arc there is a range scale (presumably for use with H.E. shell) graduated from 0 - 80 (in hundreds of metres). The range of 8000 metres corresponds approximately to 151 mils (8.5°) on the left hand scale.

Provision is made for the illumination of the bubble, but the bulb and wiring are deficient on this instrument. The bulb seems to be smaller than that normally used in German instruments and is probably a pea bulb.

An alternative position for the clinometer is provided outside the left cradle side plate, to the rear of the first position. In order to mount it here, the securing pins have to be reversed.

Auxiliary M.G.

The hull machine gun is sighted by the standard episcopic sighting telescope K.Z.F.2 (See C.I.A. Sketch No. 129 Sheet 6).

Magnification	-	x 1.75
Field of view	-	18°
Length	-	380 mm.
Weight	-	7 lbs.

FIRE CONTROL

A single dial target position indicator, similar to that on the Pz. Kw.IV with 7.5 cm. Kw.K (short), is fitted on the turret ring to the left of the gunner. It is graduated from 1 to 12 in clock hours and carries a pointer driven off the turret rack by means of a pinion and universally jointed shafts. In addition, there is a toothed indicating ring, also graduated from 1 to 12 and with 360 teeth, inside the cupola driven off the turret rack.

A sighting vane is incorporated in the front episcope in the cupola.

It is known from examination of burnt-out "Tigers" that a rangefinder is also sometimes carried, but whether this is universal or merely applies to a proportion of tanks is not known. No mention of it is made in captured stowage lists for this tank and none was found in the tank under examination, but two fixed tubular supports on the turret roof, one in front of and one behind the cupola, seem to be standard fittings, and their internal diameter corresponds to the ground mounting for this rangefinder.

From examination of a badly burnt specimen (marked Cxn. Kf 50995. E.M. 34ˣ), taken from a "Tiger", the rangefinder would appear to be the E.M. 34 , of coincidence type, with a base length of 70 cm. (27.56 ins), a magnification of x11 and giving ranges from 200 to 10,000 metres (219 to 10936 yards). Full particulars, drawing and photographs are contained in M.I.10 Summary No. 75 and Middle East A.F.V. Technical Report No. 13.

It is believed that a scissors telescope (type S.F.14.Z) is carried, and it is probable that the pivoted tubular bracket under the right hand side of the cupola is used for mounting this. Part of the mounting appears to be deficient, so the telescope could not be fitted.

AUXILIARY ARMAMENT

Smoke Generator Dischargers

These are mounted in two sets of three, one on each forward side wall of the turret. The top discharger of each set has an elevation of 30° and is on a parallel axis with the keel line of the tank. The centre dischargers have an elevation of 35° and are inclined outwards with their axes at 15° to the keel line. The bottom dischargers also have an elevation of 35°, but are inclined further outboard with their axes at 30° to the keel line.

The discharger cups are of 95 mm. internal diameter and of 150 mm. internal length. They are of Nb.K.Wg type and are electrically fired from six push buttons, in two sets of three, on the turret roof on each side and forward of the cupola.

They fire the Nb.K. 39 90 mm. smoke generator, six of which are carried, one in each discharger. No spare generators, primers or discharger spares are carried.

Machine Carbine and Ports

The machine carbine is assumed to be the 9 mm. M.P. 38 or 40, and is vertically stowed on the offside rear of the turret wall. Earlier models of the Pz. Kw. VI had two machine carbine ports, similar to those in the Italian tanks M.11/39 and M.13/40, at 4 o'clock and 8 o'clock in the turret wall.

These ports are closed by means of a rotating armoured shutter operated by a lever. The shutters contain an eccentrically positioned aperture, which may be moved into or out of register with a similar sized aperture in the turret wall.

In later models, including that under examination, the 4 o'clock port has been removed and replaced by a large circular loading or escape hatch which swings downwards and outwards and may be opened (but not closed) from the inside. It is locked by a vertically sliding bar held by two screw clamps. As it cannot be closed from the inside, it obviously cannot be used for the jettisoning of empty cases in action.

Signal Pistol

This is the 27 mm. (1.032 in.) Walther signal and grenade pistol (Kampfpistole) and is stowed on the left hand turret wall behind the commander's traverse wheel. It is rifled and carries a small dial sight for use with H.E. Grenades.

Descriptions of this pistol and its ammunition will be found as follows :-

Pistol - Enemy Weapons, Part V

Pistol and Ammunition - M.I.10 Summary No. 101

Ammunition - M.I.10 Summaries Nos. 65 and 112.

"Minenabwurfer"

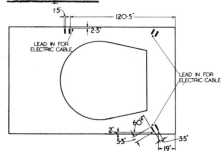

Provision appears to be made on the nearside rear, and the near and offside front of the superstructure roof for the fitting of three "Minenabwurfer" or mine-droppers. They appear to be electrically fired from the fighting compartment, the leads being connected to a switch in the centre of the rear bulkhead. The mine droppers and the switch are deficient on this vehicle.

Their exact function is unknown and no details are available, but from examination of a photograph (STT No. 4069.) they would appear to consist of a small cylinder, similar to the smoke generator dischargers on the turret. The mountings are fixed, that of the rear thrower pointing outboard at 90° and those of the forward throwers at 45°, to the keel line, and elevated at approximately 30°. The mine thrower can only be a single shot weapon, with no means of reloading in action once fired.

AMMUNITION

SUMMARY

The following ammunition is carried on this tank :-

Calibre & Type	No. of Rounds
8.8 cm. Kw. K 36	92
7.92 mm. M.G. 34	5,100 (34 - 150 rd. Belts)
27 mm. Signal Pistol	24 (12 white, 6 red, 6 green)
90 mm. Nb.K.39 Smoke Generators	6
9 mm. Machine Carbine	An unknown number, in 32-round magazines.

8.8 cm. AMMUNITION

Where Stowed		No. of Rounds
Left of driver	-	6
Offside of forward compartment	-	16
Nearside of forward compartment	-	16
Forward offside of fighting compartment	-	4
Forward nearside of fighting compartment	-	4
Aft offside of fighting compartment	-	16
Offside floor of fighting compartment	-	4
Nearside floor of fighting compartment	-	4
Under turntable, offside (may only be removed when turret is at 12 o'clock	-	6
Aft nearside of fighting compartment	-	16
TOTAL	-	92

All rounds are horizontally stowed, lying fore and aft, alternately nose and base forward, in unarmoured sheet metal bins with folding doors.

The rounds stowed on the fighting compartment floor are retained at their bases by rests, sliding vertically in grooves in the bin sides. The rests may be lifted, pushed back and dropped into grooves out of register with the rounds as the latter are removed.

The neck of each round sits on a pivoted spring loaded rest which may be swung sideways into the side of the bin when the round is removed to facilitate access to the lower rounds. As the majority of rounds are stowed high up in the vehicle, they are more vulnerable than those in British A.F.V.'s which are stowed low down in armoured bins.

Normal Flak 18 and 36 ammunition is used in this gun, fitted with C/22 electric primers instead of C/12 percussion primers. According to a captured document (M.I.10 letter A/M564) the types and proportions of ammunition in use in the N. African campaign were H.E. (25%) A.P. 38 (A.P.C.B.C.) (66%) and A.P. 40 (9%). For a total of 92 rounds these proportions give 23 rounds of H.E., 61 rounds of A.P.C.B.C. and 8 rounds of A.P. 40 per tank. In the tank under examination only A.P.C.B.C and H.E. (with percussion fuze) rounds were found. Both the A.P.C.B.C. and H.E. have smoke tracers.

Any of the undermentioned types of ammunition may be used, however, although H.E. with time fuze is not likely to be encountered.

Type	A.P.38 A.P.C.B.C	A.P.40	H.E/A.Tk (HI.Gr Patr 39)	H.E (Percussion Fuze)	H.E. (Time Fuze)
M.V.(ft/sec)	2657	3000	1968	2690	2690
Weight of Round (lbs)	33.75			32	31.75
Length of Round (ins)	34.21			36.69	36.69
Weight of Projectile (lbs)	20.75	16	16.75	20.3	20.06
Length of Projectile (ins)	14.49			15.55	15.55
Filling (lbs)	3 T.N.T		1.5	1.9 Cast Amatol	1.9 Cast Amatol
Fuze	Base 222		A.Z.38 St.	Nose (percussion) A.Z.23/28	Nose (clockwork) Zt.Z.s/30
Propellant Charge (lbs)	5.34 diglycol Nitro Cellulose	6.14 diglycol	2.6 diglycol	5.34 diglycol	5.34 diglycol
Weight of Core (lbs)		4.25			
Length of Core (ins)		5.5			
Diameter of Core (ins)		1.375			

<u>Cartridge Case</u>

Weight	–	3.06 kg. (6.75 lbs.)
Length	–	569 mm. (22.4 ins.)
Diameter at neck	–	90 mm. (3.54 ins.)
Diameter at base	–	103 mm. (4.06 ins.)
Diameter at rim	–	115 mm. (4.56 ins.)

Capacity :– 3650 cc's   Design No. 6347

These base markings are typical of those found on the ammunition in the tank at the time of examination.

An elevation scale for the Kw. K 36 firing H.E. with percussion fuze will be found at Appendix "A" to Part I of this report.

For further information on the ammunition for the Kw. K 36, see the following :–

A.P.C.B.C. (A.P. 38)	–	Enemy Weapons, Part V (Appendix "F"). M.I.10 Summaries Nos. 80/3, 98/3 and 72/3 and Appendix "E".
A.P.40	–	M.I.10 Summaries Nos. 72/3 and Appendix "E", and 107 M.I.10 Summary (14/9/43) 1/2 No. 17.
H.E./A.Tk	–	M.I.10 Summary No. 111/6.
H.E. (Percussion Fuze)	–	Handbook of Enemy Ammunition, Pamphlet No. 1 (sec.ii.) M.I.10 Summary No. 80/3 C.
H.E. Shell (Time Fuze)	–	Handbook of Enemy Ammunition Pamphlet No. 1 (sec.ii.) Enemy Weapons Part IV (Appendix "E"). M.I.10 Summary No. 72 (Appendix "D").

<u>7.92 mm. AMMUNITION</u>

<u>Fighting Compartment</u>

<u>Where Stowed</u>	<u>No. of Belt Bags (150 rds)</u>
Forward bulkhead – Offside side plate	1
Rear Bulkhead – Nearside, bottom	1
Rear Bulkhead – Nearside, higher up	5
Rear Bulkhead – Centre bottom	3
Rear Bulkhead – Offside bottom	1
Rear Bulkhead – Offside top	1
Offside turret wall (behind loader)	4
On Gun	1
Total in Fighting Compartment	17

Hull Gunner's Compartment

Where Stowed	No. of Belt Bags (150 rds).
Rear bulkhead, above pannier	4
Offside wall, above pannier	8
Front vertical plate, above pannier	4
On Gun	1
Total in hull gunner's compartment	17

Total in tank - 34 belt bags (5,100 rounds).

This total agrees with that in the captured stowage list, which gives 32 belt bags, not including one at each gun. Each belt contained a mixture of A.P. trace and A.P. incendiary rounds of 1937 and 1938 manufacture in the approximate ratio of 50 rounds of A.P.I. in each belt. Two belts, however, consisted of ball (with green annulus and varnished steel cases) and A.P. trace (with coppered steel cases) of 1942 manufacture, in the ratio of 75 : 25.

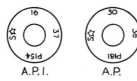

These markings on the bases of the rounds are typical.

For further data on 7.92 ammunition, See C.I.A. Foreign Ammunition Chart, Lines "C" and "D".

SMOKE GENERATORS

These are the Nb.K.39, 90 mm. generator, and use the C/23 electric primer, a miniature version of the electric C/22 fitted on the 8.8 cm. ammunition. No spare smoke generators are carried.

SIGNAL CARTRIDGES

These are stowed in two metal containers on the rear of the turret ring on the right hand side of the commander.

MACHINE CARBINE 9mm.

An unknown number of 32-round magazines are stowed in a removable container beside the machine carbine on the offside of the rear turret wall.

APPENDIX "A" TO SECTION I, PART II

OF REPORT ON PZ. KW. VI (H)

ELEVATION SCALE

-for the-

GERMAN TANK GUN 8.8 cm. Kw.K 36.

Firing H.E. with Percussion Fuze

(Taken from Clinometer)

RANGE (metres)	T.E (mils)	RANGE (metres)	T.E (mils)	RANGE (metres)	T.E. (mils)
200	1.6	3600	38.0	6550	101.6
400	3.0	3700	39.7	6600	103.1
600	4.5	3800	41.3	6650	104.8
800	6.4	3900	42.6	6700	106.3
1000	8.0	4000	44.2	6750	107.6
1100	9.3	4100	45.5	6800	109.2
1200	10.0	4200	47.4	6850	110.8
1300	11.0	4300	49.5	6900	112.2
1400	12.0	4400	51.5	6950	113.7
1500	13.1	4500	53.5	7000	115.1
1600	14.2	4600	55.5	7050	116.9
1700	15.3	4700	57.6	7100	118.2
1800	16.5	4800	59.7	7150	119.8
1900	17.5	4900	61.8	7200	121.3
2000	18.5	5000	63.9	7250	122.8
2100	19.8	5100	65.9	7300	124.3
2200	20.8	5200	68.0	7350	125.9
2300	22.0	5300	70.0	7400	127.3
2400	23.0	5400	72.0	7450	128.7
2500	24.2	5500	74.0	7500	130.3
2600	25.8	5600	76.0	7550	132.2
2700	26.8	5700	78.2	7600	134.0
2800	28.0	5800	80.5	7650	136.2
2900	29.2	5900	83.2	7700	138.0
3000	30.4	6000	86.0	7750	140.1
3100	31.5	6100	88.3	7800	142.2
3200	32.7	6200	91.3	7850	144.2
3300	34.0	6300	94.1	7900	146.3
3400	35.2	6400	97.2	7950	148.3
3500	36.6	6500	100.2	8000	150.6

RESTRICTED

The information given in this document
is not to be communicated, either directly
or indirectly, to the Press or to any person
not authorized to receive it.

REPORT ON

Pz Kw VI
(Tiger)
Model H

PART II

ARMAMENT, FIGHTING ARRANGEMENTS, STOWAGE

AND POWER TRAVERSE

SECTION II

FIGHTING ARRANGEMENTS

Military College of Science
SCHOOL OF TANK TECHNOLOGY
Chobham Lane   Chertsey

January   1944

PART II

ARMAMENT, FIGHTING ARRANGEMENTS, STOWAGE AND POWER TRAVERSE

SECTION II

FIGHTING ARRANGEMENTS

INTRODUCTION

The fighting arrangements in this vehicle are, to a large extent, of standard German design. Notable innovations are the offsetting of the commander's position and cupola to the nearside (following British practice), the rotating turret floor and the provision of a seat for the loader.

Although crew comfort has been given great consideration during design, in actual fact the commander's and gunner's positions are somewhat cramped. On the other hand the loader's position is roomy by comparison with that in recent British tanks, partly on account of the absence of ammunition stowage on the turntable.

February, 1944.   Lieut. P.L. Gudgin (R.T.R)

FIGHTING CHAMBER, LAYOUT AND CREW ACCOMMODATION

<u>Leading Dimensions of Fighting Chamber</u>

Height of roof above turret ring	$25\frac{1}{2}$ ins.
Depth of turret ring	$7\frac{1}{4}$ "
Turret platform to turret ring	$28\frac{1}{4}$ "
Headroom in turret	61 "
Additional headroom in cupola	$10\frac{1}{2}$ "
Total headroom	$71\frac{1}{2}$ "
Distance between trunnions	$54\frac{7}{8}$ "
Distance of trunnion axis from centre of turret	$49\frac{1}{2}$ "
Height of trunnion axis above top of turret ring	$9\frac{1}{2}$ "
Height of front of roof above trunnion axis	16 " (approx)
Floor to trunnion axis	45 " (")
Ground to trunnion axis	82
Offset of axis of 8 8 cm. gun to right of turret centre	4 "
Internal diameter of turret ring	$70\frac{1}{2}$ "
Diameter of turret platform	$57\frac{1}{2}$ "
Internal diameter of cupola	18 "

LAYOUT AND CREW ACCOMMODATION

For the first time, the commander's position is offset to the near-side behind the gunner. A pressed sheet metal guard plate is bolted to the roof of the turret on the commander's right hand side, which protects him from the left deflector guard side plate, and possible injury to his right elbow by the recoil of the gun.

Commander

The commander's seat is mounted on a pillar bolted to the turret ring at 7 o'clock. There are two seats on the same pillar, one above the other. The upper one (52" above the turret platform) is used for observing out of the top of the cupola, and when not in use may be folded down, to form the backrest of the lower seat, by operating a lever on the right hand side of the pillar against the compression of a spring. The lower seat (36" above the turret platform) may be folded up when not in use. Two footrests are provided, as described below.

Gunner

This seat is non-adjustable and is mounted $21\frac{3}{4}$" above the turret platform on an extension arm welded to the hollow casing of the elevating handwheel shaft.

Below the seat is welded a footrest $18\frac{1}{4}$" above the turret platform for use with the commander's lower seat. The back-rest is secured to the power traverse drive casing which also carries the footrest for the commander's upper seat, $26\frac{1}{2}$" above the turret platform.

Loader

For the first time, the Germans have in this tank, seriously considered the seating and comfort of the loader. His seat is mounted on the off-side of the fighting chamber, $22\frac{1}{2}$" above the turret platform. It is pivotally mounted on the elevation gearbox and normally faces to the rear. When not in use, however, it may be lifted and swung forwards under the gun It is not adjustable for height.

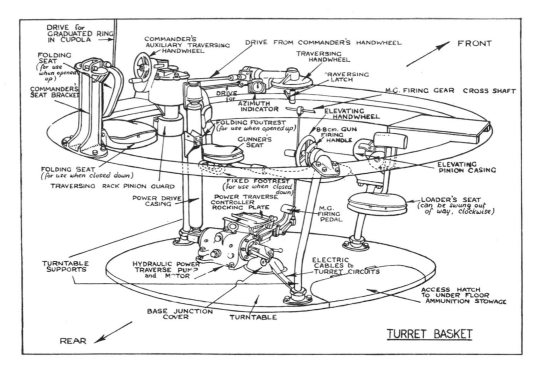

Diagram labels:

DRIVE for GRADUATED RING IN CUPOLA
COMMANDER'S AUXILIARY TRAVERSING HANDWHEEL
DRIVE FROM COMMANDER'S HANDWHEEL
FRONT
FOLDING SEAT (for use when opened up)
TRAVERSING HANDWHEEL
TRAVERSING LATCH
COMMANDERS SEAT BRACKET
DRIVE for AZIMUTH INDICATOR
M.G. FIRING GEAR CROSS SHAFT
ELEVATING HANDWHEEL
FOLDING FOOTREST (for use when opened up)
8·8 cm. GUN FIRING HANDLE
GUNNER'S SEAT
ELEVATING PINION CASING
FOLDING SEAT (for use when closed down)
TRAVERSING RACK PINION GUARD
FIXED FOOTREST (for use when closed down)
POWER DRIVE CASING
POWER TRAVERSE CONTROLLER ROCKING PLATE
M.G. FIRING PEDAL
LOADER'S SEAT (can be swung out of way, clockwise)
TURNTABLE SUPPORTS
HYDRAULIC POWER TRAVERSE PUMP and MOTOR
ELECTRIC CABLES to TURRET CIRCUITS
ACCESS HATCH TO UNDER FLOOR AMMUNITION STOWAGE
BASE JUNCTION COVER
TURNTABLE
REAR
TURRET BASKET

Driver

The driver has an orthodox seat of tubular metal construction. It is mounted on the forward near side of the hull floor, is adjustable longitudinally and has a ratchet adjustment for the backrest (see diagram).

Hull Gunner

This is a fixed non-adjustable seat of orthodox type on the off side floor of the forward compartment. The backrest is hinged to the hull side-plate and may be lifted out of the way to facilitate rapid exit from the turret through the forward compartment, or vice versa.

All seats are fitted with comfortable sponge rubber seats and back-rests.

VISION

Commander

Five vision slits (size $7\frac{1}{4}"x\frac{5}{8}"$) around the cupola. These are provided with standard fixed laminated glass blocks, 94 mm. thick; no protective shutters are fitted. A sighting vane is incorporated in the front episcope. One machine carbine port at 8 o'clock in nearside turret wall.

Turret Gunner

Binocular sight T.Z.F.9 (b)

One vision port, with slit 5" x $\frac{3}{8}$" at 10 o'clock in nearside turret wall. Both this and the loader's slit have a replaceable laminated glass block (70 mm. x 150 mm. x 94 mm.) and no B.P. shutters.

Loader

One vision port at 12 o'clock in offside turret wall (similar to gunner's).

One loading and escape hatch at 4 o'clock in offside turret wall (or one machine carbine port in earlier models). It is believed that an episcope is located in front of the loader's hatch in the latest models.

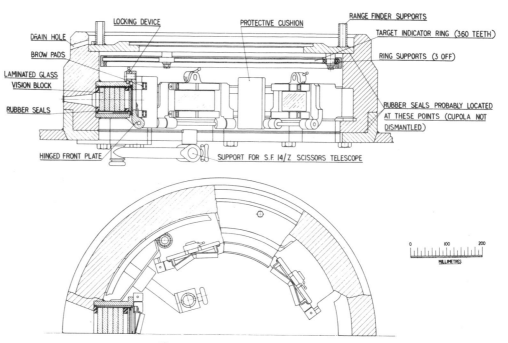

Section through Cupola

Hull Gunner

One sighting telescope K. Z. F. 2.

One episcope in a circular hatch in superstructure roof. Both this and the driver's episcope have plastic casings and renewable prisms. The windows measure 5"x1½" and the length has been increased by a rubber faced distance piece to 11". Both episcopes are fixed facing forward and outboard, at an angle of about 30° to the keel line of the tank and have armoured hoods.

Driver

One visor in the front vertical plate, with a double sliding shutter (operated by a handwheel on the right of the steering wheel) and a replaceable laminated glass block (70 mm. x 240 mm. x 94 mm.).

Two holes for the driver's episcope K. F. F. 2 in the front vertical plate have been plugged and welded. The episcope has also been deleted in a captured stowage list, though it was present on a Pz. Kw. VI. examined on the battlefield in N. Africa by the writer.

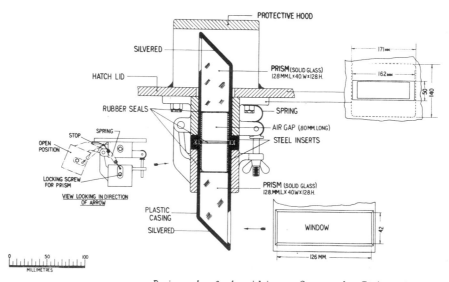

Driver's & Auxiliary Gunner's Episcope

RESTRICTED

The information given in this document
is not to be communicated. either directly
or indirectly. to the Press or to any person
not authorized to receive it.

REPORT ON
PzKw VI
(Tiger)
Model H

PART II

ARMAMENT, FIGHTING ARRANGEMENTS, STOWAGE

AND POWER TRAVERSE

SECTION III

STOWAGE

Military College of Science
SCHOOL OF TANK TECHNOLOGY
Chobham Lane   Chertsey

January   1944

PART II

ARMAMENT, FIGHTING ARRANGEMENTS, STOWAGE AND POWER TRAVERSE

SECTION III

STOWAGE

INTRODUCTION

The stores and fittings stowed in this vehicle show little variation from those previously found in British or German tanks. The chief difference is the provision of accessories for deep wading and the method of attaching fittings to the turret walls. The latter is worthy of especial note.

The items have been carefully positioned to achieve ease of access and maximum freedom of movement for the crew.

Two lists of items are given - first, a list of those fittings, stores etc. found in the tank under examination, and second, a captured enemy official kit list, with ordnance reference numbers.

This Section has been compiled in collaboration with Major Shaw, D.C.M., R.T.R., V/GD Branch, D.T.D.

February, 1944.   Lieut. P.L. Gudgin, (R.T.R.)

STOWAGE

1. INTERNAL

(a) Fighting Chamber

All stowage fittings in the turret are welded, not directly to the turret wall but to vertical strips approximately $\frac{1}{4}$" clear of the wall. These are welded at the top to the turret roof and at the bottom to the turret ring. Thus, a hit on the wall will not cause the fittings to be projected into the turret, unless directly hit by the projectile.

Item	No.	Where Stowed	Item in captured Equipment Table
Breathing tubes	2	In containers, front near-side turret roof	C. 47
Breathing tube	1	In container, front off-side turret roof	C. 47
Plug for machine gun port	1	Front offside turret roof	C. 11
Pivoted bracket (scissors telescope ?)	1	On right of cupola " "	
Container for gun history sheets	1	Nearside turret side wall	
Gunner's respirator	1	" " " "	
Signal pistol	1	" " " "	C. 43
Container for binoculars	1	Nearside rear on turret ring	
Stopper for machine carbine port	1	Nearside rear turret side wall	C. 12
Commander's respirator	1	Rear turret wall	
Water bottle	1	" " "	
W/T headset and microphone	2	In boxes on turret wall	C.52, 53 & 54
Glass blocks for vision ports	4	Rear turret wall	C. 27
Hatch keys	2	" " "	C. 36
Containers for signal cartridges	2	" " "	C. 46
Carrier for M.G. ammunition container	1	Offside " "	C. 29
Machine carbine	1	" " "	C. 40
Water bottle	1	Offside turret side wall	
Loader's respirator	1	" " " "	
Projectile ejector (Entlader)	1	" " " "	C. 57
Holder for M.G. bipod box	1	" " " "	C. 19
Water bottle	1	" " " "	
"Baggage" container	1	" " " "	
Fire extinguisher	1	Front of turret platform	63
Box	1	Front of turret platform under gunner's seat	
Box for 8.8cm Breech spares	2	Front of turret platform	C. 1
5 gallon water cans	3	Rear " " "	64 & 65
Stowed position turret M.G	1	Nearside of turret platform	
Wire basket	1	Nearside of turret platform (under commander's seat)	
M.G. spare barrels, in case	2	Offside of front bulkhead	C. 39
Spare prism	1	Nearside of front bulkhead	C. 25
Box for M.G tools	1	Rear of offside wall	C. 13

(b) <u>Auxiliary gunner's compartment.</u>

Respirator	1	Offisde pannier side wall	
Spare prism	1	" " " "	C. 25
M.G. spare barrels in case	2	" " " "	C. 39
Box for M.G. Tools	1	Offside of front bulkhead	C. 13
Breathing tube	1	Centre of front bulkhead	C. 47
Water bottle	1	Front wall, on right of M.G.	
Spare prism	1	" " " " "	C. 25
First aid kit	1	On pannier roof, offside	C. 42
M.G. spares box	2	" " "	C. 38
Clips for offside headlamp when stowed.		Offside superstructure roof.	

(c) <u>Driver's Compartment.</u>

Clips for nearside headlamp		Nearside superstructure roof	
Vision blocks (spare)	2	Offside above instrument panel	C. 26
Breathing tube	1	Offside of front bulkhead	C. 47
W/T headset & microphone	2	Offside floor, behind seat	C. 52, 53 & 54
Water bottle	1	Nearside of front bulkhead	
Spare prism	1	Nearside of front bulkhead	C. 25
Respirator	1	Nearside pannier wall behind seat	
Oil can	1	Nearside floor, behind seat	46
Box for telescope accessories (?)	1	Nearside pannier wall	
Gyroscopic direction indicator	1	Nearside front of pannier roof	C. 44
1 Bin in floor behind seat table.)		(See section II (c) of 3, Enemy Equipment	

2 <u>EXTERNAL.</u>

Towrope	2	Offside and nearside, superstructure roof	81
Crow bar	1	Nearside " "	75
Wireless Aerial	1	Offside " "	
Fire Extinguisher (hand)	1	In holder, offside rear of superstructure roof.	80
Jacking block	1	Front offside, superstructure roof	74
Axe	1	Front centre of superstructure roof	76
Wire cutters	1pr	Front nearside of superstructure roof	77
Blanking off plate	1	" " "	83
Shovel	1	" " "	79
Spade	1	Centre of front glacis plate	78
Sledge hammer	1	Front centre of superstructure roof	82
Track pulling cable	1	Nearside side plate	73
Track tool box	1	" " rear of track guard	28
Inertia starter handle	1	Offside, rear vertical plate	71
15-ton jack	1	Offside, rear track guard	72
Towing shackles	2	Offside and nearside, rear vertical plate	86
Track links	12	Front vertical plate	
Stowage bin	1	On rear of turret.	

The five or six section cleaning rod for the 8.8 cm gun, when carried is secured externally in the tow rope clips on the superstructure roof. No rods were present on this vehicle. Variations in stowage positions for most of the above mentioned items may be encountered, as, from examination of various photographs, no standard layout would appear to have been fixed as yet.

Certain fittings have been seen on the turret sides arranged vertically in pairs, 5 pairs a side. The purpose of these is unknown and none were found on the tank under examination.

EQUIPMENT TABLE FOR Pz.Kw.VI, MODEL H, MARK H1. (Translation of a captured document).

Serial No.	Description	No. per veh.	Indent Ref & Drawing No.
	I. TOOLS AND SPARE PARTS		
	A. Carried inside vehicle.		
	1. In tank tool box		
1.	Tool box, tank pattern	1	21 B 7641
2.	List of contents for tool box	1	021 St 37083
3.	Spanners DE (8 x 9)	1	)
4.	" (10 x 11)	1	)
5.	" (14 x 17)	1	) DIN 839
6.	" (19 x 22)	1	)
7.	" (24 x 27)	1	)
8.	Spanners, box, hexagonal DE (8 x 9)	1	R 9 5322
9.	" (10 x 11)	1	R 2 5323
10.	" (14 x 17)	1	R 5326
11.	" (19 x 22)	1	R 5331
12.	" (24 x 27)	1	R 5334
13.	Tommy Bar	1	R 5335
14.	Spanner, adjustable, 70 mm.	1	R 5292
15.	Half-round file, bastard, 200 mm. long	1	R 2103
16.	File handle with guard, diam. of handle 23mm.	1	R 2324
17.	Hammer, fitters, wt. 500 g. with handle	1	R 4586
18.	Screwdriver, with handle, blade .05 mm.	1	R2 5152
19.	" blade 1.2 mm.	1	R6 5152
20.	Roll of insulating tape in sealed packing width 15 mm. length 5 m.	1	Commercial Pattern
21.	Fire-point elements.	10	DIN 72581
	2. In engine tool box (Maybach) (attached to engine) Spare parts (incl in tool box)		
22.	Gauge, valve adjustment, contact breaker and point clearance	1	225084/1
23.	Spanner, sparking plug and jet	1	
24.	Sparking plugs	3	W 225 T 1
25.	Washers for sparking plugs (14 x 20)	3	DIN 7603
26.	Spare bowl for petrol pump	1	351 192/1
27.	Washer for above	1	351 193/1
	B. Secured outside vehicle		
	3. In track tool box on tailplate		
28.	Tool box complete	1	021 B 2799 U6
29.	List of contents	1	021 D 2799-49
30.	Track puller	1	021 C 39399 U9
31.	Hammer, fitters, wt. 1500 g. with handle	1	R 45 89
32.	Spanner for track tensioning and for removing covers over track adjusting spindles	1	021 D 2799-6

33.	Drifts for track-pins	1	021 E 2799-8
34.	Steel wire, diam. 1 mm., wt. 100 g. (on wooden fork 021 F 8999-12)	1	021-41099
35.	Pliers, combination 160 mm. long	1	R 4406
36.	Chisel, flat 25 x 16, 200 mm. long	1	R 4145
37.	Securing rings for track-pins	100	HE 2996-4
38.	Spanner for air pipe	1	021 C 2743 U14
39.	Spanner (box) for bogie wheels and sprockets	1	021 E 2799-5
40.	Hollow drift for track	1	021 E 2799-7

4. In bin on back of turret

41.	Track links	10	HB 3008-1
42.	Track pins	10	HE 2996-3

II. AUXILIARY EQUIPMENT

1. Carried inside vehicle

(a) In container on left under driver

43.	"Magnet" inspection lamp 12 V 15 W with protective wire grid and 20' flex	1	021 E 8999-38
44.	Box for above	1	021 E 8999-39

(b) On floor to left of driver

46.	Oil can, capacity 15 litres	1	U 481
47.	Grease gun with flex piping capacity 500 cu.cms.	1	U 548
48.	Coupling (for grease gun nozzle)	1	021 F 9399-64

(c) Behind driver's seat under floor

49.	Cotton waste, 1 lb.	1	
50.	Weather shield (hung on instrument panel)	1	
51.	Spanner, hexagonal for screw filler on power traverse 22 mm. diam., and for screw filler on radiator 32 mm. diam.	1	021 D 2799 U17
52.	Spanner for engine cover plates	1	021 D 2799 U16
52a.	Spanner, hexagonal, for internal engine bolts	1	14 DIN 911
53.	Spanner, for watertight seat on engine cover plates	1	021 E 2799 U14
54.	Filler, oil	1	U 574
55.	Filler, power traverse oil	1	021 E 2799-51

(d) In bin on back of turret

56.	Tarpaulins 1200 x 1800 mm. (6' x 4')	2	HSK No. J 3003

(e) In box (apparatus carried on tank for use in cold weather)

57.	Hose for transfer of warm water with holder	1	R10-104/4-14
58.	Heating equipment with handpump	1	HSK No.J 2838 U1
59.	Blow lamp	1	R 1 5882
60.	Connecting hose for heating equipment, 1200 mm (4' long)	1	HSK No.J 2838 U2
61.	Connecting hose for heating equipment, 1800 mm (6' long)	1	HSK No.J 2838 U2

(f) In satchel

62.	Instructional satchel containing:		
	Maintenance handbook incl. description and working instructions, circuit and layout diagrams		HSK No.J 2713
	Diagram of auto-fire extinguisher circuit		021 C 2727-17
	Drawing of warm water transfer equipment		HSK No.J 2933
	Drawing of pre-heater equipment		HSK No.J 2932
	Drawing of heating arrangement for fighting compartment		HSK No.J 2934
	Lubricating and maintenance points		HSK No.J 3056
	Lubrication chart		HSK No.J 3076
	Equipment table for chassis		
	Equipment table for superstructure and turret		

(g) On turret turn-table

63.	Fire extinguisher (C.T.C), 2 litres,(4 pints) with holder	1	U 1705
64.	Water container, standard Army pattern, capacity 20 litres (5 gals)*	2	574/Army
65.	Container for distilled water, standard Army pattern, contents 20 litres*	1	574/Army

(h) Beside headlamp holder

67.	Screwdriver for headlamp, unstowed	1	021 E 2799-2
68.	Locking ring	1	F 8999-86
69.	Ignition key, Bosch	1	S.A.A3/7*
70.	Cover for ignition key	1	021 F 9299-202

2. Stowed outside vehicle

(a) On tail plate

71.	Handle for inertia starter	1	021 B 2799 U13
72.	Steel jack 15 tons, with ratchet drive	1	U1684/5 at present 3767/6341

(b) On left side-plate

73.	Steel cable, 14 mm. diam x 15 m long with eye	1	021E 2799 U12

(c) On roof

74.	Jacking pad	1	021E 29399 U4
75.	Crowbar 1800 mm. (5' 10") long	1	R 1843
76.	Axe *	1	R 24
77.	Wire cutters * /	1	28 B 41
78.	Spade *	1	29 C 46
79.	Shovel /	1	R 4284 DIN betn 120
80.	Fire extinguisher (C.T.C) (2 litres, with holder)	1	U1705
81.	Steel cable, 8.2 m. long 32 mm diam.	2	021 D 2799-45
82.	Sledge-hammer 6 kg (13¼ lbs.) with handle	1	R 4605
83.	Blanking off plate for air split over engine compartment	1	HSK No.J 3032
84.	Duct for warm air	1	HSK No.J 2743 U 1 in box
85.	Transfer hose for warm air	1	HSK No.J 2743 U5 in box
86.	Shackles (on tank)	4	

C. Equipment lists for superstructure and turret of Pz.Kw.VI, Model H1.

1.	Spares box (No.1) for breech of 8.8 cm.Kw.K 36	1	
2.	Cleaning rod head	1	5D 6899-115 U4
3.	Cleaning rod (in 5 or 6 parts) 4 rods 1238mm long	4	HSK J2669 U1
	1 rod 1240mm long	1	HSK J2669 U2
4.	Cover for cleaning rod	1	5C 6899-205
5.	Breech cover for 8.8 cm. Kw.K 36 (canvas)	1	5B 3899-2
6.	Lanyard for fuze key	1	8353
7.	Fuze key for percussion fuze (type A.Z.23)	1	13 E 6615
8.	(deleted) Muzzle Cover (canvas or artificial leather) for Kw. K 36	1	5C 3899-6
8a.	Muzzle covers (expendable)	10	5B 3899-5
9.	Canvas bag for muzzle covers	1	605 C 490
10.	Deflector bag	1	5B 3854 U2
11.	Plug for M.G opening	1	021 D 869
12.	Stopper for pistol port	1	per 021 SE875
13.	M.G spares boxes	2	21 St 7614
14.	Cover for M.G 34	1	021 C 57499-230
15.	Cover for gun mantlet	1	021 C 39099-80
16.	Cover for M.G. mantlet	1	in accordance with Model 4 St.ARF 31441
17.	Cartridge belt bags	32	021 St.39150
18.	Holders for above	2	021 St.37462
19.	Containers for M.G. spares (bipod, butt, foresight bracket) 1 in turret 1 in hull	)))	021 B 7622
20.	Sighting telescope (type TZF 9b)	1	027 Gn 185
20a.	Cover for above	1	027-265-267
21.	(deleted) Driver's episcope KFF2 (1 set binoculars)	1 set	027 Gr. 3539
21a.	Dust covers for above	2	021 St.33999-21
22.	M.G sighting telescope, type KZF2	1	027 Gr 5075
23.	Cover for ball mounting, '100'	1	According to Model Wa. proof 6.
24.	Cap for ball mounting	1	HSK J 3098
25.	Prism holders	8	021 D 2746-1
26.	Bullet-proof glass 70 x 240 x 94	3	021 St. 9296
27.	Bullet-proof glass 70 x 150 x 94	11	021 St. 9280
28.	Cover for machine carbine	1	021 C 37499-255
29.	Case for machine carbine magazines	1	01 B 3321
30.	Extraction fan (in fighting compartment) capacity 12-13 cu. in. (approx. 450 cu.ft) per min.	1	
31.	Extraction fan cover (watertight)	1	021 C860 U51
32.	"Out of action" flag (yellow and black)	1	021 D 33477
33.	Smoke discharger, left	1	021 St 41406
34.	" " , right	1	021 St 41407
35.	Switch boxes for Smoke dischargers	2	21 St 7642
36.	Hatch keys	2	6 AKF 31406-1
37.	M.G.34 with tank type barrel sleeve	2	
38.	Ammunition Boxes - M.G	3	
39.	Holders for M.G barrels (each containing 2 barrels)	3	
40.	Machine carbine	1	
41.	M.G spares (butt and bipod)	1	set
42.	First Aid kit	1	
43.	Signal Pistol	1	
44.	Gyro-direction indicator with lead	1	
45.	Transformer for above	1	
46.	Signal pistol ammunition, 24 rounds	12 white, 6 red, 6 green	
47.	Flexible hose for gas masks	4	
48.	Belt tags for M.G.34	32	
49.	Belt links for M.G. 34	96	
50.	Carrying slings (complete) for M.G.34	2	
51.	Belts filler 34 with box	1	

115

52.	Headsets, W/T, type B, soundproof	2	
53.	Throat microphone, type A, with 2-point plug and switch	2	
54.	Throat microphone, type B, with 3-point plug and switch	2	
55.	Twin lead, 25 cm. long with cross-piece and three double 20 mm. non-interchangeable plugs	1	
56.	Grease gun with tube, contents 140 cu.cm ($8\frac{1}{2}$ c.in.)	1	U547
57.	Ejector, projectile for 8.8 cm. gun	1	5E 6899-40
58.	Clinometer for 8.8 cm. gun	1	
59.	Spanner for M.G. 34	2	
60.	Muzzle covers for M.G. 34, expendable	4	
61.	Brushes for cleaning M.Gs.	2	
62.	" " "	4	
63.	Grease box for 2 oz. lubricating grease	1	J/9441/35 1099-210
64.	Sealing covers	2	4/VI/E 03479
65.	Air pump with tube)	–	4AKF 31406-50
66.	Air pressure gauge in leather case)	–	5AKF 31406-51
67.	Hexagonal box-spanner) Ø	–	5AKF 31406-52
68.	Tension device for compensating spring)	–	
69.	Padlocks	2	

*:	Supplied by unit.
≠	Fitted by Unit.
Ø	One of each for five turrets.
≠≠	On indent from C.O.O., Kassel.

RESTRICTED

The information given in this document
is not to be communicated. either directly
or indirectly, to the Press or to any person
not authorized to receive it.

REPORT ON

Pz Kw VI

(Tiger)

Model H

PART II

ARMAMENT, FIGHTING ARRANGEMENTS, STOWAGE

AND POWER TRAVERSE

SECTION III

STOWAGE

Military College of Science

SCHOOL OF TANK TECHNOLOGY

Chobham Lane   Chertsey

January   1944

117

PART II

ARMAMENT, FIGHTING ARRANGEMENTS, STOWAGE AND POWER TRAVERSE

SECTION III

STOWAGE

INTRODUCTION

The stores and fittings stowed in this vehicle show little variation from those previously found in British or German tanks. The chief difference is the provision of accessories for deep wading and the method of attaching fittings to the turret walls. The latter is worthy of especial note.

The items have been carefully positioned to achieve ease of access and maximum freedom of movement for the crew.

Two lists of items are given - first, a list of those fittings, stores etc. found in the tank under examination, and second, a captured enemy official kit list, with ordnance reference numbers.

This Section has been compiled in collaboration with Major Shaw, D.C.M., R.T.R., V/GD Branch, D.T.D.

February, 1944.   Lieut. P.L. Gudgin, (R.T.R.)

STOWAGE

1. INTERNAL

(a) Fighting Chamber

All stowage fittings in the turret are welded, not directly to the turret wall but to vertical strips approximately $\frac{1}{4}$" clear of the wall. These are welded at the top to the turret roof and at the bottom to the turret ring. Thus, a hit on the wall will not cause the fittings to be projected into the turret, unless directly hit by the projectile.

Item	No.	Where Stowed	Item in captured Equipment Table
Breathing tubes	2	In containers, front near-side turret roof	C. 47
Breathing tube	1	In container, front off-side turret roof	C. 47
Plug for machine gun port	1	Front offside turret roof	C. 11
Pivoted bracket (scissors telescope ?)	1	On right of cupola " "	
Container for gun history sheets	1	Nearside turret side wall	
Gunner's respirator	1	" " " "	
Signal pistol	1	" " " "	C. 43
Container for binoculars	1	Nearside rear on turret ring	
Stopper for machine carbine port	1	Nearside rear turret side wall	C. 12
Commander's respirator	1	Rear turret wall	
Water bottle	1	" " "	
W/T headset and microphone	2	In boxes on turret wall	C.52, 53 & 54
Glass blocks for vision ports	4	Rear turret wall	C. 27
Hatch keys	2	" " "	C. 36
Containers for signal cartridges	2	" " "	C. 46
Carrier for M.G. ammunition container	1	Offside " "	C. 29
Machine carbine	1	" " "	C. 40
Water bottle	1	Offside turret side wall	
Loader's respirator	1	" " " "	
Projectile ejector (Entlader)	1	" " " "	C. 57
Holder for M.G. bipod box	1	" " " "	C. 19
Water bottle	1	" " " "	
"Baggage" container	1	" " " "	
Fire extinguisher	1	Front of turret platform	63
Box	1	Front of turret platform under gunner's seat	
Box for 8.8cm Breech spares	2	Front of turret platform	C. 1
5 gallon water cans	3	Rear " " "	64 & 65
Stowed position turret M.G	1	Nearside of turret platform	
Wire basket	1	Nearside of turret platform (under commander's seat)	
M.G. spare barrels, in case	2	Offside of front bulkhead	C. 39
Spare prism	1	Nearside of front bulkhead	C. 25
Box for M.G tools	1	Rear of offside wall	C. 13

(b) <u>Auxiliary gunner's compartment.</u>

Respirator	1	Offsdie pannier side wall	
Spare prism	1	" " " "	C. 25
M.G. spare barrels in case	2	" " " "	C. 39
Box for M.G. Tools	1	Offside of front bulkhead	C. 13
Breathing tube	1	Centre of front bulkhead	C. 47
Water bottle	1	Front wall, on right of M.G.	
Spare prism	1	" " " "	C. 25
First aid kit	1	On pannier roof, offside	C. 42
M.G. spares box	2	" " "	C. 38
Clips for offside headlamp when stowed.		Offside superstructure roof.	

(c) <u>Driver's Compartment.</u>

Clips for nearside headlamp		Nearside superstructure roof	
Vision blocks (spare)	2	Offside above instrument panel	C. 26
Breathing tube	1	Offside of front bulkhead	C. 47
W/T headset & microphone	2	Offside floor, behind seat	C. 52, 53 & 54
Water bottle	1	Nearside of front bulkhead	
Spare prism	1	Nearside of front bulkhead	C. 25
Respirator	1	Nearside pannier wall behind seat	
Oil can	1	Nearside floor, behind seat	46
Box for telescope accessories (?)	1	Nearside pannier wall	
Gyroscopic direction indicator	1	Nearside front of pannier roof	C. 44
1 Bin in floor behind seat		(See section II (c) of 3, Enemy Equipment table.)	

2 <u>EXTERNAL.</u>

Towrope	2	Offside and nearside, superstructure roof	81
Crow bar	1	Nearside " "	75
Wireless Aerial	1	Offside " "	
Fire Extinguisher (hand)	1	In holder, offside rear of superstructure roof.	80
Jacking block	1	Front offside, super-structure roof	74
Axe	1	Front centre of superstructure roof	76
Wire cutters	1pr	Front nearside of super-structure roof	77
Blanking off plate	1	" " " "	83
Shovel	1	" " " "	79
Spade	1	Centre of front glacis plate	78
Sledge hammer	1	Front centre of super-structure roof	82
Track pulling cable	1	Nearside side plate	73
Track tool box	1	" " rear of track guard	28
Inertia starter handle	1	Offside, rear vertical plate	71
15-ton jack	1	Offside, rear track guard	72
Towing shackles	2	Offside and nearside, rear vertical plate	86
Track links	12	Front vertical plate	
Stowage bin	1	On rear of turret.	

The five or six section cleaning rod for the 8.8 cm gun, when carried is secured externally in the tow rope clips on the superstructure roof. No rods were present on this vehicle. Variations in stowage positions for most of the above mentioned items may be encountered, as, from examination of various photographs, no standard layout would appear to have been fixed as yet.

Certain fittings have been seen on the turret sides arranged vertically in pairs, 5 pairs a side. The purpose of these is unknown and none were found on the tank under examination.

EQUIPMENT TABLE FOR Pz.Kw.VI, MODEL H, MARK H1. (Translation of a captured document).

Serial No.	Description	No. per veh.	Indent Ref & Drawing No.
	I. TOOLS AND SPARE PARTS		
	A. Carried inside vehicle.		
	1. In tank tool box		
1.	Tool box, tank pattern	1	21 B 7641
2.	List of contents for tool box	1	021 St 37083
3.	Spanners DE (8 x 9)	1	)
4.	" (10 x 11)	1	)
5.	" (14 x 17)	1	) DIN 839
6.	" (19 x 22)	1	)
7.	" (24 x 27)	1	)
8.	Spanners, box, hexagonal DE (8 x 9)	1	R 9 5322
9.	" (10 x 11)	1	R 2 5323
10.	" (14 x 17)	1	R 5326
11.	" (19 x 22)	1	R 5331
12.	" (24 x 27)	1	R 5334
13.	Tommy Bar	1	R 5335
14.	Spanner, adjustable, 70 mm.	1	R 5292
15.	Half-round file, bastard, 200 mm. long	1	R 2103
16.	File handle with guard, diam. of handle 23mm.	1	R 2324
17.	Hammer, fitters, wt. 500 g. with handle	1	R 4586
18.	Screwdriver, with handle, blade .05 mm.	1	R2 5152
19.	" blade 1.2 mm.	1	R6 5152
20.	Roll of insulating tape in sealed packing width 15 mm. length 5 m.	1	Commercial Pattern
21.	Fire-point elements.	10	DIN 72581
	2. In engine tool box (Maybach) (attached to engine) Spare parts (incl in tool box)		
22.	Gauge, valve adjustment, contact breaker and point clearance	1	225084/1
23.	Spanner, sparking plug and jet	1	
24.	Sparking plugs	3	W 225 T 1
25.	Washers for sparking plugs (14 x 20)	3	DIN 7603
26.	Spare bowl for petrol pump	1	351 192/1
27.	Washer for above	1	351 193/1
	B. Secured outside vehicle		
	3. In track tool box on tailplate		
28.	Tool box complete	1	021 B 2799 U6
29.	List of contents	1	021 D 2799-49
30.	Track puller	1	021 C 39399 U9
31.	Hammer, fitters, wt. 1500 g. with handle	1	R 45 89
32.	Spanner for track tensioning and for removing covers over track adjusting spindles	1	021 D 2799-6

33.	Drifts for track-pins	1	021 E 2799-8
34.	Steel wire, diam. 1 mm., wt. 100 g. (on wooden fork 021 F 8999-12)	1	021-41099
35.	Pliers, combination 160 mm. long	1	R 4406
36.	Chisel, flat 25 x 16, 200 mm. long	1	R 4145
37.	Securing rings for track-pins	100	HE 2996-4
38.	Spanner for air pipe	1	021 C 2743 U14
39.	Spanner (box) for bogie wheels and sprockets	1	021 E 2799-5
40.	Hollow drift for track	1	021 E 2799-7

4. In bin on back of turret

41.	Track links	10	HB 3008-1
42.	Track pins	10	HE 2996-3

II. AUXILIARY EQUIPMENT

1. Carried inside vehicle

(a) In container on left under driver

43.	"Magnet" inspection lamp 12 V 15 W with protective wire grid and 20' flex	1	021 E 8999-38
44.	Box for above	1	021 E 8999-39

(b) On floor to left of driver

46.	Oil can, capacity 15 litres	1	U 481
47.	Grease gun with flex piping capacity 500 cu.cms.	1	U 548
48.	Coupling (for grease gun nozzle)	1	021 F 9399-64

(c) Behind driver's seat under floor

49.	Cotton waste, 1 lb.	1	
50.	Weather shield (hung on instrument panel)	1	
51.	Spanner, hexagonal for screw filler on power traverse 22 mm. diam., and for screw filler on radiator 32 mm. diam.	1	021 D 2799 U17
52.	Spanner for engine cover plates	1	021 D 2799 U16
52a.	Spanner, hexagonal, for internal engine bolts	1	14 DIN 911
53.	Spanner, for watertight seat on engine cover plates	1	021 E 2799 U14
54.	Filler, oil	1	U 574
55.	Filler, power traverse oil	1	021 E 2799-51

(d) In bin on back of turret

56.	Tarpaulins 1200 x 1800 mm. (6' x 4')	2	HSK No. J 3003

(e) In box (apparatus carried on tank for use in cold weather)

57.	Hose for transfer of warm water with holder	1	R10-104/4-14
58.	Heating equipment with handpump	1	HSK No.J 2838 U1
59.	Blow lamp	1	R 1 5882
60.	Connecting hose for heating equipment, 1200 mm (4' long)	1	HSK No.J 2838 U2
61.	Connecting hose for heating equipment, 1800 mm (6' long)	1	HSK No.J 2838 U2

(f) In satchel

62.	Instructional satchel containing:
	  Maintenance handbook incl. description and
	    working instructions, circuit and layout
	    diagrams
			HSK No.J 2713

	Diagram of auto-fire extinguisher circuit		021 C 2727-17
	Drawing of warm water transfer equipment		HSK No.J 2933
	Drawing of pre-heater equipment		HSK No.J 2932
	Drawing of heating arrangement for fighting compartment		HSK No.J 2934
	Lubricating and maintenance points		HSK No.J 3056
	Lubrication chart		HSK No.J 3076
	Equipment table for chassis		
	Equipment table for superstructure and turret		

(g) On turret turn-table

63.	Fire extinguisher (C.T.C), 2 litres,(4 pints) with holder	1	U 1705
64.	Water container, standard Army pattern, capacity 20 litres (5 gals)*	2	574/Army
65.	Container for distilled water, standard Army pattern, contents 20 litres*	1	574/Army

(h) Beside headlamp holder

67.	Screwdriver for headlamp, unstowed	1	021 E 2799-2
68.	Locking ring	1	F 8999-86
69.	Ignition key, Bosch	1	S.A.A3/7*
70.	Cover for ignition key	1	021 F 9299-202

2. Stowed outside vehicle

(a) On tail plate

71.	Handle for inertia starter	1	021 B 2799 U13
72.	Steel jack 15 tons, with ratchet drive	1	U1684/5 at present 3767/6341

(b) On left side-plate

73.	Steel cable, 14 mm. diam x 15 m. long with eye	1	021E 2799 U12

(c) On roof

74.	Jacking pad	1	021E 29399 U4
75.	Crowbar 1800 mm. (5' 10") long	1	R 1843
76.	Axe *	1	R 24
77.	Wire cutters * ≠	1	28 B 41
78.	Spade *	1	29 C 46
79.	Shovel ≠	1	R 4284 DIN betn 120
80.	Fire extinguisher (C.T.C) (2 litres, with holder)	1	U1705
81.	Steel cable, 8.2 m. long 32 mm diam.	2	021 D 2799-45
82.	Sledge-hammer 6 kg (13¼ lbs.) with handle	1	R 4605
83.	Blanking off plate for air split over engine compartment	1	HSK No.J 3032
84.	Duct for warm air	1	HSK No.J 2743 U 1 in box
85.	Transfer hose for warm air	1	HSK No.J 2743 U5 in box
86.	Shackles (on tank)	4	

C. Equipment lists for superstructure and turret of Pz.Kw.VI, Model H1.

1.	Spares box (No.1) for breech of 8.8 cm.Kw.K 36	1	
2.	Cleaning rod head	1	5D 6899-115 U4
3.	Cleaning rod (in 5 or 6 parts) 4 rods 1238mm long	4	HSK J2669 U1
	1 rod 1240mm long	1	HSK J2669 U2
4.	Cover for cleaning rod	1	5C 6899-205
5.	Breech cover for 8.8 cm. Kw.K 36 (canvas)	1	5B 3899-2
6.	Lanyard for fuze key	1	8353
7.	Fuze key for percussion fuze (type A.Z.23)	1	13 E 6615
8.	(deleted) Muzzle Cover (canvas or artificial leather) for Kw. K 36	1	5C 3899-6
8a.	Muzzle covers (expendable)	10	5B 3899-5
9.	Canvas bag for muzzle covers	1	605 C 490
10.	Deflector bag	1	5B 3854 U2
11.	Plug for M.G opening	1	021 D 869
12.	Stopper for pistol port	1	per 021 SE875
13.	M.G spares boxes	2	21 St 7614
14.	Cover for M.G 34	1	021 C 57499-230
15.	Cover for gun mantlet	1	021 C 39099-80
16.	Cover for M.G. mantlet	1	in accordance with Model 4 St.ARF 31441
17.	Cartridge belt bags	32	021 St.39150
18.	Holders for above	2	021 St.37462
19.	Containers for M.G. spares (bipod, butt, foresight bracket) 1 in turret 1 in hull	)))	021 B 7622
20.	Sighting telescope (type TZF 9b)	1	027 Gn 185
20a.	Cover for above	1	027-265-267
21.	(deleted) Driver's episcope KFF2 (1 set binoculars)	1 set	027 Gr. 3539
21a.	Dust covers for above	2	021 St.33999-21
22.	M.G sighting telescope, type KZF2	1	027 Gr 5075
23.	Cover for ball mounting, '100'	1	According to Model Wa. proof 6.
24.	Cap for ball mounting	1	HSK J 3098
25.	Prism holders	8	021 D 2746-1
26.	Bullet-proof glass 70 x 240 x 94	3	021 St. 9296
27.	Bullet-proof glass 70 x 150 x 94	11	021 St. 9280
28.	Cover for machine carbine	1	021 C 37499-255
29.	Case for machine carbine magazines	1	01 B 3321
30.	Extraction fan (in fighting compartment) capacity 12-13 cu. in. (approx. 450 cu.ft) per min.	1	
31.	Extraction fan cover (watertight)	1	021 C860 U51
32.	"Out of action" flag (yellow and black)	1	021 D 33477
33.	Smoke discharger, left	1	021 St 41406
34.	" " , right	1	021 St 41407
35.	Switch boxes for Smoke dischargers	2	21 St 7642
36.	Hatch keys	2	6 AKF 31406-1
37.	M.G.34 with tank type barrel sleeve	2	
38.	Ammunition Boxes - M.G	3	
39.	Holders for M.G barrels (each containing 2 barrels)	3	
40.	Machine carbine	1	
41.	M.G spares (butt and bipod)	1	set
42.	First Aid kit	1	
43.	Signal Pistol	1	
44.	Gyro-direction indicator with lead	1	
45.	Transformer for above	1	
46.	Signal pistol ammunition, 24 rounds	12 white, 6 red, 6 green	
47.	Flexible hose for gas masks	4	
48.	Belt tags for M.G.34	32	
49.	Belt links for M.G. 34	96	
50.	Carrying slings (complete) for M.G.34	2	
51.	Belts filler 34 with box	1	

52.	Headsets, W/T, type B, soundproof	2	
53.	Throat microphone, type A, with 2-point plug and switch	2	
54.	Throat microphone, type B, with 3-point plug and switch	2	
55.	Twin lead, 25 cm. long with cross-piece and three double 20 mm. non-interchangeable plugs	1	
56.	Grease gun with tube, contents 140 cu.cm ($8\frac{1}{2}$ c.in.)	1	U547
57.	Ejector, projectile for 8.8 cm. gun	1	5E 6899-40
58.	Clinometer for 8.8 cm. gun	1	
59.	Spanner for M.G. 34	2	
60.	Muzzle covers for M.G. 34, expendable	4	
61.	Brushes for cleaning M.Gs.	2	
62.	" " "	4	
63.	Grease box for 2 oz. lubricating grease	1	J/9441/35 1099-21G
64.	Sealing covers	2	4/VI/E 03479
65.	Air pump with tube)	–	4AKF 31406-50
66.	Air pressure gauge in leather case)	–	5AKF 31406-51
67.	Hexagonal box-spanner) ∅	–	5AKF 31406-52
68.	Tension device for compensating spring)	–	
69.	Padlocks	2	

˸	Supplied by unit.
⟋	Fitted by Unit.
∅	One of each for five turrets.
⟋⟋	On indent from C.O.O., Kassel.

RESTRICTED

The information given in this document
is not to be communicated, either directly
or indirectly, to the Press or to any person
not authorized to receive it.

REPORT ON
PzKw VI
(Tiger)
Model H

PART II

ADDENDA TO SECTIONS I, II AND III.

AND REPORT ON GUNNERY TRIALS

Military College of Science
SCHOOL OF TANK TECHNOLOGY
Chobham Lane   Chertsey

November   1944

PART II

ADDENDA TO SECTIONS I, II AND III.

AND REPORT ON GUNNERY TRIALS.

INTRODUCTION

The Tiger tank was sent for brief Gunnery Trials by Experimental Wing, A.F.V. School.   This section contains the substance of their reports: E.O. No. 37/1/157 dated 17th March 1944 and 37/1/171 dated 14th April 1944, together with a few additional points which have come to light since Sections I, II and III of Part II were published.

November 1944.   Major W. de L. Messenger, R.T.R.

ADDENDUM TO SECTION I

8.8 cm. GUN Kw.K.36

AND MOUNTING

BREECH MECHANISM.

The accessibility and ease of stripping are noteworthy. All moving parts can be removed without the use of tools. During firing the action of the semi-automatic gear was extremely smooth and silent.

RECOIL GEAR.

During firing, recoils averaged as follows:-

Projectile	Recoil	
	mm.	ins.
H.E.	520	20.5
A.P.C.B.C.	530	20.9
(Maximum working	580	22.8)

From this it is concluded that the system was functioning correctly. Recoil and run-out were very smooth, the gun coming gently to rest.

FIRING GEAR.

The trigger for the electric firing gear is remarkably light.

MOUNTING.

Studs are provided on the rear face of the mantlet to act as elevation stops.

BALANCE GEAR.

There is a certain amount of "spring" in the linkage, while the various pivots introduce considerable friction when elevating or depressing the gun. Working against the "spring" only, the trunnion friction was $\frac{1}{2}$ to 1 lbs measured at the rim of the elevating wheel, but when the "spring" was taken up the load rose to 23 - 24 lbs due to pivot friction.

ELEVATING GEAR.

Backlash was 16 - 19 minutes at the gun or $\frac{3}{8}$ in. at the rim of the elevating wheel.

TRAVERSE GEAR.

Hand Traverse.   The force required to rotate the turret with the tank 0° 56' down at 12 o'clock and 1° 2' down at 3 o'clock was:-

Position of turret.	Traversing.		Note:
	Right.	Left.	
12	½ lbs.	16 lbs.	There is a foul caused
1	12 "	14 "	by damage between 9 and
2	16 "	12 "	10 o'clock when the
3	22 "	6 "	loads rose to 60 lbs.
4	22 "	1 "	right and 45 lbs. left,
5	28 "	1½ "	and the turret jammed.
6	20 "	1½ "	At this point it could
7	28 "	1½ "	not be rotated owing to
8	15 "	1½ "	the clutch slipping.
9	28 "	9 "	
10	3 "	9 "	
11	10 "	17 "	

CO-AXIAL MACHINE GUN

CRADLE.

The gun is mounted so close to the 8.8 cm. buffer cylinder that re-arming with a new belt is very difficult.

SIGHTS

MAIN ARMAMENT.

Telescope T.Z.F.9b.   The illuminating lamp plugs into a socket in the turret roof, and is controlled by a switch on the board to the gunner's left.   The intensity shutter control is too far forward for the gunner to reach.   (This difficulty is also experienced on the Pz Kpfw III.)

Experimental Wing, A.F.V.S. suggest that the aiming mark in the left telescope is for use with A.P. composite rigid shot (Pzgr 40).

No jump is allowed for the 8.8 cm. gun, but there is an allowance for +6 mins. with the M.G.

Clinometer.   This has the same dimensions as that for the 7.5 cm. Kw. K (short) in Pz Kpfw IV (see report by D.T.D. on Pz Kpfw IV Model E) being 16.4 ins. long and curved at a radius of about 24 ins.   The only difference is the scale.

The range of the bubble between the marks on the glass is ½ mil.

FIRE CONTROL.

The approximate characteristics of the S.F.14Z stereo binocular are:-

Magnification	x10	Field of view	5°	
Exit pupil	5mm.	Eye relief	½ inch.	
Interocular distance	)	57 mm. or more - as stereo		
	)	58 mm. or more - as periscopic.		

Graticule, right eyepiece, in 10 mil squares with 2 mil gaps at 5 mil intervals. Interrupted cross at centre for datum point.

The graticule is illuminated.

A small clinometer graduated in mils is also incorporated.

The S.F.14Z was provided with an adapter by Experimental Wing A.F.V.S. and used during the firing trials.

With the binoculars properly mounted and using the auxiliary hand traverse, the commander has an excellent means of accurately aligning the gun onto a target which the gunner cannot see.

When mounted on an ordinary tripod the performance was very similar to that of the British Stereoscopic Binoculars but the light transmission appeared to be slightly inferior.

It is believed that the instrument should be mounted on a rotating azimuth dial, if so this might explain the absence of a proper azimuth indicator on the turret ring of the tank.

AUXILIARY ARMAMENT

"S" MINE DISCHARGERS.

Examination of further photographs and subsequent inspection of the tank reveal that two further dischargers were at one time mounted on the rear corner of the hull, directed outwards at 45° to the keel line.

AMMUNITION

SUMMARY.

The ammunition capacity is re-stated as follows:-

8.8 cm.

Where stowed.	No. of rounds	Type
Left Pannier.		
Beside driver	6	A.P. or H.E.
Centre	16	A.P. or H.E.
Rear	16	A.P. or H.E.
Right Pannier.		
Centre	16	A.P. or H.E.
Rear	16	A.P. or H.E.
Fighting Compartment.		
Left front	4	A.P.
Left rear	4	A.P.
Right front	4	A.P.
Right rear	4	A.P.
Under Turntable.		
Right	6	A.P. or H.E.
Total	92	

Possible proportions lie between:-

(a) 92 (100%) A.P. and

(b) 16 (17½%) A.P. and 76 (82½%) H.E.

Intelligence reports indicate that about 50% of each is carried.

The armour piercing projectiles are low capacity A.P.C.B.C. shell (white tip), not "A.P.38" as stated in Section I of Part II.

7.92 mm.

Where stowed.	No. of 150 rd belt bags.	No. of Rds.
Fighting Compartment.		
On gun	1	
Turret - right wall	4	
Forward bulkhead - right	1	
Rear bulkhead	16	
Total	22	3300
Forward Compartment.		
On gun	1	
In right pannier - vision plate	3	
- side plate	8	
- front bulkhead	4	
Total	16	2400
Grand total	38 belts	5700

This is more than given in the German kit list, but represents the maximum capacity of the stowage fittings.

ADDENDUM TO SECTION II

FIGHTING ARRANGEMENTS

LAYOUT AND CREW ACCOMMODATION.

The shield on the right of the commander protects him from back-flash if flashing ammunition is used.

The flush turntable without coaming and the absence of shielding around it improve access to and ease of handling the ammunition. On the other hand the loader is somewhat handicapped by having no ready use ammunition stowed on the turntable.

COMMANDER.

The commander has three alternative positions:-

(a) Sitting on upper seat - head out.

(b) Sitting on lower seat - closed down.

(c) Standing on turntable -. closed down.

Nevertheless, his position is cramped and uncomfortable.

GUNNER.

The gunner is cramped by the legshield and has the most uncomfortable position in the tank. However, the position of the laying controls is good.

DRIVER.

The driver's seat folds back to allow exit into the fighting chamber.

VISION

The fields of view from the vision devices have been mapped by the M.R.C. Physiological Laboratory, and in consequence the section on "VISION" has been re-written to include the gist of their report, and to expand the information previously given in Part II Section II. The original text should therefore be ignored, but reference should be made to the section drawings of the commander's cupola and of the driver's episcope.

It should be noted that all the vision devices are made watertight with rubber seals. All glass blocks and prisms are readily changed, and spares are carried.

COMMANDER.

Provided with a fixed cupola with <u>five vision slots</u> $(7\frac{1}{4}" \times \frac{5}{8}")$ backed by 94mm laminated glass blocks; there are no shutters. A sighting vane is incorporated with the front slot.

A machine carbine port is provided at 8 o'clock in the turret wall.

The cupola field of view on the ground is shown in Fig. I. The firm line represents the nearest point on the ground that is visible from the cupola, moving the head if necessary. The part of the turret structure that limits near vision in a particular direction is indicated on the line. The radiating dotted lines give the boundaries of the field from each slot with the head held centrally opposite the glass blocks without moving. The blocks are numbered clockwise (C1), (C2), etc.

In the Pz Kpfw III and IV commander's vision was outstandingly good (especially when compared with contemporary Allied vehicles), particularly in that he could see near ground all round the vehicle. The distance between the vision device and the edge of the turret, the slope of the turret roof and the height of the device above the general level of the turret roof, are the main factors determining whether or not ground will be seen near the vehicle in any given direction. These various factors were all well balanced in the Pz Kpfw III and IV. The cupola was centrally placed at the rear and narrowest part of the turret and allowed good vision to the rear and sides of the vehicle. Vision forwards was less good because the whole length of the turret was in front of the cupola, but this was mitigated to some extent by sloping the roof downwards from the cupola and further by raising the cupola above the roof. Compared with vision in other directions, commander's near vision forwards is not so important, as vision in this direction is also covered by the driver and hull gunner. In contemporary Allied vehicles the commander's vision device was placed to one side of a square flat-topped turret. This meant that on the whole vision was good in one direction (over the nearest turret edge) and liable to be bad in other directions, because of the distance between vision device and turret edge. The blind zone in the commander's field on the Churchill extended to within 120 feet of the right hand side of the turret. Also, because of the lowness of the periscopes on the turret roof, visual fields were badly obstructed by fixtures such as fans which projected above the general roof level.

In the early models of the TIGER, it appears that the designers did not consider near vision to be so important. The commander's cupola is placed not centrally behind, but to one side of the gun. Vision to the left and rear of the turret is good, but bad to the right and right rear. It should, however, be noted that part of the blind area to the right in the commander's field can be seen through the loader's slot (see Fig. I).

Using the head movement necessary to get the maximum field from each of the constituent vision blocks, a continuous view of the ground round the vehicle is obtained with a slight overlap between the peripheral fields of each block. If one only looks through the centre of each block without head movement, there is a blind zone of 15-20° between it and the next block. The fact that the commander sees through a narrow fixed aperture in front of each block does not mean that the vertical field is reduced, but that the whole available field cannot be seen at once, vertical head movement being needed to cover it all.

The generally cramped position of the commander makes it difficult to turn round and look to the rear. Vision to the right rear is limited by the stowage bin, this limitation could have been reduced by sloping its top surface more steeply as was done on the Pz Kpfw III and IV.

Fig. 1. shows clearly that the best approach for tank hunters is from the right and right rear of the turret. If close to the ground they should be invisible when within 100-120 feet of the vehicle.

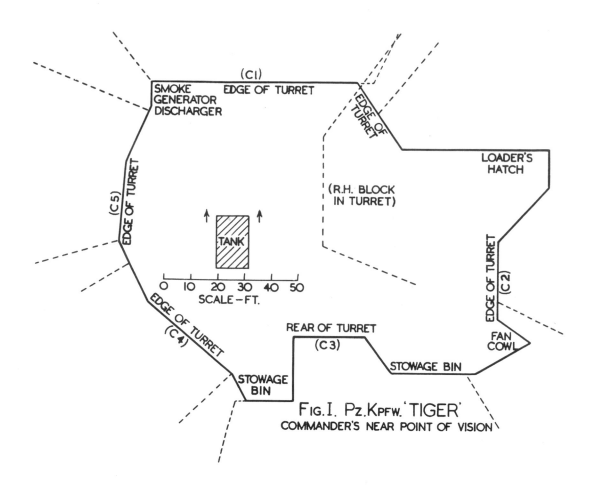

FIG. I. Pz.Kpfw. 'TIGER'
COMMANDER'S NEAR POINT OF VISION

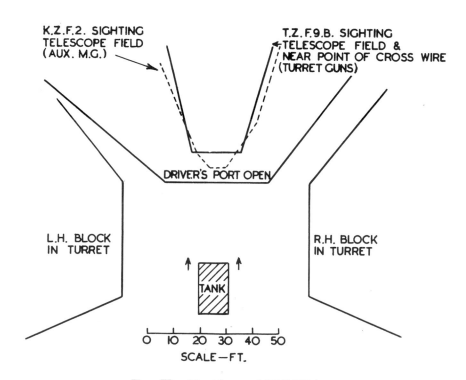

FIG. II. Pz.Kpfw. 'TIGER'
NEAR POINT OF LOADER'S, GUNNER'S, DRIVER'S &
HULL GUNNER'S VISION.

It would, however, appear from recent photographs that re-design of the cupola to improve observation of the ground near the vehicle has been necessary. It is interesting to note that the new design, as far as can be seen from the photographs, involves the use of eight high episcopes in place of the direct vision blocks. Episcopes have not been used in cupola design by the Germans since the Pz Kpfw II.

TURRET GUNNER (See Fig. II).

Besides the binocular sighting telescope T.Z.F.9b (field of view 23°) in the co-axial mounting (elevation 17°, depression 7°), there is a slot, 5" x $\frac{3}{8}$", at 10 o'clock in the turret wall backed by a replaceable laminated glass block (70mm x 150mm x 94mm thick). There is no shutter. This aperture allows a good view to the left, but considerable head movement is required to cover the whole field of view.

The nearest point fire of the gun is 35 feet to the front and sides and 70 feet over the tail.

LOADER (See Figs. I and II).

The loader has a slot similar to the gunner's at 2 o'clock in the turret wall. This covers part of the commander's blind area, but the loader is restricted in obtaining a full field of view rearwards by the kit bin which prevents him moving his head.

Photographs show that later models incorporate what appears to be a fixed episcope, similar to those used in the forward compartment, in front of the loader's hatch. In the present model the loader is uncomfortably blind.

Early models of the tank had a second machine carbine port in place of the loading and escape hatch.

DRIVER (Fig. II).

The normal driving vision aperture is a port in the front plate which may be closed down as much as required by a balanced pair of rising and falling shutters, operated by a handwheel on the right. This is backed by a laminated glass block (70mm x 240mm x 94mm thick). It gives good and adequate vision.

The front plate is bored with two holes for the normal driver's episcope, consisting of a pair of K.F.F.2 cranked telescopes, but the holes have been plugged and welded, and the episcope carrier fittings removed. The K.F.F.2 telescopes have also been crossed out on the stowage list.

There are no side ports, but the hatch carries a fixed episcope facing 45° to the left of the keel line of the tank. The "windows" measure 5" x 1$\frac{1}{2}$" and the height is 11" with a 3.2" air gap. Top and bottom prisms are identical and interchangeable. As this was out of order, its field of view could not be mapped, but it is probable that it is partly masked to the front by the upward projection of the edge of the superstructure front plate.

AUXILIARY GUNNER (Fig. II).

Besides the K.Z.F.2 Telescope (field of view 18°) in the ball mounting (elevation 20°, depression 10°, traverse 15° left and 15° right) the auxiliary gunner has a fixed episcope identical to the driver's, but facing outwards to the right. The same remarks apply to this as to the driver's episcope and, unfortunately, its field of view could not be plotted either.

GUNNERY TRIALS.

<u>8.8 cm. AMMUNITION.</u>

A.P.C.B.C./H.E.   Length   34.21 ins.
                  Weight   33.75 lbs.
                  Point of balance 19.75 ins. from base.

H.E. fuzed AZ 23/28 Length   36.69 ins.
                     Weight   32.0 lbs.
                     Point of balance 19.75 ins. from base.

The balance of the rounds was bad when picked up in the most convenient way from the bins, being projectile heavy.

Both types were fitted with a smoke trace and use flashless propellent. This gave a large quantity of smoke but no flashes were observed firing in daylight.

FUMES FROM 8.8 cm. GUN.

It was only possible for the M.R.C. Physiological Laboratory to take two snap samples of the fumes in the commander's cupola which were collected in 565 cc. vacuum bottles after firing the 2nd and 3rd rounds in a 5 round burst of H.E. ammunition. These were analysed for carbon monoxide and ammonia. During the trial all hatches were closed, the engine was off but the ventilation fan was running.

RESULTS.

Trial.	Rounds fired.	Conc. NH_3 in parts per million in atmosphere.	%CO in atmosphere.	%CO per 100 parts per million NH_3.
Blank	-	-	.029	-
8.8 cm.	2	150	.850	.565
8.8 cm.	3	191	1.015	.530

This does not provide sufficient data on which to issue a report and M.R.C. merely comment as follows:-

"Under the exceptional conditions of this trial the fumes drifted slowly through the fighting compartment and contained a dangerous amount of CO. The ammonia was irritating. These results give no information about the gun fumes in a properly ventilated Tiger tank".

BACKFLASH.

Owing to shortage of ammunition available for firing during subsequent demonstrations, electric primers were fitted to the H.E. ammunition which had been supplied with the tank to make up the stowage. This was stated to be Flak ammunition though it was fuzed percussion.

138

The markings on it were indistinct but it bore the date 1941, and the projectiles were fitted with copper driving bands as opposed to iron.

This ammunition was, as expected, not flashless but gave considerable muzzle flash and large backflashes occurred with 3 out of 4 rounds fired.

The conditions were not conducive to backflash as there was a following wind and the hatches were opened up without the fan or engine running.

This confirms the supposition that the deflector guard fitted on the Commander's side was placed there to protect him against backflash and also may be one of the reasons why the Germans have adopted flashless propellant for their tank guns.

ASSEMBLY OF AMMUNITION.

During trials one round was noticed to hang fire and one misfire occurred. This latter round was broken down and revealed that

(a) the primer had fired.
(b) the silk sleeve and igniting charge had been incorrectly assembled or shaken off.

The silk sleeve showed a good deal of charring where it was folded over the primer opening and had prevented the flash reaching the igniter or propellent.

A further point of interest was noticed in the base fuze and tracer assembly. The fuze is assembled into the shell with a right hand thread and the tracer screws into it with a left hand thread, while the rifling has a right hand twist.

STABILITY.

The tank provides a very stable gun platform for either head-on or broadside stationary firing.

The gun tends to rise due presumably to the suspension settling down for the first two or three rounds fired, but after this remains constant.

During the firing trials a hornet target was engaged at 1100 yards. Correction was given to the gunner for the first round, after which he fired a further 5 rounds without having any observation or moving either the traverse or elevating controls, and secured 5 consecutive hits.

OBSERVATION.

The flashless propellant produces a very large smoke cloud which is dispersed to some extent on each side of the gun by the muzzle brake. There was a following wind throughout the firing trials so that the smoke prevented observation of strike by the gunner at range up to 1600 yards. In most cases, however, the commander was able to observe by seeing over the smoke cloud.

ACCURACY.

The gun appeared to be remarkably consistent.

A shoot of 5 rounds taking a constant aim at a screen target at 1200 yards gave all the shots in an area 16" by 18".

Owing to a fracture of the offside front suspension arm, the tank could not be taken to the new range and firing could only be carried out at ranges up to 1600 yards.

RATE OF FIRE.

The highest timed rate of fire during these limited trials was 4 rounds in 39 seconds. (1st round loaded and timed from firing).

The normal rate of fire is estimated to be from 5 - 8 rounds per minute.

Over a great number of rounds, the availability of a large quantity of ammunition should give this tank a higher rate of fire than in our own heavy gun tanks where the bulk of the ammunition is not so readily accessible.

MOVING TARGETS.

Tracking of moving targets at 1000 yards up to speeds of 15 m.p.h. was done with the tank on level ground.

Hand traverse was easy for all speeds.

Powered traverse on "low" was the best for ease of tracking at all speeds but had a very wide neutral zone.

On "high", speeds appeared a little irregular and it was unsuitable for speeds of 5 m.p.h. or lower. At 10 m.p.h., correction by the hand traverse was necessary.

Five rounds were fired at a target moving at 15 m.p.h., range 1500 yards. Although smoke obscured direct observation by the gunner, 3 hits were scored after corrections had been given by the commander. Laying was done on Low Speed with hand traverse assistance.

CLINOMETER.

A target at 1800 yards was engaged by normal bracketting methods. A hit was obtained with the 4th round.

SUMMARY.

The design has been well thought out and it embodies a number of distinctly original features such as the heavy armament and armour, turret and hull construction, powered traverse layout and facilities for total submersion.

It appears that the user has not had the same influence on it as on British tanks since so many of the items, whilst basically good, are unsatisfactory and could well be improved from the user aspect by slight modification.

The outstanding features would appear to be:-

GOOD POINTS.

1. 8.8 cm gun with its smooth action and easily stripped breech mechanism.
2. Heavy armour and method of construction (welding and front plates projecting above the roof plates).
3. Stability as a gun platform.
4. Ammunition stowage - quantity and accessibility.
5. Electrical firing gear with safety interlocks and novel trigger switch.
6. Flush turret floor without coaming or shields.
7. Binocular telescope with fixed eyepiece.
8. Mounting for periscopic binoculars in cupola and commander's hand traverse.
9. Ability to superimpose hand on power traverse and absence of oil pipes and unions.
10. Ample space for loader.
11. Method of attaching stowage to turret walls (flexible strips).
12. Spring assisted hatches.
13. S-mine dischargers.
14. 2-position commander's seat and backrest.
15. Electrically fired smoke generator dischargers.
16. Handholds on roof to assist gunner.

BAD POINTS.

1. Out-of-balance of gun and turret.
2. Obscuration by smoke from flashless propellent.
3. Ventilation of gun fumes.
4. Lack of intercommunication for loader.
5. Cramped positions of gunner and commander.
6. Powered traverse control - lack of definite neutral position and awkward range of movement.
7. No armouring on bins.
8. Small gun deflector bag.
9. Awkward re-arming of co-axial M.G.
10. Gunner's exit via commander's cupola.
11. Head pad on auxiliary M.G.

The Pz Kpfw VI with its heavy armour, dual purpose armament and fighting ability is basically an excellent tank, and, in spite of the defects noted, constitutes a considerable advance on any tank that we have tried.

Its greatest weakness is probably the limit imposed on mobility owing to its weight, width and limited range of action.

Taking it all round, it presents a very formidable fighting machine which should not be under-rated.

ADDENDUM TO SECTION III

STOWAGE

REMARKS BY EXPERIMENTAL WING, A.F.V.S.

A large amount of kit is carried on the tank and yet the interior does not appear unduly cluttered up. The points of particular interest are :-

Internal

1.   All fittings are labelled - similar to British practice.

2.   Crew equipment is stowed near to their position in the tank and consists of (a) waterbottle, (b) gasmask container and (c) breathing tube.

3.   Each M.G. has :-
(i) Its own spare parts box with shaped wooden compartments for the accessories carried therein.
(ii) A box containing bipod and butt for dismounted use.
(iii) Two spare barrels in container.

4.   Only one machine carbine is carried. This is understandable since both turret and hull M.G. can be used dismounted.

5.   One bin is provided in the turret R.H. top corner for kit and L.H. turret sill plate has a raised coaming forming a "loose" container for use by both the commander and gunner.

6.   Ammunition (see also Part II, Section I).
No immediate supply is carried on the turntable but the floor and pannier bins are very accessible for most turret positions.
The method of securing the rounds in the floor bins is simple, quick and accessible. The projectile is held by a separator which swings out of the way; the round is prevented from moving forward by its rim engaging a lip and the rear separators lift up quickly and park in special grooves at the end of the bin. They cannot be removed and so are not lost.
The turntable necessitates the rounds in the rear bins being stowed with the projectiles facing 12 o'clock which is the wrong way round for loading. A changeover of hands is therefore necessary.
The pannier bins, too, work quite well but the outermost rounds require a knack for quick removal. In fact, rapid withdrawal of ammunition necessitates learning the optimum procedure for each batch of rounds. This comes quickly with experience.
Six rounds are held in reserve under the floor and are accessible with the turret at 12 o'clock.
A total of 36 150rd. belt bags (5400 rounds) of M.G. ammunition appear to be carried. This excludes any on the M.G's and is four in excess of that given in the German list. Of the 36 bags, 21 are in the main turret and 15 in the front compartment. The normal British stowage requirement. is 15 225-rd liners for the co-axial M.G. and 10 liners for Hull M.G. - total 3625 rounds.
No cross country work was done so we were unable to check the security of the German method of stowing the "Gurtsacke" (belt bag) on rails. The bags were quite easy to handle and would seem to provide an effective dust protector-cum-collector bag.
The belt filling machine was complicated in construction but worked most efficiently when its operation was understood.

<u>External</u>

Gun cleaning rods, spades, axes, shovels are stowed in clips or straps and some of the track tools in a partitioned box.

The general impression was of tidiness in front but a conglomeration of kit and fittings all over the engine compartment.

No track plates were attached to the visor plate.

Some models may be fitted with track plates round the turret between 3 and 5 o'clock, and 9 and 7 o'clock.

The stowage diagrams which follow are based on those by Experimental Wing, A.F.V.S.

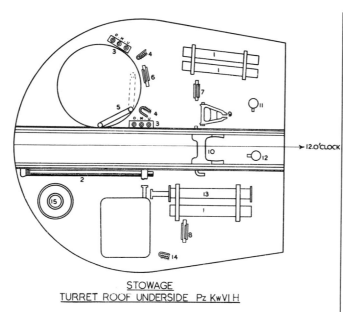

→ 12.O'CLOCK

STOWAGE
TURRET ROOF UNDERSIDE Pz Kw VI H

KEY TO DIAGRAM

1. BREATHING TUBES. (ATEMSCHLAUCH)
2. PLUG FOR COAXIAL M.G. APERTURE.
   DURING SUBMERSION.(DICHTSTOPFEN
   BEZW M.G.)

FITTINGS
3. SMOKE GENERATOR DISCHARGER SWITCHES.
   (NEBELKERZEN)
4. COMMANDERS HANDHOLDS.
5. CMDRS SCISSORS PERISCOPE HOLDER.
6. CMDRS FESTOON LAMP.
7. GUNNERS FESTOON LAMP.
8. LOADERS FESTOON LAMP.
9. TELESCOPE SUPPORT BRACKET.
10. GUN ELEVATION CRAMP.
11. SOCKET FOR TELESCOPE &
    CLINOMETER ILLUMINATION.
12. SOCKET FOR ELECTRIC FIRING CIRCUIT.
13. BALANCE GEAR LOADERS HATCH.
14. LOADERS HANDHOLD
15 EXTRACTOR FAN. 12 V. 10 A. GOOO

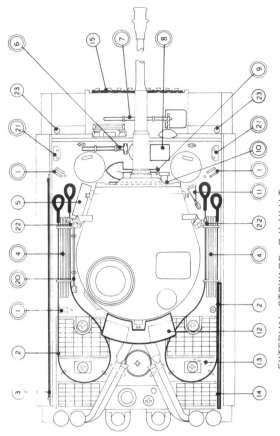

EXTERNAL STOWAGE PzKwVI.H.Tiger.

KEY TO DIAGRAM

1: ANTI-PERSONNEL MINE ATTACHMENTS.
2: TOW ROPE.
3: 15 WIRE ROPE.
4: GUN CLEANING RODS.
5: BLANKING OFF PLATE FOR AIRSLIT ENGINE COMP'T.
6: SLEDGE HAMMER.
7: SHOVEL.
8: JACKING BLOCK.
9: SPADE.
10: AXE.
11: WIRE CUTTERS.
12: TURRET BIN
   (10 TRACK LINKS, 10 TRACK PINS)
13: TETRA FIRE EXTINGUISHER.
14: WIRELESS AERIAL STOWAGE.
15: SPARE TRACK LINKS.
20: CROW BAR 5'10"
21: HEAD LAMP POSITIONS.
22: SMOKE GENERATOR DISCHARERS.
23: HOLE FOR POLE SUPPORTING CAMOUFLAGE
   (CAMOUFLAGED AS LORRY OR BUS)

ITEMS THUS ◯ TAKEN FROM EXISTING ON VEHICLE.

ITEMS THUS ◯ TAKEN FROM W O PHOTOGRAPH M 2OI8I.

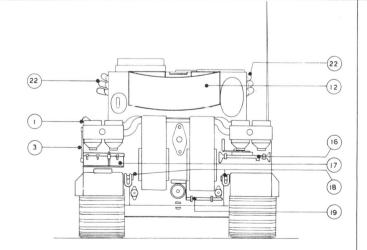

EXTERNAL STOWAGE - REAR.
Pz Kw VI.H. TIGER.

KEY TO DIAGRAMS
EXTERNAL STOWAGE

1. ANTI PERSONNEL MINE ATTACHMENTS.

3. 15 m. WIRE ROPE FOR PULLING TRACKS.

12. TURRET STOWAGE BIN. (10 TRACK LINKS AND 10 TRACK PINS)

16. 15 TON JACK.

17. TRACK TOOL BOX.

18. TOWING SHACKLES.

19. HANDLE FOR INERTIA STARTER.

22. SMOKE GENERATOR DISCHARGERS.

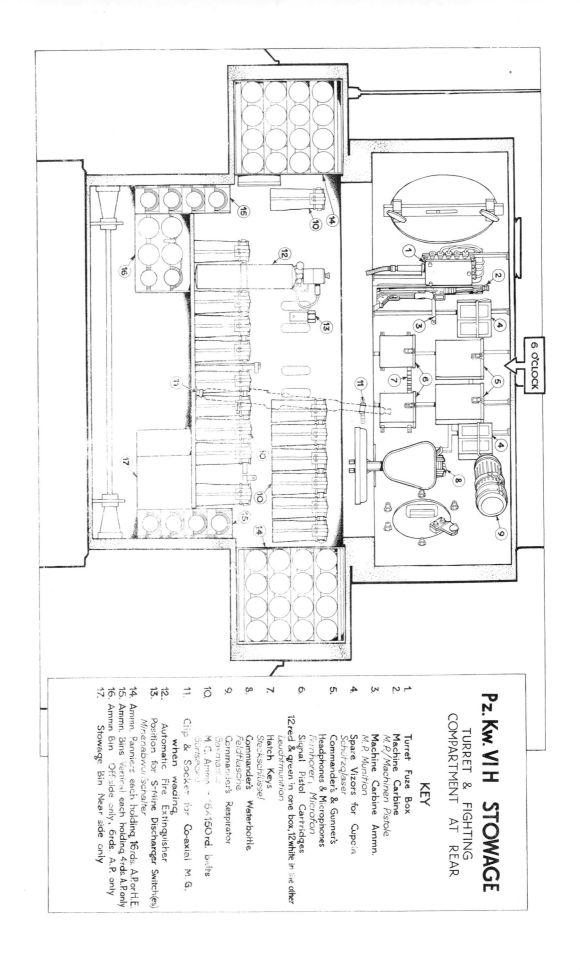

Pz. Kw. VIH STOWAGE

TURRET & FIGHTING
COMPARTMENT AT REAR

KEY

1. Turret Fuze Box
2. Machine Carbine
   M.P./Machinen Pistole
3. Machine Carbine Ammn.
   M.P. Munition
4. Spare Vizors for Cupola
   Schutzglaser
5. Commander's & Gunner's
   Headphones & Microphones
   Fernhorer; Microfon
6. Signal Pistol Cartridges
   12 red & green in one box, 12 white in line other
   Leuchtmunition
7. Hatch Keys
   Steckschlüssel
8. Commander's Waterbottle
   Feldflasche
9. Commander's Respirator
   Gasmaske
10. M.G. Ammn. - 6×150 rd. belts
    Gurtsacke
11. Clip & Socket for Co-axial M.G.
    when waeding.
12. Automatic Fire Extinguisher
13. Position for S-Mine Discharger Switch(es)
    Minenabwurfschalter
14. Ammn. Panniers each holding 16 rds. A.P. or H.E.
15. Ammn. Bins Vertical each holding 4 rds. A.P. only
16. Ammn Bin Offside only, 6 rds. A.P. only
17. Stowage Bin Near side only

145

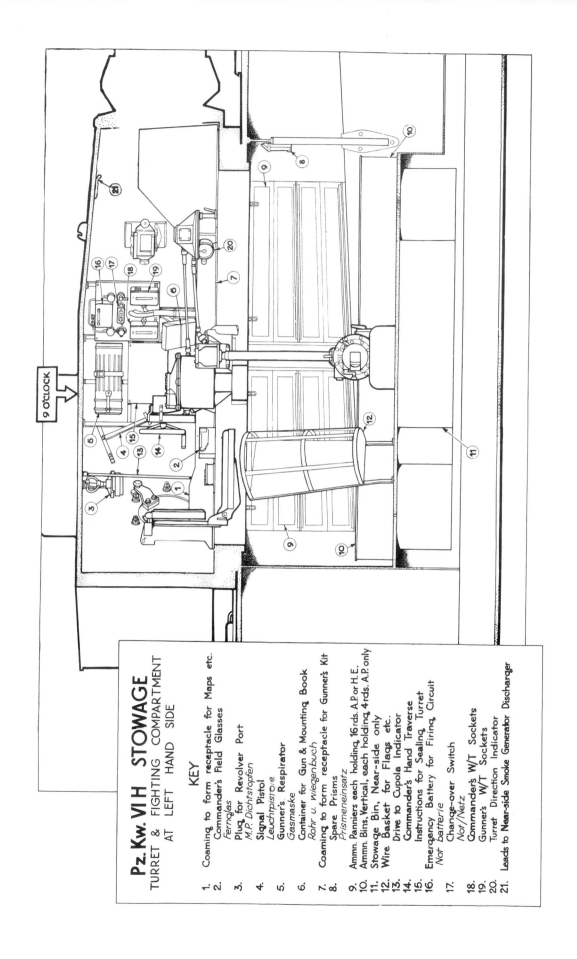

9 O'CLOCK

Pz.Kw. VI H STOWAGE
TURRET & FIGHTING COMPARTMENT
AT LEFT HAND SIDE

KEY

1. Coaming to form receptacle for Maps etc.
2. Commander's Field Glasses
   Fernglas
3. Plug for Revolver Port
   M.P. Dichtstopfen
4. Signal Pistol
   Leuchtpistole
5. Gunner's Respirator
   Gasmaske
6. Container for Gun & Mounting Book
   Rohr u. wiegenbuch
7. Coaming to form receptacle for Gunner's Kit
8. Spare Prisms
   Prismeneinsatz
9. Ammn. Panniers each holding 16 rds. A.P. or H.E.
10. Ammn. Bins.Vertical, each holding 4 rds. A.P. only
11. Stowage Bin, Near-side only
12. Wire Basket for Flags etc.
13. Drive to Cupola Indicator
14. Commander's Hand Traverse
15. Instructions for Sealing Turret
16. Emergency Battery for Firing Circuit
    Not batterie
17. Change-over Switch
    Not/Netz
18. Commander's W/T Sockets
19. Gunner's W/T Sockets
20. Turret Direction Indicator
21. Leads to Near-side Smoke Generator Discharger

146

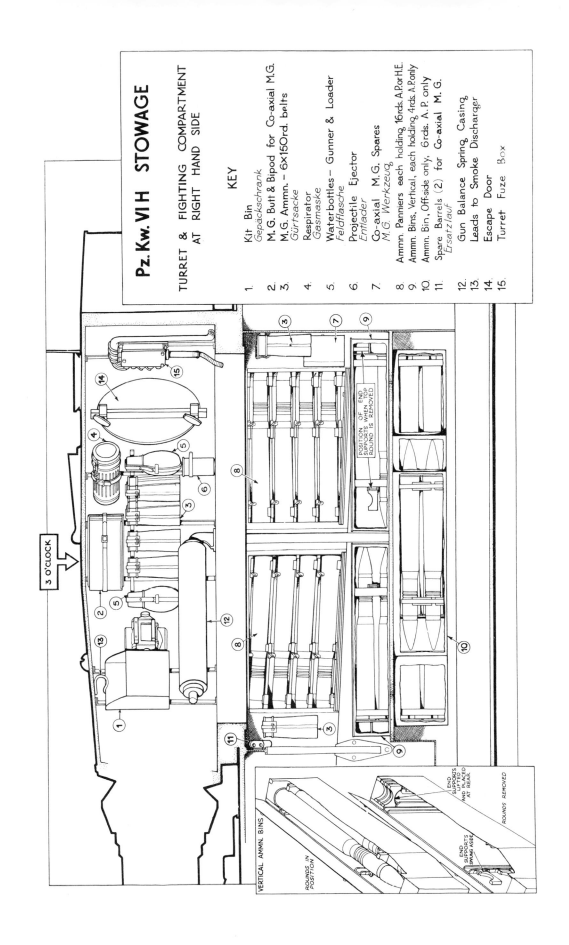

Pz.Kw.VI H STOWAGE

TURRET & FIGHTING COMPARTMENT AT RIGHT HAND SIDE

KEY

1. Kit Bin
   Gepäckschrank
2. M.G. Butt & Bipod for Co-axial M.G.
3. M.G. Ammn. – 6×150rd. belts
   Gürtsacke
4. Respirator
   Gasmaske
5. Waterbottles – Gunner & Loader
   Feldflasche
6. Projectile Ejector
   Entlader
7. Co-axial M.G. Spares
   M.G. Werkzeug
8. Ammn. Panniers each holding 16rds. A.P.or H.E.
9. Ammn. Bins, Vertical, each holding 4rds. A.P.only
10. Ammn. Bin, Off-side only, 6rds. A.P. only
11. Spare Barrels (2) for Co-axial M.G.
    Ersatzlauf
12. Gun Balance Spring Casing
13. Leads to Smoke Discharger
14. Escape Door
15. Turret Fuze Box

3 O'CLOCK

POSITION OF END SUPPORTS WHEN TOP ROUND IS REMOVED

VERTICAL AMMN. BINS

ROUNDS IN POSITION

END SUPPORTS LIFTED AND PLACED AT REAR

END SUPPORTS SWUNG ASIDE

ROUNDS REMOVED

147

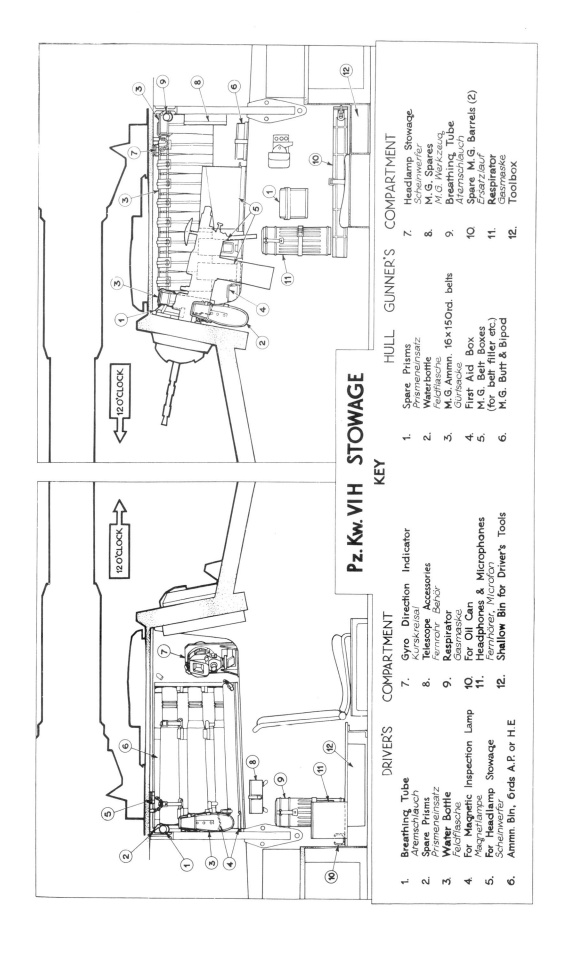

Pz. Kw. VIH STOWAGE

KEY

DRIVER'S COMPARTMENT

1. **Breathing Tube**
   Atemschlauch
2. **Spare Prisms**
   Prismeneinsatz
3. **Water Bottle**
   Feldflasche
4. **For Magnetic Inspection Lamp**
   Magnetlampe
5. **For Headlamp Stowage**
   Scheinwerfer
6. **Ammn. Bin, 6rds A.P. or H.E**

7. **Gyro Direction Indicator**
   Kurskreisal
8. **Telescope Accessories**
   Fernrohr Behör
9. **Respirator**
   Gasmaske
10. **For Oil Can**
11. **Headphones & Microphones**
    Fernhörer, Microfon
12. **Shallow Bin for Driver's Tools**

HULL GUNNER'S COMPARTMENT

1. Spare Prisms
   Prismeneinsatz
2. Waterbottle
   Feldflasche
3. M.G. Ammn. 16×150rd. belts
   Gürtsacke
4. First Aid Box
5. M.G. Belt Boxes
   (for belt filler etc.)
6. M.G. Butt & Bipod

7. Headlamp Stowage
   Scheinwerfer
8. M.G. Spares
   M.G. Werkzeug
9. Breathing Tube
   Atemschlauch
10. Spare M.G. Barrels (2)
    Ersatzlauf
11. Respirator
    Gasmaske
12. Toolbox

148

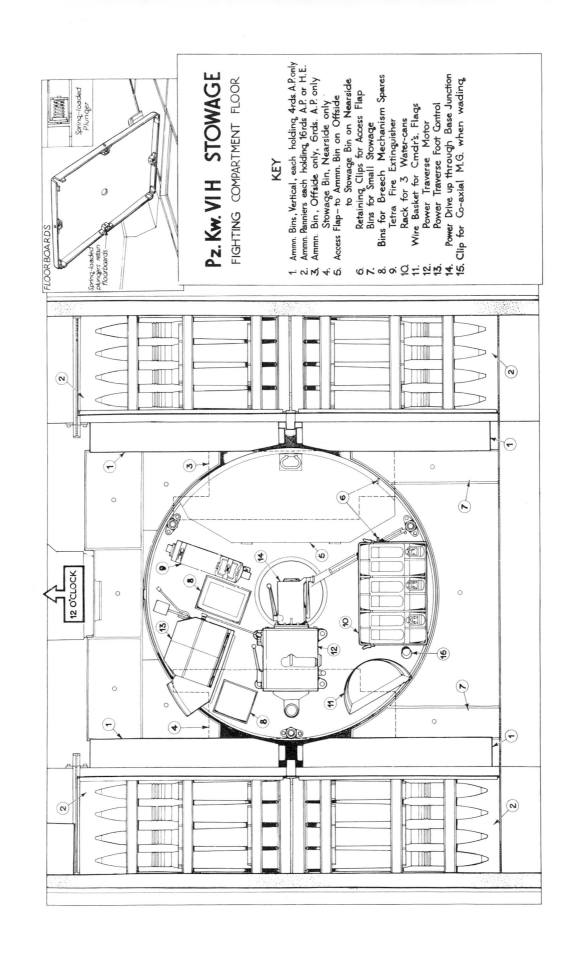

Pz.Kw.VIH STOWAGE
FIGHTING COMPARTMENT FLOOR

KEY

1. Ammn. Bins, Vertical, each holding 4 rds. A.P. only
2. Ammn. Panniers each holding 16 rds A.P. or H.E.
3. Ammn. Bin, Offside only, 6 rds. A.P. only
4. Stowage Bin, Nearside only
5. Access Flap – to Ammn. Bin on Offside
   to Stowage Bin on Nearside
6. Retaining Clips for Access Flap
7. Bins for Small Stowage
8. Bins for Breech Mechanism Spares
9. Tetra Fire Extinguisher
10. Rack for 3 Water-cans
11. Wire Basket for Cmdr's. Flags
12. Power Traverse Motor
13. Power Traverse Foot Control
14. Power Drive up through Base Junction
15. Clip for Co-axial M.G. when wading

FLOORBOARDS

Spring-loaded Plunger

Spring-loaded plungers retain floorboards

12 O'CLOCK

PART IV

POWER PLANT

SECTION I

GENERAL DESCRIPTION OF ENGINE.

INTRODUCTION

In addition to the engine installed in the tank, two spare power units and a quantity of spare parts were shipped from North Africa. The report which follows is based mainly on examination of one of the spare engines, both of which were in a damaged condition.

In one case, failure of big end bearings had caused considerable damage to the crank pins, whilst the other engine had suffered a similar failure with additional damage to one piston and cylinder liner caused by the fracture of a connecting rod. Whilst the tank was undergoing firing trials at Lulworth, its engine also failed in a similar manner, and the recurrence of this trouble would seem to indicate an inherent weakness in design. A composite engine is being built by F.V.P.E., from the spares available with a view to field trials and this may give a better indication of the reliability factor.

The particular engine which was examined in detail, had one or two features which rather suggested that it was an early prototype built before quantity production had commenced.

Various components have been submitted to specialist manufacturers for examination and will therefore be reported upon separately.

A number of parts have also been subjected to material analysis and the results of these investigations are not included in this section.

September 1944.

J.D. BARNES Major, R.T.R.
D.M. PEARCE B.A.(Cantab).
G. BOYD Lieut., R.A.C.

LEADING DATA

Type	HL 210 P 45
Date of manufacture	1942
Engine No.	46064
Bore	125 mm. (4.92 ins.)
Stroke	145 mm. (5.71 ins.)
Stroke/bore Ratio	1.16 :1
Capacity	21.353 litres (1301.2 cu.ins.)
Capacity per cylinder	1.779 litres (108.43 cu.ins.)
Compression Ratio	7 : 1
Rated maximum B.H.P.	650 metric B.H.P. (641 British B.H.P.) at 3000 R.P.M.
Maximum R.P.M.	3000
Mean piston speed at 3000 R.P.M.	2854 ft/min.
Firing order	1 - 12 - 5 - 8 - 3 - 10 - 6 - 7 - 2 - 11 - 4 - 9
Overall length	1220 mm. (4ft. 0 ins.)
Overall width	975 mm. (3ft. 2¼ ins.)
Overall height (excluding air cleaners)	940 mm. (3ft. 1 in.)

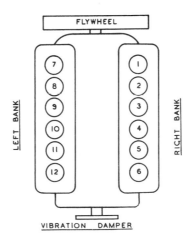

Cylinder numbering diagram.

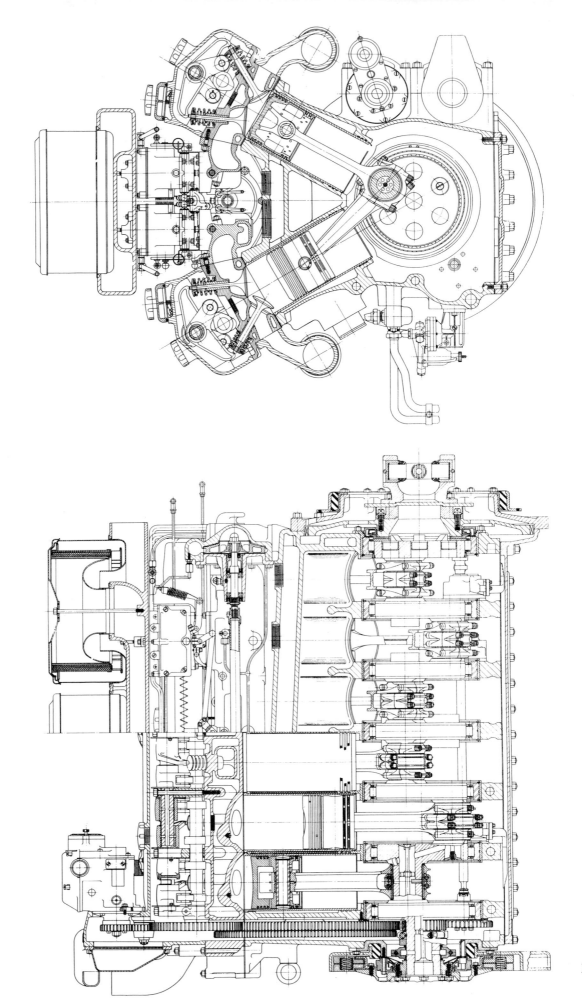

153

GENERAL DESCRIPTION

The Maybach, type HL.210-P.45, petrol engine of 21 litres, is a 60 degree, Vee - 12 cylinder. The cylinder blocks and crankcase are a single light alloy casting and the cylinders are fitted with wet liners. Cast iron cylinder heads carry one inlet and one exhaust valve per cylinder. The valves are inclined and both inlet and exhaust are driven by a single overhead camshaft to each bank. The inlet valves are of large diameter tulip form, whilst the exhaust are sodium filled.

The camshafts are gear driven from the rear end of the crankshaft. A six cylinder Bosch magneto is provided for each bank, and gear driven from the camshafts. Also driven from the timing gears is a two-speed take-off for the cooling fans, immediately behind which is situated the governor. The governor shaft extends between the banks to drive the water pump which is mounted at the front end of the engine. Four Solex type 52 JFF 2 carburettors are installed between the cylinder banks. Aluminium pressed pistons are carried on forged "H" section rods and copper lead big end bearings are employed. The forged crankshaft has circular webs which form the inner races of the seven large diameter roller main bearings. A friction type vibration damper is carried on the "free" end of the crankshaft. Dry sump lubrication is employed, two gear type scavenge and one delivery pump of similar pattern being driven by a shaft in the crankcase from the timing gears. This same shaft drives the four diaphragm type fuel pumps. The dynamo, also driven from the timing gears, and the electric and inertia starters are carried on the side of the crankcase.

DESIGN

It is at once apparent that the engine was specifically designed by Maybach for use in a heavy tank. It closely follows this maker's previous tank engine practice, and may generally be regarded as a scaled up version of the type HL. 120 as used in the Pz.Kpfw. III and IV.

The chief feature of the design is its compactness, and this aim has no doubt influenced the designer to use roller main bearings, resulting in close pitching of the cylinders and consequent small overall length.

It is considered that the design is generally excellent, achieving small bulk, with high output, and that the apparent unreliability is due to the engine being over-rated. It is significant in this connection that the later Tiger tanks are powered with an engine similar to that of the Panther with an increased swept volume of 23 litres. The larger engine, though very similar in design to the HL 210-P.45, incorporates one or two major changes, notably the substitution of cast iron for aluminium for the cylinder block and crankcase, possibly in an attempt to improve crankcase rigidity.

The installation is very neat, internal drillings and the mounting of the oil tank on the engine have enabled the number of external oil pipes to be reduced to the minimum.

The engine runs in a sealed compartment - to allow the tank to be submersible - and consequently particular attention has been paid to the forced draught over the exhaust manifolds and the direction of air around the front and rear of the engine.

The rubber engine mounting is of a somewhat unusual design, but appears sound. The combustion chamber is of near hemispherical form and an accessible central position of the sparking plug has been achieved by off-setting the single overhead camshaft. The use of sodium cooled exhaust valves is interesting, though the rather unusually heavy section rocker arms are somewhat inconsistent with the generally high standard of finish of the valve gear. Attention is directed to the very unusual arrangement of the forked connecting rod - the web being parallel to the crankshaft axis. The use of four big end bolts on the blade rod is also noteworthy.

The very unusual mounting of the master timing pinion to arrange for setting of the valve timing was only present on the one engine examined in detail and this together with other small modifications seem to indicate that this particular engine was an early prototype manufactured before large scale production had begun.

The finish and workmanship is everywhere of a high order.

PART IV

POWER PLANT

SECTION II

DETAILED DESCRIPTION OF ENGINE.

CRANKCASE AND CYLINDER BLOCKS.

Left hand side ¾ view showing liner partially withdrawn

The crankcase and cylinder blocks are a single aluminium alloy casting closed at the base by a simple flat cover. The crankcase extends well below the centre line of the crankshaft. The crankshaft is assembled through the front end wall, and the structure is extremely rigid.

The timing case is cast integrally with the crankcase which is internally divided into seven compartments formed by the walls of the timing case and webs which support the main bearings.

The webs incorporate oilways and are machined to receive steel bands which form the housings for the main bearings. The bands have grooves and circlips to locate the roller main bearings. Nos. 1, 2 and 5 webs are internally drilled and have machined faces to receive the three oil pumps. Nos. 3 and 6 webs and the front end wall are drilled and bushed to support the oil pump driving shaft. A drilling on the rear end of the block face delivers lubricant to the overhead valve gear.

Right hand side ¾ view showing timing case

There are external machined surfaces on the left hand side for four petrol pumps, oil filter (with connections to internal drillings), and unions for external oil pipes. The oil tank is bolted to the right hand side of the crankcase and a machined surface with three drillings in line provides the necessary connections. The central drilling passes to the sump, while the other two continue through Nos. 4 and 5 bearing webs.

Wet cast iron cylinder liners are employed; they are spigotted into the crankcase at their bases and located at the top by a flange seating in an annular groove in the top face of the cylinder block. Water sealing is by three rubber rings.

There are 18 water passages which communicate with appropriate holes in the cylinder head. It is noted that four additional holes in each bank have been blanked off. The timing case has two water passages cored in it for two outlet pipes, whilst at the other extremity of the block there are two passages for the centrifugal pump.

Two water hose connections are provided on the left side of the cylinder block, one to the rear at the base and the other central at the top. Two sets of brackets are cast on this side of the crankcase for the oil cooler and dynamo. Similarly on the right hand side the bracket for the electric starter is cast, whilst that for the inertia starter is bolted. This rather confirms the report that an inertia starter was not fitted to the first 50 Pz.Kpfw.VI tanks.

14 main bolts hold down each cylinder head and the same bolts serve to secure the valve rocker gear. A steel threaded sleeve, screwed and caulked into the cylinder block, locates each bolt.

Core plugs are threaded and have squared recesses for the insert - ion of a tool for fitting or removal. Jointing material is used with the plugs.

Four lifting eyes are provided, one on the top front corner of each side and two on the rear wall.

Underside view of crankcase

DATA AND DIMENSIONS

Overall height	685mm
" length	1100mm
Angle between banks	60°
Centre line of crankcase to block face	420mm
Centres of cylinders	142mm
Distance of sump plate from centre line of crankshaft	190mm
No. of cylinder head studs	14
Diameter of studs	14mm

Cylinder Liners

Depth of liners	267mm
Thickness of liners	4mm
Internal diameter	125mm
External diameter	133mm
Diameter over flange	142mm
Depth of water passages	202mm

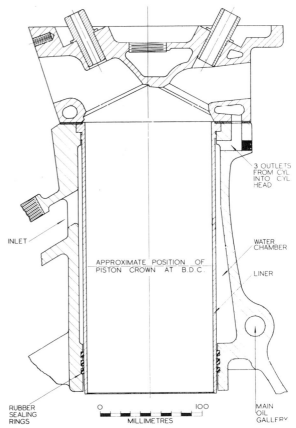

Section of cylinder liner

159

Engine compartment

The engine is flexibly mounted at either end by rubber rings which locate on flanges concentric with the crankshaft. The rings are carried between two pressed steel sections and the whole is bonded together to form a composite flexible structure. At the forward end, the circular housing rests in a cutaway section in the bulkhead and is secured to it by a ring of twelve bolts.

At the rear the framework rests upon two pillars. These pillars are welded to the belly plates of the tank and are strutted.

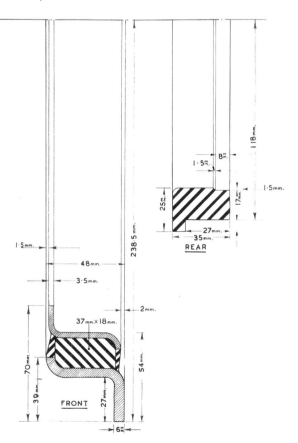

Scrap section of rubber mounting

160

CYLINDER HEADS

Cylinder heads with camshaft and rocker gear removed

A single cast iron cylinder head is used on each bank of six cylinders. Hemispherical combustion chambers are machined in the head and each valve is inclined at an angle of 60° to the head face. The valves seat directly on the head metal and each is provided with a single port, the inlets being to the inside of each bank and the exhausts to the outside. A single 14mm. plug is situated in each combustion chamber. The bore of the plug hole lies parallel to the inlet valve and breaks into the side of the combustion chamber on the longitudinal centre line.

The sections of the casting are fairly heavy and the machining operations comparatively few and simple. Ample water passages are cored round the valve seats and ports and round the plug bosses. A metal and asbestos gasket is used and as the cylinder liners stand 1.5mm. above the cylinder top face, a high localised pressure is obtained around each cylinder joint. Cooling water passes into the head through holes in the head face below the valve ports. A single water outlet is situated at the timing case end of the head at the side of the rectangular hole accommodating the camshaft driving gear. Each head is secured by 14 bolts.

The top face of the head is milled flat to receive the pedestal bearings for the camshaft and rocker gear, and the cast aluminium valve cover. A tubular extension, on the inside of the valve cover, forms a joint round each plug hole in the head and communicates with a trough in the top of the cover which accommodates the ignition leads. This trough is provided with a separate cast aluminium cover which is removed for access to the plugs.

DATA AND DIMENSIONS

Inlet port dimensions	65mm x 50mm
Exhaust port dimensions	70mm x 37mm
Volume of combustion chamber	211 c.c.
Proportion of combustion chamber volume to total clearance volume	70.5%
Depth of head	93mm.

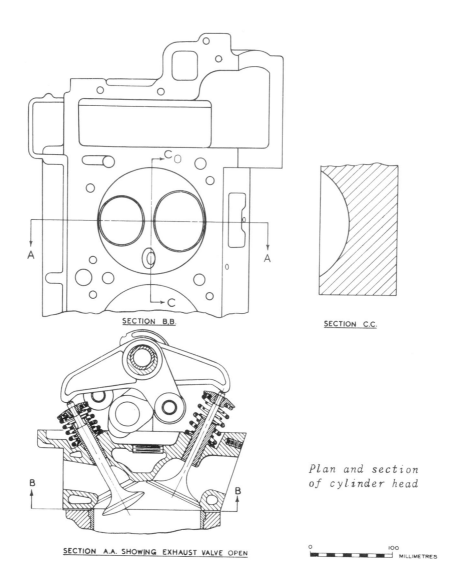

SECTION B.B.

SECTION C.C.

SECTION A.A. SHOWING EXHAUST VALVE OPEN

Plan and section of cylinder head

0   100
|_|_|_|_|_|_|_|_|_|_|
                     MILLIMETRES

Pistons and connecting rod assembly

PISTONS.

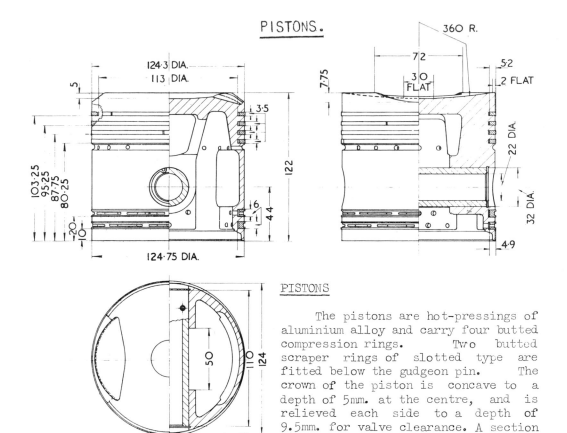

PISTONS

The pistons are hot-pressings of aluminium alloy and carry four butted compression rings. Two butted scraper rings of slotted type are fitted below the gudgeon pin. The crown of the piston is concave to a depth of 5mm. at the centre, and is relieved each side to a depth of 9.5mm. for valve clearance. A section of the skirt at gudgeon pin level is turned elliptically.

A groove 5mm. wide immediately below the 4th compression ring has 14 oil return holes, $3\frac{1}{2}$mm. diameter. The holes are evenly spaced in groups of 7 each side of the gudgeon pin bosses. Each scraper ring groove has ten 5mm. holes.

The gudgeon pin bosses are supported from the crown by two lateral webs. Two 5mm. holes are drilled in each boss for lubrication.

The gudgeon pins are fully floating, parallel bored and located by circlips.

DATA AND DIMENSIONS

Piston

Overall length	122mm.
Diameter	124.5mm.
Centre of gudgeon pin to crown (highest point)	78mm.
Width of ring groove (compression)	3.5mm.
" " " (scraper)	6.0mm.
Width of lands	4.0mm.
Distance from top of ring to crown (highest point)	15.25mm.

Gudgeon Pin

Outside diameter	32.0mm.
Inside diameter	22.0mm.

Weights

Piston (bare)	3.219 lbs
Four compression rings	.418 "
Two scraper rings	.246 "
Gudgeon pin (with circlips)	.812 "

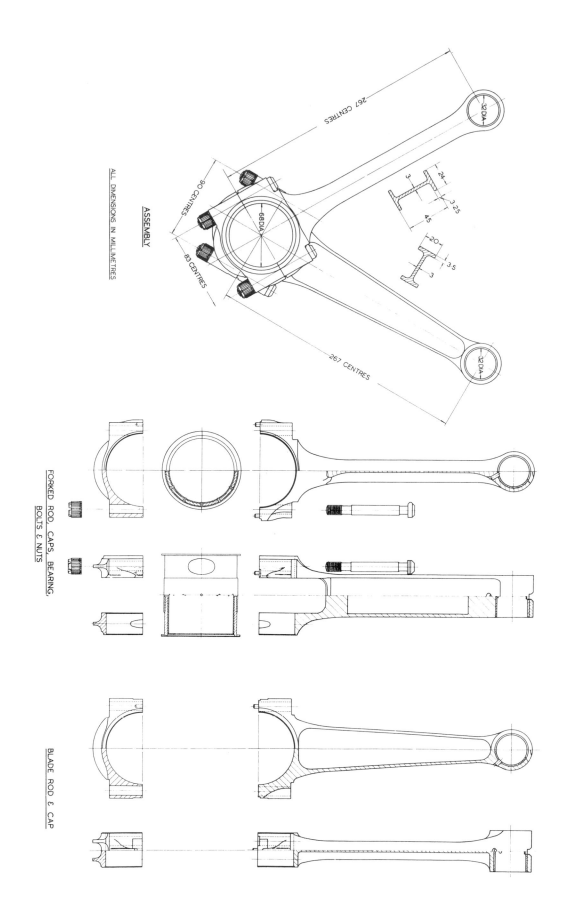

ASSEMBLY

ALL DIMENSIONS IN MILLIMETRES

267 CENTRES

68 DIA

90 CENTRES

83 CENTRES

32 DIA

32 DIA

267 CENTRES

24

3

3.25

45

20

3.5

3

FORKED ROD, CAPS, BEARING,
BOLTS & NUTS

BLADE ROD & CAP

164

CONNECTING RODS

<u>CONNECTING ROD ASSEMBLY</u>

A forked and blade rod arrangement is employed.   The stamped steel rods are of "H" section, machined all over.   A high degree of surface finish is apparent on the more highly stressed areas.   An unusual feature is that the "H" section of the forked rod is at right angles to   that of the blade rod, i.e. the web is parallel to the crankshaft axis.

Four big end bolts are provided for each rod.   The heads are shaped to prevent turning and their undersides bevelled to clear the con rod radius.   The castellated nuts are of serrated barrel type.

The steel big end bush, which is copper lead lined, is in two halves and is dowelled into one of the forked caps.   The blade rod bears centrally upon a copper lead lined surface on the outside of the bush and lubrication is by 12 radially drilled holes.   The big end caps of each rod are located by two dowels.

A phosphor bronze bush is used in the small end.   A rectangular slot in the bush registers with a similar slot machined in the top of the rod for lubrication.   In addition, two holes are drilled through the rod and bush for the same purpose.

DATA AND DIMENSIONS

<u>Connecting Rods</u>

Centres   267 mm.

	Blade Rod	Forked Rod
Flange width	20mm	24mm.
Web thickness	3mm	3mm.
Flange thickness	3.25mm	3.5mm.
Diameter of bolts	10 mm.	

<u>Big End Bush</u>

Width over flange	87mm.
Effective bearing width	81.5mm.
Inside diameter	68mm.
Outside diameter	77mm.
Outside diameter over blade rod bearing.	78mm.
Outside diameter over flanges	82mm.
Width of blade rod bearing	35.5mm.
Diameter of oil holes	2mm.

<u>Small End Bearing</u>

Outside diameter	35mm.
Inside diameter	32mm.
Length, effective	44mm.

<u>Weights</u>

Weight of forked rod (less big end bearings)	4lbs	$6\frac{1}{2}$oz
Weight of blade rod	3lbs	$11\frac{1}{2}$oz
Weight of big end bearings (worn)	1lb.	$8\frac{3}{4}$oz

Circular web crankshaft

The six throw forged crankshaft has circular webs, is machined all over and supported in seven large diameter roller bearings. The circular webs form the inner races for the main bearings. This bearing arrangement results in a very short crankshaft. The crank pins and bearing surfaces of the webs are hardened.

Each web has seven drillings and balance of the shaft is effected by bolting weights through these holes, with the exception of No. 4 web which has a semi-circular weight secured each side by three bolts passing through the drillings. One of the drillings in each web is concentric with a crankpin and an oil seal is formed by conically seated caps secured by a single bolt. Where the drillings are not blanked by balance weights they are left clear with the exception of those on No. 1 web which have light metal dished caps pressed into them.

A band is fitted over the diameter and flush with the side of No. 1 web and is secured in position in six places by tack welding. This band butts against the main bearing rollers and takes care of end thrust in one direction. A plate bolted to the outside of the crankshaft takes the thrust in the reverse direction. The end thrust is very light, as the clutch thrust is not taken by the crankshaft, the main clutch being incorporated in the gearbox. It is noteworthy that in every case the welds have failed.

Oil control at the front bearing is by a somewhat elaborate assembly comprised of light metal dished pressings. This feature has all the appearances of a "one off" job.

On the face of the front web are six tapped holes to receive the flywheel studs.

The free end of the crankshaft incorporates a flange carrying a frictional type torsional vibration damper. It consists of two flywheels, two fibre friction discs, two presser plates and eighteen springs.

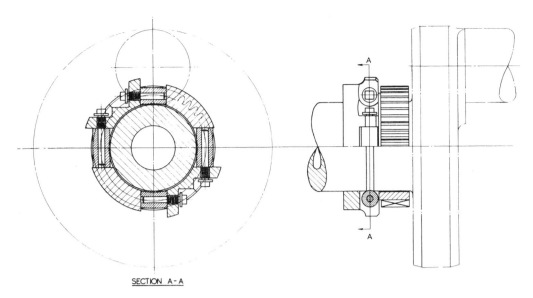

SECTION A-A

Timing adjustment

The master timing pinion is located on the shaft by lugs locked together by radial bolts passing through distance pieces.

Oil is delivered to the crankshaft by an oil muff at the rear end and circulates through the radially drilled webs and hollow crankpins. Three radial holes are drilled in each crankpin, the outer one of which has an internally protruding copper tube to act as a sludge trap.

DATA AND DIMENSIONS

Overall length of crankshaft   1029 mm.
Weight   194.5 lbs.

Pins

Outside diameter	68 mm
Inside diameter	40 mm
Length of pin	88 mm
Radius crank pin to web	3.18 mm
Oil holes diameter	5 mm
Diameter copper tubing inserted in one hole	3.5 mm
Projection copper tubing internally in crank pin	8 mm

Webs

Diameter	215 mm
Wdith Nos. 1 - 6	40 mm
No. 7	33 mm
Diameter of drillings in webs	40 mm
" " oilway through webs	20 mm
" " circular balance weights	68 mm

Oil Muff

Diameter of oil holes	10 mm

Flywheel Studs

Number	6
Diameter	12 mm
P.C. Diameter	164 mm

167

Damper Studs

Number	8
Diameter	12 mm
P.C. Diameter	120 mm

Roller Main Bearings

Number	7
Outside diameter of race	270 mm
Inside diameter of race	215 mm
Width	40 mm
No. of rollers	34
Diameter of rollers	6 mm. approx.
Length of rollers	22 mm
Annular groove on circumference of race	3 mm
Diameter of 3 radial holes in above groove	3 mm

Roller main bearing

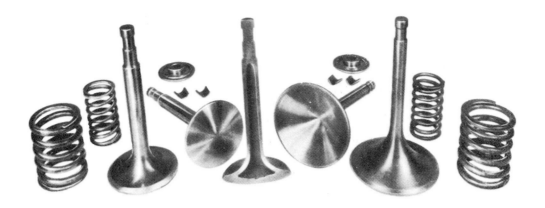

Valve assemblies showing sectioned exhaust.

A single gear driven camshaft to each bank operates one inlet and one exhaust valve per cylinder through rocker arms with roller followers. The inlet valves are of tulip form of unusually large diameter whilst the exhausts have sodium cooled heads and stems.   The valves are filled through the head, the filling holes being closed by welding.   Double valve springs are fitted in each case; the springs appear to be ground and are lacquered.   By contrast with the high degree of finish and light construction found elsewhere on the valve gear, the rocker arms are heavy machined steel forgings.   The valve guides are cast iron.

The camshaft, which is slightly off-set from the centre line of the cylinder head, is supported in seven bearings in pedestals dowelled into the cylinder head.   The bearings are split, the two halves being dowelled and secured by two screws.   The bearing surface is white metal run on direct.   A thrust bearing is formed in the rear pedestal by machined faces, white metalled, running against the flange of the camshaft driving gear and a machined step on the first cam.

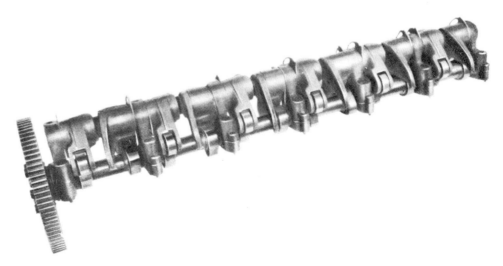

Rocker and camshaft assemblies

The rocker shaft is supported on the centre line of the head in the same seven pedestals which carry the camshaft, and is bored throughout its length and blanked off at the ends by metal plugs.   Radial drillings communicate with the rocker arm bushes.

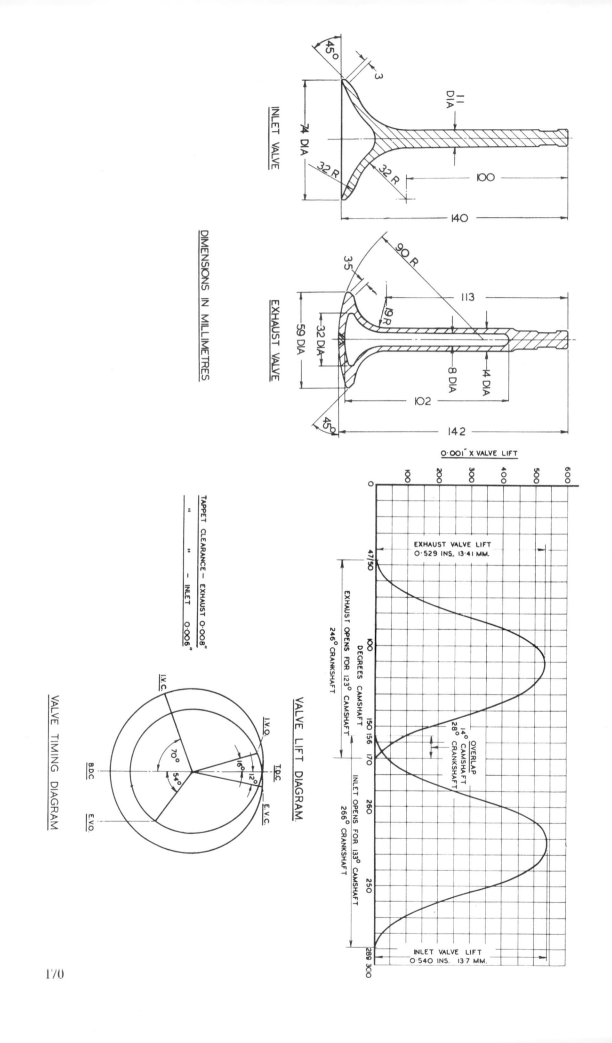

INLET VALVE

EXHAUST VALVE

DIMENSIONS IN MILLIMETRES

VALVE LIFT DIAGRAM.

VALVE TIMING DIAGRAM

TAPPET CLEARANCE — EXHAUST 0.008"
        "   " — INLET   0.006"

0.001" X VALVE LIFT

EXHAUST VALVE LIFT
0.529 INS. 13.41 MM.

EXHAUST OPENS FOR 123° CAMSHAFT
246° CRANKSHAFT

INLET OPENS FOR 133° CAMSHAFT
266° CRANKSHAFT

14° CAMSHAFT
28° CRANKSHAFT
OVERLAP

INLET VALVE LIFT
0.540 INS. 13.7 MM.

DEGREES CAMSHAFT

The rocker arm is slotted to receive the pedestal securing bolts, which thereby serve as cotters to prevent the shaft rotating in its bearings. Seven of the cylinder head holding down bolts each serve also as one of the pedestal fixing bolts.

The rockers are mounted on eccentric bronze bushes which are a light push fit in the rockers and on the shaft and which have a slotted flange on one side. Tappet adjustment is obtained by rotation of the bush and is locked by a bolt passing through the flange of the bush into the pedestal.

Rocker, pedestal and eccentric bush

DATA AND DIMENSIONS

Camshaft

Length of shaft	892.5 mm
Diameter of shaft	31.0 mm
No. of bearings	7
Diameter of bearings	32.0 mm
Width of six bearings	33.0 mm
Width of front end thrust bearing	35.0 mm

Cams

Base circle diameter of cam	46.0 mm
Width of cam	17.0 mm
Lift of cam	8.5 mm

Rocker Arms

Diameter of housing for bush	35.0 mm
Width " " " "	51.0 mm
Diameter of roller	38.0 mm
Width of roller	14.0 mm
Effective leverage of rocker	1 : 1.57

Eccentric Bronze Bush

Outside diameter	35.0 mm
Inside diameter	30.0 mm
Maximum eccentricity	3.0 mm
Effective bearing surface on outside diameter	49.0 mm
Diameter of oil holes in bush	4.0 mm

Rocker Shaft

Length of shaft	875.0 mm
Outside diameter of shaft	30.0 mm
Inside diameter of shaft	20.0 mm
Diameter of oil holes	4.0 mm

Valves

	Inlet	Exhaust
No. per cylinder	1	1
Diameter of head	74.0 mm	59.0 mm
Stem diameter	11.0 mm	14.0 mm
Length of valve	141.0 mm	142.0 mm
Angle of seat	45°	45°
Minimum area through valve	38cm^2	23cm^2
Valve lift	13.7 mm	13.4 mm
Mean gas velocity through valve at 3,000 R.P.M.	238ft/sec.	334ft/sec.

Weights

	Inlet	Exhaust
Valve	.551 lbs	.551 lbs
Inside and outside springs	.370 lbs	.384 lbs
Cap and cotters	.099 lbs	.099 lbs
Rocker arm and roller	2.094 lbs	2.094 lbs

Springs (Inside)

	Inlet	Exhaust
Free length	55.37 mm	54.86 mm
Wire diameter	3.5 mm	3.5 mm
Mean coil diameter	25.0 mm	25.0 mm
No. of active coils	5.5	5.5
Rate	109 lb/in.	108 lb/in.

Springs (Outside)

	Inlet	Exhaust
Free length	58.42 mm	58.67 mm
Wire diameter	5.5 mm	5.5 mm
Mean coil diameter	4.0 mm	4.0 mm
No. of active coils	4	4
Rate	234 lb/in.	228 lb/in.

Valve Guides

Overall length	57 mm
Inside diameter	13 mm
Outside diameter	19 mm
Length (in block)	30 mm
Diameter of flange	30 mm
Width of flange	2 mm
Length projecting in port	25 mm

TIMING AND AUXILIARY DRIVE GEAR

All the gears are housed in the timing case, which is part of the main crankcase casting.

The drive is taken from the master timing pinion on the crankshaft to a large triple intermediate gear supported from the crankcase by two taper roller bearings on a hollow shaft. The outer diameter of this gear drives the camshafts, also through an idler gear, the oil and petrol pump shaft. The magneto for each bank is driven via an idler from the camshaft gear. A two speed fan drive is provided for by movement of a selector rod which engages gears either with the outer diameter of the intermediate gear, or with a second gear cut on a smaller diameter. Also driven from this smaller gear, through an idler, is the pinion on the dynamo. The smallest diameter gear on the intermediate timing wheel drives the governor and water pump situated centrally between the cylinder banks and mounted respectively at each end of the engine. All the gears are steel of straight cut pattern.

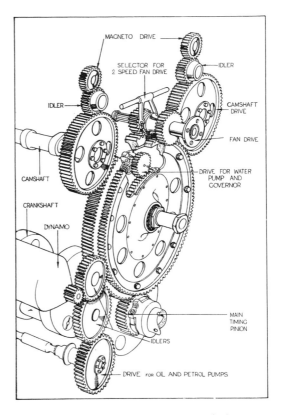

Timing gears and auxiliary drives

The magneto for each bank, together with its idler gear, is carried on the valve cover, consequently removal of the cover upsets the ignition timing. Scribe marks on the wheels facilitate replacement. The various pinions are generally supported on ball races.

DATA AND DIMENSIONS

Gear	No. of teeth	P.C. Diam.	Face Width	Module
Main timing pinion	42	103mm	24mm	2.4mm
Oil pump	52	129mm	15mm	2.5mm
Intermediate oil pump gear	59	146mm	15mm	2.5mm
Intermediate dynamo drive	43	106.5mm	15mm	2.5mm
Camshaft	84	214mm	22mm	2.5mm
Intermediate Mag idler	30	72.5mm	15mm	2.4mm
Magneto	28	70mm	15mm	2.5mm
Governor & water pump drive	24	59mm	15mm	2.5mm
Fan drive (1)	39	96.5mm	15mm	2.5mm
(2)	28	70mm	25mm	2.5mm
Intermediate gear (Main)				
(1) Large gear	182	456mm	25mm	2.5mm
(2) Middle gear	173	429mm	15mm	2.5mm
(3) Small gear	104	259mm	13mm	2.5mm

SPEED X ENGINE R.P.M.

Camshaft	.5	Magnetos	1.5	Fuel pumps	.8077
Oil pumps	.3077	Governor	1.75	Water pump	1.75

LUBRICATION SYSTEM.

General Description and Circulation

The lubrication system is of the dry sump type employing one pressure and two scavenge pumps. An external filter and an oil cooler are mounted on the left side of the engine, whilst the oil tank is bolted to the right hand side.

External pipe lines have been reduced to the minimum and the crankcase has extensive oilways both in the walls and the webs. Crankcase ventilation is via the timing case, and gauze protected breathers are fitted to the valve covers adjacent to the magneto mountings.

The accompanying diagram shows the circuit. Oil is drawn from the tank by the pressure pump mounted on No.2 web through a drilling in No.4 web and is pumped to a three-way junction box. External pipes convey the oil through the cooler, back to the junction box and to the filter. A spring loaded valve incorporated in the junction box isolates the cooler when the oil is cold.

The filter is bolted to a machined boss and the oil passes through a drilling in this boss to an internal gallery which runs the whole length of the crankcase and across No.6 main bearing web. A pressure relief valve is fitted in this boss. Piped to the main gallery is a muff on the rear end of the hollow crankshaft for the lubrication of main and big end bearings.

Two drillings from the main oil gallery, into which reducer nipples are fitted, lead to the block face of each cylinder bank. Oil then passes up around cylinder head fixing bolts, via the pedestals into the hollow rocker shaft. From the rocker shafts oil is distributed by holes, drillings and the pedestal fixing bolts to the valve rockers, roller followers and camshaft bearings. Excess oil then drains back down the timing case, and also through a hole at the opposite end of each block.

Oil Pumps

The three gear type oil pumps, mounted on the main bearing webs, are driven in tandem by splined shafts from the timing gears.

All the pumps are similar in design but the pressure pump is of slightly smaller capacity than either of the scavenge pumps.

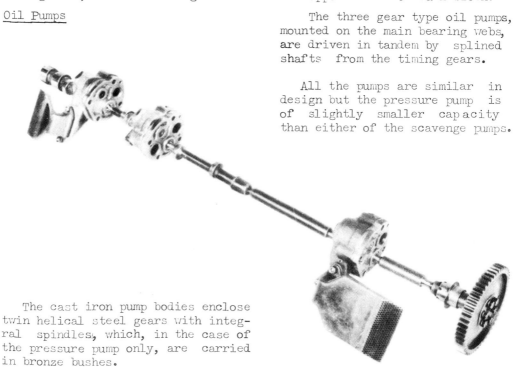

The cast iron pump bodies enclose twin helical steel gears with integral spindles, which, in the case of the pressure pump only, are carried in bronze bushes.

The driving gears are splined to receive the driving shaft.

Oil pumps and drive shaft

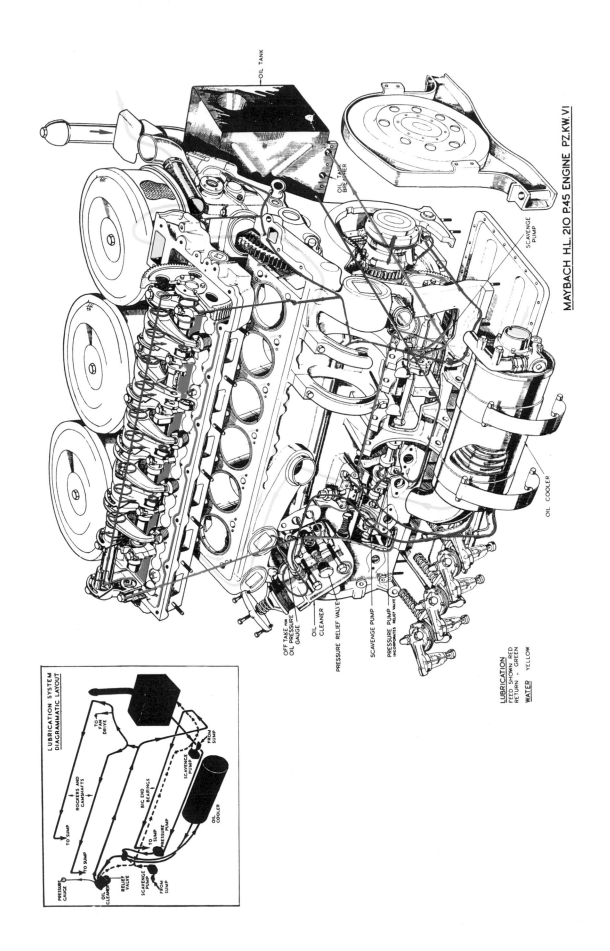

OIL TANK

OIL TANK BREATHER

SCAVENGE PUMP

OIL COOLER

OFF TAKE FOR OIL PRESSURE GAUGE

OIL CLEANER

PRESSURE RELIEF VALVE

SCAVENGE PUMP

PRESSURE PUMP
INCORPORATES RELIEF VALVE

MAYBACH H.L. 210 P.45 ENGINE PZ.KW.VI

LUBRICATION
FEED SHOWN RED
RETURN - GREEN
WATER - YELLOW

LUBRICATION SYSTEM
DIAGRAMMATIC LAYOUT

TO FAN DRIVE

ROCKERS AND CAMSHAFTS

TO SUMP

TO SUMP

BIG END BEARINGS

FROM SUMP

SCAVENGE PUMP

TO SUMP

PRESSURE PUMP

OIL COOLER

PRESSURE GAUGE

OIL CLEANER

RELIEF VALVE

SCAVENGE PUMP

FROM SUMP

175

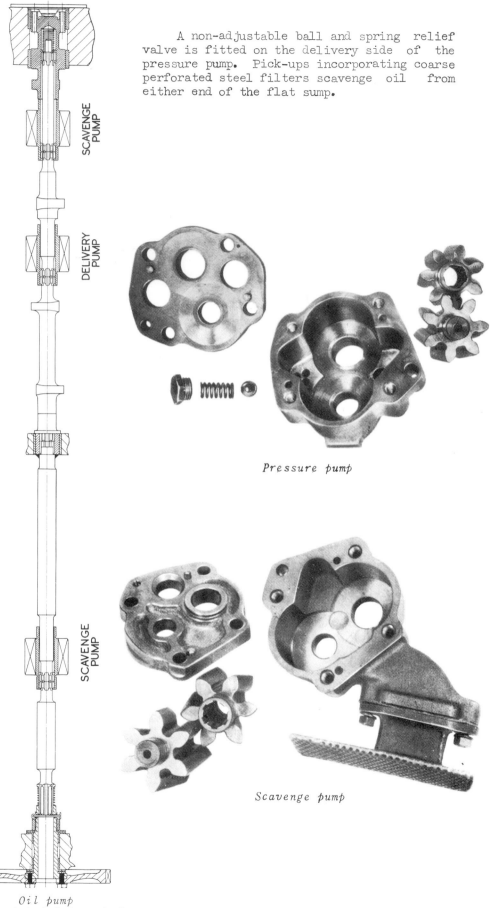

A non-adjustable ball and spring relief valve is fitted on the delivery side of the pressure pump. Pick-ups incorporating coarse perforated steel filters scavenge oil from either end of the flat sump.

SCAVENGE PUMP

DELIVERY PUMP

SCAVENGE PUMP

Pressure pump

Scavenge pump

Oil pump articulated drive shaft

Oil Tank

The oil tank which has a capacity of approximately 4 gallons is bolted directly on the crankcase. Three short elbow pipes leading from the bottom of the tank are welded to a machined flange which is bolted to a corresponding machined surface on the crankcase. The two outer elbow pipes register with drillings through Nos. 4 and 5 main bearing webs and serve as delivery and return lines respectively. The central elbow is extended inside the tank to form a standpipe and a breather to the crankcase. It would therefore be possible to flood the sump by careless overfilling of the tank.

A dipstick is contained in the long filler tube, the cap of which has a fine thread and a "bolt head" top.

Lengthwise in the tank is a cylindrical hole through which pass the input shaft and engagement rod of the inertia starter.

Oil Cooler

The oil cooler consists of a close coil contained in a cylindrical sheet metal jacket, through which water is circulated. It is installed together with the filter on the pressure side of the system. In cold climates it is enemy practice to introduce hot water from an outside source, and under these conditions the installation would serve to warm up the cold lubricant.

Filter

The oil filter has an element of gauze discs separated with spacer plates. Feed is from the outside of the element to the centre. If the filter becomes choked, the whole element moves against a spring and allows the oil to by-pass. A pipe for the oil gauge is taken from the outlet side of the filter.

Oil filter

DATA AND DIMENSIONS

Approximate capacity of system   6.2 gallons.

	Pressure Pump	Scavenge Pump
No.	1	2
No. of teeth on gear	7	6
Outside diameter of gear	47 mm.	47 mm.
Root diameter of gear	26 mm.	$22\frac{1}{2}$ mm.
Face width of gear	45 mm.	38 mm.
Clearance between teeth	.33 mm.	.30 mm.
Theoretical delivery at 100% efficiency at 1000 pump RPM	11.3 gals/min	14.37 gals/min (One pump)
Theoretical delivery at 100% efficiency at 3000 engine RPM (2423.1 pump RPM)	27.38 gals/min	69.638 gals/min (both pumps)

Ratio one pressure to two scavenge pumps   1 : 2.54

Filter

No. of spacer plates	29
No. of gauze discs	30
Total effective area of gauze	2050 sq. cm.

ENGINE COOLING SYSTEM

The system, which is sealed, comprises two radiators, and two pairs of fans, and the water is circulated by a centrifugal pump.

The cooling system incorporates several unusual features which fulfil the requirements of submerged running, and these will be described in detail in a separate section. The following description is therefore confined to the engine only.

Water enters the cylinder block via the oil cooler on the left side and returns to the radiators through a single pipe at the rear of each cylinder head. From the oil cooler the water enters a passage cored round the left side to the front of the block, thence via the pump, into a further passage cored between the banks. This passage communicates with the top of the cylinders through small ports, one to each cylinder; these ports are situated to one side of their respective cylinders, thus imparting a swirl to the water on entry. All the cylinders of each bank are interconnected by cored holes at the bottom. A small hole in the rear cylinder of the left bank communicates with a coring which circulates water round the rear wall of the block which forms the casing for the timing gears. Water enters the cylinder heads through holes below the valve ports.

Water Pump

The centrifugal pump is mounted on the forward top end of the crankcase between the cylinder banks.

It is connected to the corings through curved machined faces.

The body of the pump and the impeller are of cast iron. The latter is keyed on a shaft supported in two taper roller bearings. Seals are fitted at either end and lubricant is introduced into the space between the seals through a nipple in the housing.

DATA AND DIMENSIONS

No. of vanes	9
Tip diameter of vanes	146 mm.
Heel diameter of vanes	70 mm.
Width of vane at tip	8 mm.
Width of vane at heel	15 mm.
Inclination of vanes to tangent at tip	30°
Inclination of vanes to tangent at heel	110°

WATER PUMP.

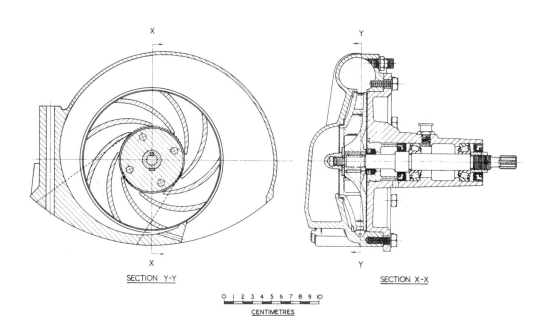

SECTION Y-Y   SECTION X-X

0 1 2 3 4 5 6 7 8 9 10
CENTIMETRES

RESTRICTED

The information given in this document
is not to be communicated. either directly
or indirectly, to the Press or to any person
not authorized to receive it.

REPORT ON

PzKw VI
(Tiger)
Model H

PART IV

POWER PLANT

SECTION V

ELECTRICAL EQUIPMENT (ENGINE)

BOSCH DYNAMO. TYPE GUL 1000/12/1000 LS 26

Military College of Science
SCHOOL OF TANK TECHNOLOGY
Chobham Lane   Chertsey

April 1944

PART IV

POWER PLANT

SECTION V

ELECTRICAL EQUIPMENT (ENGINE)
BOSCH DYNAMO. TYPE GUL 1000/12/1000 LS26

INTRODUCTION

The dynamo was tested and examined by Messrs. C.A.V. Ltd. who provided the subject matter for this report.

The performance of the machine was found to be good. Its main dimensions are comparable with the C.A.V. Model D8C dynamo although its output is higher and its working temperature lower. With regard to the performance, however, comparison is not justified, as the Bosch dynamo has obviously been designed as a 12 volt machine whereas the D8C was primarily designed for 24 volts.

The commutation of the machine at full load is very good over the working speed range. The reactance voltage, calculated from the usual formula is reasonable for a non-interpole machine, viz., 1.9 volts at 2000 R.P.M x 100 amps.

The light construction and efficient working of the fan are points of interest, particularly so in this installation, as the air in the engine compartment is relatively stagnant, the radiators and fans being housed in separate compartments.

The method of joining the field coils before taping, and the brush box construction are interesting design features.

The ball races are of French manufacture. In view of the date of manufacture, it is noteworthy that the construction of the machine shows no attempt at economy in the use of copper.

April, 1944.

Major J.D. Barnes,R.T.R.
D.M. Pearce, B.A. (Cantab)

GENERAL DESCRIPTION

The dynamo is strapped to the side of the crankcase and is gear driven at engine speed in an anticlockwise direction. It is a 12 volt machine with a maximum output of 1300 watts (maker's rating). The maximum charging rate is stated to be 100 amps. The date of manufacture is 1942.

The dynamo is ventilated by a radial flow fan, which draws air over the commutator through a flexible pipe which opens into the fighting compartment.

Yoke and Field System

View with End Cover and Fan Removed

Armature

Commutator End Shield

Ventilating Fan

CONSTRUCTIONAL DETAILS AND DIMENSIONS

Overall length of Machine .. .. 480 mm.
Weight.. ... ... 114 lbs.

Yoke

Outside Diameter ... ... 203 mm.
Thickness... ... ... 10 mm.
Length, excluding brush gear ... ... 218 mm.

Field System

The yoke carries six poles secured by set screws. The field is split,
each field consisting of three coils in series. Two parallel field
resistances are wound on two of the field coils. The poles are
slightly skewed, and no interpoles are fitted. It was noted that the
ends of the field inter-connectors were soldered close to the coils
before the coils were taped - this gives the effect of a one piece
field inter-connector.

Pole face . ... 145mm. long (gross)
Pole chord ... ... 43mm.
Width of winging .. .. 8mm.
Pole core, width .. .. 25.7mm.
   "   "   depth .. .. 23mm.
Resistance of field ... ... 5.5 ohms per field
Parallel field resistance . ... 16 ohms per
                                                       resistance

Armature & Commutator

The armature windings are of single turn, single coil, strip, wave
wound. The slots are slightly skewed in an opposite direction to the
poles.

The commutator is of rivetted construction with mica inter-bar insula-
tion.

Length of core ... ... 143 mm.
Diameter of core .. .. 135 mm.
No. of slots... 49
Width of slot . ... 2 mm.
   "   " tooth ... ... 7 mm.

Approximate dimensions of strip winding ... ... 6mm. x 2.5 mm.
Commutator length (excluding risers) .. .. 65mm.
   "   "   (overall) ... ... 75mm.
   "   Diameter ... ... 100mm.
No. of commutator bars 49

End Shields

Both end shields are of aluminium. The driving end shield is not fitted with a lubricator and the ball race is held in by an aluminium
clamping plate. This plate carries the armature earthing brushes,
which are situated between the armature and the bearing and bears on a
copper slip ring.

The commutator end shield carries the terminal box. The ball race is
housed in a brass liner and is held in by a steel clamping plate.
Earthing brushes are fitted between the shield and the fan.

Driving End ball race - O.D. .. .. 80 mm.
Commutator End "   " - O.D. .. .. 62 mm.

Brush Gear

The brush box is of rivetted brass construction. Two sets of four brushes are fitted, the brushes being of the usual German construction. Clock type brush springs are employed.

Brush size ... ...25 x 8 mm.
Spring pressure .. ..3.25 lb.

Fan

The radial flow ventilating fan is keyed to the armature shaft. It is constructed of light sheet steel welded together.

Fan Diameter (mean) .. ..180 mm.
Fan width ... ... 33 mm.
No. of blades. 30
Blade dimensions . ... 33 x 18 mm.

TEST RESULTS

The machine was placed on the test bench and the cutting in and maximum load speeds determined. These were :-

Cutting in speed . ... 720 r.p.m.
Maximum load speed ... ... 870 r.p.m. at 100 amps 13.5 volts

The dynamo was then given heat runs at 1,000, 2,000, and 3,000 r.p.m.; on full load, these gave the following results :-

Speed.	Amb. Temp.	Rise in field after $\frac{1}{2}$ hour	Rise in field after 1 hour	Final Temp. (after 1 hr.) Field	Comm.
1000	23°C.	22.5°C.	40°C.	63°C.	83°C.
2000	19°C.	20.5°C.	36°C.	55°C.	77°C.
3000	25°C.	22°C.	35°C.	60°C.	78°C.

The machine was then run at full load and 2,000 r.p.m. when a steady temperature in the field of 69.5°C was reached in 2.1/2 hours, the corresponding commutator temperature being 84°C (ambient temperature 25°C).

The performance of the fan was then tested, and the delivery was found to vary directly with the speed within the working range.

Speed	Delivery
1000 R.P.M	10.5 cub.ft/min.
2000 R.P.M	21.6 cub.ft/min.
3000 R.P.M	33.0 cub.ft/min.

Efficiency tests were then carried out and the following curves plotted :-

Speed - Efficiency curve at constant load 1200 W   Fig.1
Load - Efficiency curve at constant voltage 1000 r.p.m. Fig.2

The following tables were extracted from these results :-

Output Watts	H.P. Input	Efficiency
600 (Half load)	1.3 H.P.	62.5%
1200 ($\frac{1}{1}$ load)	2.42 H.P.	67%
1800 ($\frac{3}{2}$ load)	3.82 H.P.	63.5%

Speed	H.P. Input	Efficiency	
1,000 r.p.m.	2.42 H.P.	67%)	At max.
2,000 r.p.m.	2.55 H.P.	63%)	load of
3,000 r.p.m.	2.86 H.P.	56%)	100 amps.

The iron, windage and friction losses were then separated for 1,000 r.p.m. by the following method :-

The machine was separately excited, and the field current varied from 0 to 5 amps., the corresponding values of watts input and O.C. volts being noted. Since the speed is constant the windage and friction losses will remain constant and correspond to the watts input at zero excitation.

A curve showing variation of watts input and O.C. volts with excitation is plotted at Fig.3

The armature and field resistance were found to be .0075 ohm and 4 ohms (total, including parallel field).

From these figures and foregoing results the following analysis of losses at 1200 watts output and 1000 r.p.m. was extracted :-

Efficiency at F.L. 67% Output 1200 watts.
∴ Total losses = 580 watts

Armature copper loss	75 watts
Field copper loss...	64 watts
Brush contact loss	200 watts
Iron losses.	96 watts
Brush friction, windage and other friction losses	120 watts
Unaccounted loss	25 watts
	580 watts

The brush contact losses were estimated from figures obtained with EGO brushes.

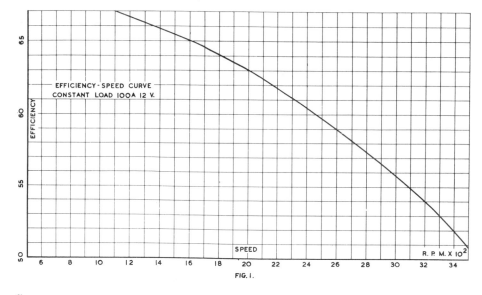

EFFICIENCY-SPEED CURVE
CONSTANT LOAD 100A 12 V.

EFFICIENCY

SPEED

R. P. M. X 10²

FIG. 1.

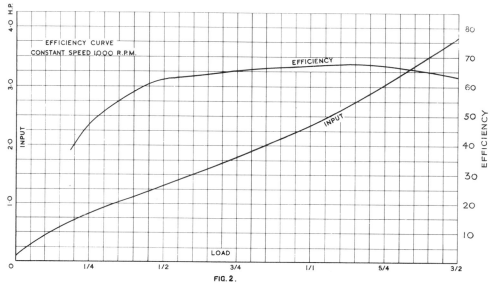

EFFICIENCY CURVE
CONSTANT SPEED 1,000 R.P.M.

EFFICIENCY

INPUT

LOAD

FIG. 2.

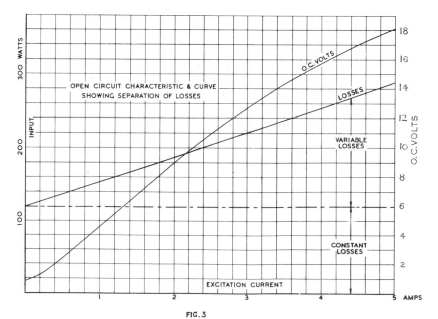

OPEN CIRCUIT CHARACTERISTIC & CURVE
SHOWING SEPARATION OF LOSSES

O.C. VOLTS

LOSSES

VARIABLE
LOSSES

CONSTANT
LOSSES

EXCITATION CURRENT

AMPS

FIG. 3

PART IV

POWER PLANT

SECTION VI.

BOSCH INERTIA STARTER
(Type AL/ZMJ)

INTRODUCTION

The Bosch Inertia Starter is fitted as standard equipment on all German tank engines with the exception of that in the Pz.Kw. I now virtually obsolete.

The starter is hand operated only, and is mounted on the engine in a similar manner to an orthodox electric starter and engages with the flywheel ring gear. It may only be operated from outside the tank through the tail plate. The hand crank drives through two sprockets and a roller chain to a shaft provided with a universal joint and attached to the starter input shaft.

The type AL/ZMJ fitted to this tank differs from the type AL/ZMA found on the smaller German tanks (Pz.Kw. II, III and IV) only in detail design. In the main it is very similar, and certain parts are interchangeable. The chief differences are found in the input gear train and the clutch engaging mechanism. It is interesting to note that the capacity of the two types - as measured by the total energy stored in the flywheel - is approximately the same, whereas the engine capacity of the Pz.Kw. VI (approximately 21 litres) is very nearly double that of the Pz.Kw. III and IV (approximately 12 litres). The geared reduction from the starter flywheel to the engine crankshaft is, however, very much greater in this case, and the engine is therefore turned over at rather more than half the speed.

The limitations of size imposed by its location necessitate a small flywheel running at a high speed and consequently the precision of design and workmanship must be of a high order. The use of a separate output gear train from the flywheel to the starting pinion appears to be an unnecessary complication, as, with a little ingenuity, a section of the input train could have been used as the output.

Messrs. Rotax and C.A.V. Ltd., have examined one of these starters and we are indebted to them for the "Run-down" Time Curve.

Major J.D. Barnes, R.T.R.
D.M. Pearce, B.A. (Cantab.)

March, 1944

189

STARTER WITH CASINGS REMOVED

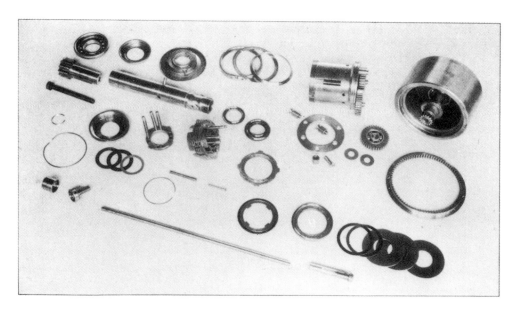

EXPLODED VIEW WITH CLUTCH, OUTPUT GEARS AND FLYWHEEL

190

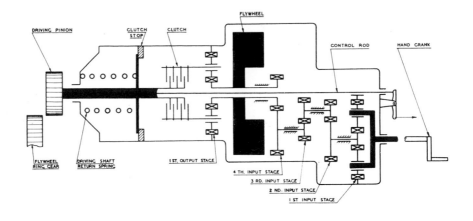

DRIVING PINION   CLUTCH STOP   CLUTCH   FLYWHEEL   CONTROL ROD   HAND CRANK

FLYWHEEL RING GEAR   DRIVING SHAFT RETURN SPRING   1 ST. OUTPUT STAGE   4 TH. INPUT STAGE   3 RD. INPUT STAGE   2 ND. INPUT STAGE   1 ST INPUT STAGE

Diagramatic Layout

PRINCIPLE OF OPERATION

The mechanism is basically a simple form of hand operated inertia starter consisting of a step-up input gear train from the handcrank to the flywheel and a reduction output gear train from the flywheel to the engine crankshaft via a starting pinion which axially engages with the flywheel ring gear. Incorporated in the reduction gear train is a clutch which is engaged manually when the flywheel is rotating at the required speed and which slips during the period when the engine is being accelerated.

From the diagram it will be seen that the first input stage consists of a simple epicyclic train, the planet carrier being the input, the annulus fixed and the sun wheel the output. The second, third and fourth stages each consist of a pair of spur gears, the output of one being integral with the input of the following stage.

The output gear train is quite separate from that of the input, being on the opposite side of the flywheel. The first stage consists of an epicyclic train, the sun wheel, which is attached to the flywheel, is the input, the annulus fixed, and the planet carrier forms the output. The output drives through the clutch the external driving pinion which engages with the flywheel ring gear, the pair forming the second and final output stage. Thus the final stage of the output gear train is outside the starter itself.

The multiplate clutch is engaged by a manually operated control rod which at the same time engages the driving pinion with the flywheel ring gear. The clutch is self energised when a torque is transmitted in one direction and acts as a free wheel when the torque is reversed.

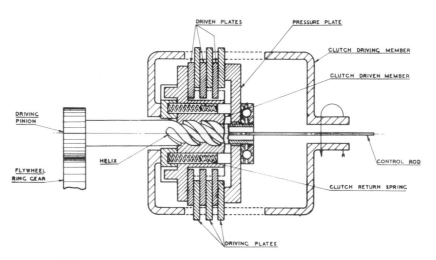

Diagramatic Layout showing clutch operation

The driving member of the clutch is a cylindrical cage slotted to receive the external serrations of the driving plates. These plates are free to slide axially in the slots. The driven member is in the form of a circular sleeve located concentrically within the driving member and grooved to receive the internal serrations of the driven plates. The outer edge of this member (as assembled) is provided with a flange against which the outer clutch plate abuts when the clutch is engaged. The member is free to slide on helical splines on the driving pinion shaft, the inner end of which is provided with a thrust race to limit the movement. A pressure plate disc is interposed between the thrust race and the driven member.

The direction of the helical splines is such that when a torque is transmitted through the clutch, in the right direction for starting the engine, the driven member tends to screw itself in on the shaft thus wedging the clutch plates between the flange and the pressure plate. As soon as the torque is reversed, i.e. when the engine fires, the action is reversed, and the clutch is automatically disengaged.

Light springs normally hold the driven member away from the pressure plate. When the driving pinion shaft is moved out to engage the pinion with the flywheel ring gear, the driven member of the clutch is pressed against a circular plate attached to the outer end of the driving member. This compresses the springs and closes the plates until sufficient torque is transmitted to the driven member to bring about the self wedging action. It will be seen therefore, that, provided the driving pinion shaft is moved far enough to start the clutch engagement, the slipping torque of the clutch is quite independant of force on the control rod but depends upon :-

      1. The dimensions of the clutch.
      2. The angle of the helical splines.

It will further be seen that the clutch is not engaged until the driving pinion is meshing with the flywheel ring gear.

The control rod passes through the axis of the flywheel and forces the driving pinion shaft outwards to engage with the flywheel ring gear. When the pressure on the control rod is released, a coil spring around the shaft returns it to its normal disengaged position. In this position a flange on the shaft is held against a stationary brake ring, thereby preventing the driving pinion from rotating through the drag in the clutch whilst the flywheel is being speeded up.

METHOD OF CONSTRUCTION

In external appearance the starter resembles an orthodox type of electric axial starter. The cylindrical casing is strapped against the side of the crankcase and a sliding driving pinion engages the flywheel ring gear. A considerable geared reduction is therefore obtained outside the starter itself. This, together with the high speed of flywheel rotation (9,000 - 10,000 R.P.M.) permits of a very compact and light design. In common with other Bosch products the workmanship is of a very high standard, and it is evidently a costly piece of mechanism to manufacture.

CASINGS.

The housing may be split into four main casings; a cylindrical aluminium casting housing the clutch, a steel sleeve surrounding the flywheel, an aluminium casting housing the shafts of the flywheel and third and fourth input gear stages, and a cast aluminium cover for the first two input stages.

The clutch casing is provided with a cast iron end plate which houses a white metal bush supporting the driving pinion shaft, and a synthetic rubber oil seal. This bearing is lubricated from a grease nipple and a felt ring surrounds the bush. The casing is provided with a flange at one end which fits into the steel flywheel casing and is held up against a shoulder in the latter by a ring nut. Between this flange and the shoulder on the flywheel casing is the annulus for the first output gear stage which is held by dowels and set screws on the flange. Pressed into the casing are the two outer races of the ball bearings supporting the cylindrical clutch driving member.

The flywheel casing consists of a length of steel tubing threaded internally at one end to take the ring nut, and provided with an internal flange at the other. Fitting inside this casing and held against the internal flange is the aluminium casting which carries the ball races for the flywheel shaft and for the two shafts carrying the third and fourth trains of spur gears. An external flange on the casting is held between the internal flange of the flywheel casing and the cast aluminium cover for the first two input stages. Long screws threaded into the flywheel casing secure these three components.

The cover for the first two input stages has an extension at one side to accommodate the first epicyclic train, the annulus of which is pressed into the cover and secured by set screws and dowels. The extension of this cover is provided with a felt oil seal through which the starting handle shaft passes. The control rod protrudes through a hole in the centre of the cover.

The aluminium casings appear to be gravity die castings.

GEAR TRAINS AND FLYWHEEL

Straight toothed spur gears are employed throughout. With the exception of the two annuli, which are soft, the gears are hardened but the tooth profiles are not ground. The pinions are made progressively lighter and the tooth face width and module decrease from the low speed to the high speed stages in the gear trains as the transmitted torque decreases.

All the pinions are supported on orthodox caged ball races with the exception of the sunwheel output of the first input stage and, integral with it, the driving pinion of the second input stage; these run on a bronze bush on an extension of the input shaft. In some cases the ball races are housed directly in the aluminium casings, in others steel housings are shrunk in.

Both epicyclic trains are of similar construction. In each case the carrier is in the form of a disc drilled to receive the three planet wheel shafts. Shoulders are turned at each end of the shafts which are held against the disc by a flat ring drilled to receive the other ends of the shafts.

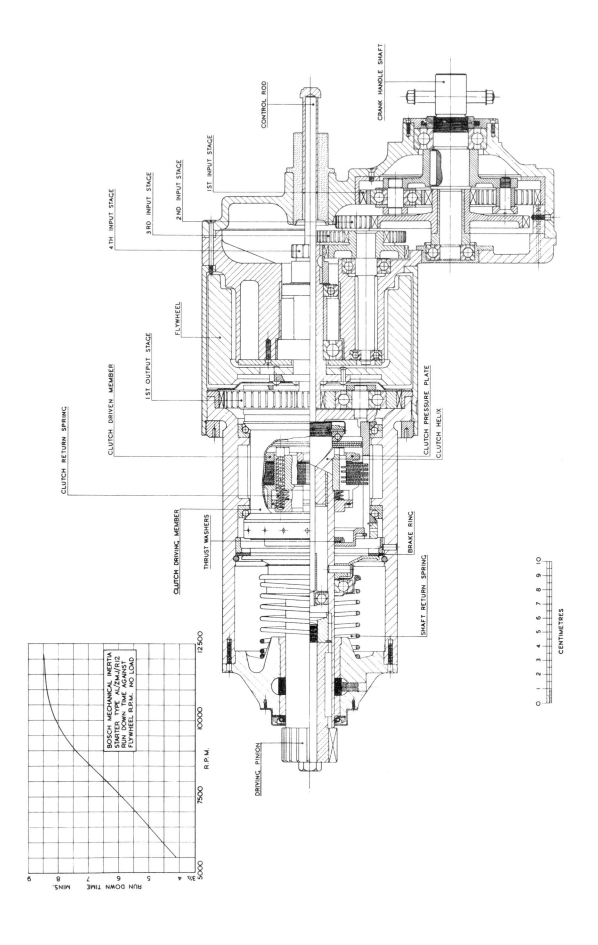

CRANK HANDLE SHAFT

CONTROL ROD

1ST INPUT STAGE

2ND INPUT STAGE

3RD INPUT STAGE

4TH INPUT STAGE

FLYWHEEL

1ST OUTPUT STAGE

CLUTCH DRIVEN MEMBER

CLUTCH RETURN SPRING

CLUTCH PRESSURE PLATE

CLUTCH HELIX

CLUTCH DRIVING MEMBER

THRUST WASHERS

BRAKE RING

SHAFT RETURN SPRING

DRIVING PINION

BOSCH MECHANICAL INERTIA
STARTER TYPE AL/ZM J/R12
RUN DOWN TIME AGAINST
FLYWHEEL R.P.M. NO LOAD

RUN DOWN TIME MINS.

R.P.M.

5000   7500   10000   12500

3¾ 4 5 6 7 8 9

CENTIMETRES

0 1 2 3 4 5 6 7 8 9 10

194

This ring is bolted to the disc by three set screws and distance pieces situated midway between the planet wheels and on the same P.C.D. Each planet wheel is pressed over a ball race, the pinion metal being nipped over the radius on the outer race in six places on each side to secure it.

The flywheel shaft is integral with the sunwheel of the first output stage, and is provided with a flange to which the flywheel is rivetted and dowelled. The steel flywheel, which is machined all over, has a wide rim on one side which surrounds the aluminium casting carrying the shafts of the flywheel and of the third and fourth input stages.

GEAR DATA

INPUT TRAIN		NO. OF TEETH	FACE WIDTH (mm.)	MODULE
1st stage	(Planet	23	12	2
	(Annulus	63	12	2
	(Sun	15	12	2
2nd stage	(Driver	55	9	2
	(Driven	12	9	2
3rd stage	(Driver	34	8	2
	(Driven	13	8	2
4th stage	(Driver	38	8	1.5
	(Driven	15	9	1.5
OUTPUT TRAIN				
1st stage	(Sun	12	13	1.5
	(Annulus	84	12	1.5
	(Planet	36	12	1.5

CLUTCH

The clutch driving member consists of a steel cylinder secured to the planet carrier of the first output stage by set screws and dowels. Fitting over this sleeve are two hardened steel conical section rings which form the inner races of two large crowded ball bearings supporting the sleeve and planet carrier. A ring nut on the outer end of the sleeve adjusts the clearance in the races.

Four slots are machined in the sleeve to receive the bronze driving plates which are arranged in pairs alternately between single steel driven plates. Eight chordal slits are cut in the outer diameter of each driving plate. The small tabs formed by these slits are turned alternately outwards and inwards so that the planes of their surfaces lie at a small angle to the plane of the surface of the rest of the plate. The purpose of this is presumably to cushion the take up and free the plates when the clutch is disengaged.

The driven member is of hardened steel, slotted to receive the driven plates and provided with three internal helical splines. Eight holes are drilled axially around the bore to receive the springs which normally keep the clutch out of engagement. These springs are provided with hardened steel pads at their inner ends.

The inner end of the driving pinion shaft is threaded to receive the clutch ball thrust race. Between this race and the innermost clutch plate is the pressure plate, two shim washers and three large washers. The outer end of the driven member is extended in the form of a sleeve with four axial slots. Fitting into this sleeve and sliding on the shaft is a steel ring serrated on its outer diameter to engage with the four slots. Eight holes are drilled a short way into the inner face of this ring to receive the clutch spring pads.

On the outer side of the ring and fitting over the shaft is a bronze, a steel and a fibre thrust washer. The outermost thrust washer bears against the circular plate attached to the outer end of the driving member and thus compresses the clutch springs when the shaft is moved outwards. The circular plate is located against a shoulder in the end of the clutch driving member and is secured by a circlip.

The driving pinion shaft is supported at its inner end on a spigot on the output planet carrier and a bronze bush is pressed into the bore of the shaft. The outer end of the shaft is supported in the white metal bush previously referred to. A steel flange is secured to the driving pinion shaft by three pins. A combined radial and end thrust ball race is held against the outer face of this flange by a coil spring, the other end of which seats on the inner face of the cast iron end plate. This spring holds the flange against a fibre ring secured by a circlip in the bore of the clutch casing.

The steel control rod passes through the casing for the first input stages, through the hollow flywheel shaft and presses against a small ball race located by a circlip in the bore of the driving pinion shaft. The driving pinion is of bronze and is keyed internally to the end of the shaft.

DATA

Make	Bosch
Type	AL/ZMJ/R.12
Weight of Complete Starter	52 lb.
Overall Length	490 mm.
Maximum Diameter	157 mm.

GEAR RATIOS

Geared reduction from Flywheel to Handcrank

1st input stage	5.2 : 1
2nd " "	4.58 : 1
3rd " "	2.62 : 1
4th " "	2.53 : 1
Total	157.9 : 1

Geared reduction from Flywheel to Crankshaft

1st output stage (Flywheel to Starter Pinion)..	8 : 1
2nd " " (Starter Pinion to Crankshaft)	16 : 1
Total	128 : 1

Estimated normal R.P.M. of Handcrank (before engagement)	60
" " " " Flywheel	9474
" " " " Starter Pinion	1184
" peak " " Crankshaft (neglecting clutch slip)..	74
" " " " " (clutch slipping)	60

FLYWHEEL
Weight	10.25 lb.
Outside Diameter	145 mm.
Calculated Moment of Inertia	0.0127 ft.lb.sec^2
Energy stored at 9474 R.P.M.	6270 ft.lb.

CLUTCH
Number of Driving Plates	5 pairs
" " Driven Plates	5
Mean diameter frictional surface	59 mm.
Total frictional Area	100 cm^2
Helix Angle	45°
Slipping Torque	82 lb.ft.
Maximum Torque capable of being transmitted to crankshaft	1376 lb.ft.

PART IX

SPECIAL DEVICES AND EQUIPMENT

SECTION I

AUTOMATIC FIRE EXTINGUISHER

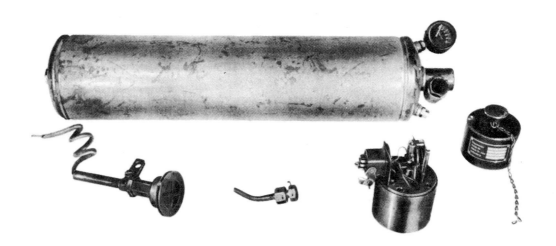

C.T.C. Container, Time Switch and Solenoid,
Spray Nozzle and Thermostatic Switch.

INTRODUCTION

The automatic fire-fighting equipment fitted to this vehicle appears to be an innovation since it has not been noted on any other German A.F.V. Normal practice is to carry only portable hand extinguishers.

The origin of the equipment is obscure, and it has probably been improvised from a variety of parts, as the spray nozzles are almost certainly aero-engine equipment and correspond with those seen on enemy aircraft.

The thermostatic switches are not, as far as can be ascertained, used in any form of aircraft. They are, however, of a very common bimetallic disc type such as could be used for a variety of purposes wherein closing an electric circuit gives an alarm or starts an electric mechanism.

The solenoid and time switch mechanism have probably been adapted mainly from standard industrial components; the escapement mechanism in particular has evidently not been made specifically for this job, and may be part of a time fuze for a shell or bomb.

The Pyrene Co., Ltd., have examined the apparatus and we acknowledge their assistance in preparing this report.

January, 1944

Major J.D. Barnes, R.T.R.
D.M. Pearce, B.A., Cantab.

A cylindrical container holding approximately 5 litres of carbon tetra-chloride is carried vertically on the engine bulkhead in the fighting compartment. When full, the container is under an air pressure of 6 Kg/cm^2 imposed by a handpump; the pressure is not maintained constant but is renewed after use.

A spring loaded valve in the neck of the container communicates via a pipe to a distributor manifold leading to four spray nozzles, two of which are directed on the carburettors, one on the petrol pumps and one on the underside of the crankcase.

The valve is opened by a solenoid mounted on top of the container, and energised by current from the starter batteries. In series with the solenoid circuit are four thermostatic switches, coupled in parallel and each situated close to a spray nozzle. The thermostatic switches close the solenoid circuit when subjected to a temperature above approximately 95°C and thus open the valve on the C.T.C. container.

Mounted over the solenoid is a time switch which ensures that once the solenoid is energised, it remains so for at least seven seconds, thus limiting the minimum quantity of C.T.C. ejected. It is presumed that without this time switch, the initial flow of C.T.C. would sufficiently cool the thermostatic switch(es), that the circuit would be opened, and the flow terminated before the fire was extinguished. If a thermostatic switch remains closed for more than seven seconds, the solenoid remains energised until the temperature is sufficiently reduced to re-open the switch.

In the event of the thermostatic switches failing, the solenoid may be energised by pressing down a button on top of the switch gear. The solenoid will then automatically remain energised until after seven seconds the time switch is tripped. In the event of a complete breakdown of the electrical system, the button may be pressed hard down to engage with the end of the solenoid rod, and thus open the valve manually.

The driver has no control over the extinguisher mechanism, but is warned by a red light, coupled in parallel with the solenoid, situated just below his vision slit. The light carries the warning "Fire in engine – immediately throttle down to idling speed."

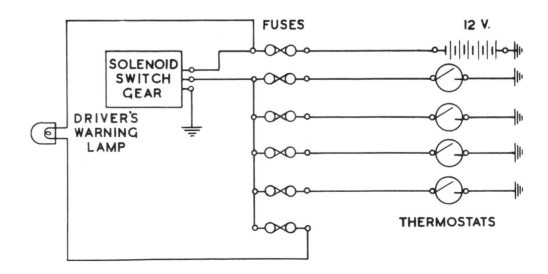

Electrical Circuit

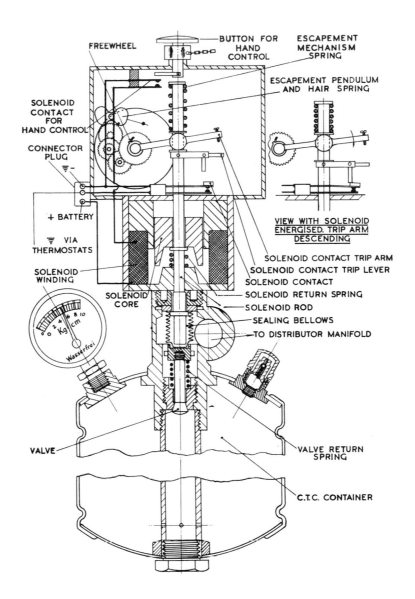

FREEWHEEL

BUTTON FOR HAND CONTROL

ESCAPEMENT MECHANISM SPRING

ESCAPEMENT PENDULUM AND HAIR SPRING

SOLENOID CONTACT FOR HAND CONTROL

CONNECTOR PLUG

+ BATTERY

VIA THERMOSTATS

SOLENOID WINDING

SOLENOID CORE

VIEW WITH SOLENOID ENERGISED. TRIP ARM DESCENDING

SOLENOID CONTACT TRIP ARM
SOLENOID CONTACT TRIP LEVER
SOLENOID CONTACT
SOLENOID RETURN SPRING
SOLENOID ROD
SEALING BELLOWS
TO DISTRIBUTOR MANIFOLD

VALVE

VALVE RETURN SPRING

C.T.C. CONTAINER

Diagram of Solenoid,
Valve and Time Switch.

METHOD OF CONSTRUCTION

In general the method of construction of the components follows orthodox lines and calls for no particular comment.

The container is similar to an ordinary hand fire extinguisher and is made of sheet steel welded together and tin or zinc plated. It is provided with a pressure gauge, a small ball-valve and connection for a hand pump and the main valve.

The main valve is of mushroom type and is spring-loaded. It opens into a pipe which extends to the base of the container, thus ensuring that liquid only is forced through the valve. On top of the valve stem is a small copper bellows which takes the place of a stuffing box and above the bellows is a short push rod.

On top of the main valve is mounted the solenoid, the windings of which are housed in a steel tube which forms part of the armature. The solenoid core is attached to a rod which extends down on to the push rod and up into the casing for the time switch gear.

The time switch consists of a pair of contacts which are held closed when the solenoid is energised by a small bell-crank on an arm attached to the solenoid rod. The downward movement of the solenoid rod compresses a coil spring which forces down a lever. This lever, at the end of its downward travel, presses on the free arm of the bell crank and trips the switch. The lever is attached at its fulcrum to an escapement mechanism which limits its downward speed, and allows the contacts to remain closed for about seven seconds.

The escapement mechanism is constructed on similar lines to a watch and consists of four stages of gears from the lever spindle to an escapement wheel, rotary pendulum, and straight hair spring. The speed of the escapement wheel is adjusted by sliding the hair spring anchorage in or out and thus altering the rate. A free wheel is incorporated on the lever spindle so that the lever can return freely to its top position when the solenoid is de-energised.
The free wheel consists of a coil spring, passing over a shaft, which when turned in one direction tends to tighten and grip the shaft, but in the other direction tends to unscrew and ride over the shaft.

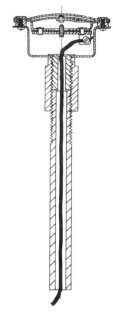

The whole time switch mechanism is enclosed in a light pressed steel cover which incorporates the manually operated button and contact switch. A standard three pole plug socket is provided at one side.

Thermostatic Switch

The thermostatic switches are of the bimetal disc type. The disc appears to be made of steel and brass. It is slightly dished and a contact is attached to the centre. The disc is earthed and at a temperature of approximately 95°C the centre of the disc snaps over and makes contact with an insulated contact, which is connected with the solenoid. The disc and contact are housed in a two piece circular steel pressing attached to a length of steel conduit which protects the solenoid lead.

In common with modern German aircraft practice the spray nozzles are made of bronze lacquered aluminium. A tapered nipple is brazed on the end of the copper feed pipe and the nozzle is held on with a union nut. The nozzle is provided with an orifice of 1.5 mm. diameter behind which is a small swirl chamber. Behind the swirl chamber is screwed a small brass plug with two diagonal grooves across the threads; these grooves impart a rotational motion to the liquid before it reaches the swirl chamber.

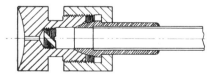

The solenoid circuit, each thermostatic switch circuit, and the driver's warning lamp circuit are protected by standard Bosch fuzes.

Spray Nozzle

PART IX

SPECIAL DEVICES AND EQUIPMENT

SECTION II

VENTILATION

REFERENCES

It appears likely that the enemy have made additions and modifications to the ventilating installation from time to time.

M.I.10 Technical Summary No. 116 dated 8th November 1943, Section 14, makes reference to a method of warming the fighting compartment by air directed from the left hand radiator outlet louvre.   This was not fitted to the tank examined.

A further report by M.I.10, dated 11th August, 1943 - (para. 26, under "Preparations for Submersion" makes reference to an apparatus for dealing with carbon-monoxide).   An order published by the enemy has forbidden submersion, and it seems likely, therefore, that subsequent vehicles have been substantially modified.

J. D. BARNES, Major, R.T.R.

D. M. PEARCE, B.A. (Cantab.)

G. BOYD, Lieut., R.A.C.

SEPTEMBER 1944.

For normal running air is drawn through two mushroom vents, one situated in the hinged engine cover plate, and one in the front top plate between the driver's and hull gunner's access hatches. This latter ventilator provides an air flow over the transmission, and rectangular section ducts conduct the air to the upper end of a cowling surrounding the gearbox. Both mushroom ventilators are screwed down to close when submerged.

An electric fan is mounted in the turret roof above the loader, and expels the fumes resulting from the firing of the turret armament.

Air supply for carburation is passed through two pre-cleaners mounted on the tail plate of the tank, and is taken to the pre-cleaners by two flexible metallic hoses mounted on the top of the engine cover plate, their open ends being provided with gauze protectors. From the cleaners air is supplied via flexible metallic hoses to a manifold bolted on the engine cover.

Circulation of air inside the tank is induced by a Sirocco fan, driven at engine speed, secured through flanges by eight bolts to the engine flywheel. The fan is contained within a volute housing bolted to the forward bulkhead of the engine compartment. The induction branch of the volute housing connects to a trunk situated on the floor of the vehicle. One end of the trunk terminates at the rear of the vehicle beneath the engine, and is open-ended. The other end leads forward into the cowling surrounding the gearbox in the driver's compartment.

Sirocco fan

A manually operated sliding valve is fitted in the trunk, immediately below the induction branch, which controls quantity and direction of air flow. For normal running the valve is moved fully forward and the fan then draws its major supply of air from the bottom of the engine compartment; the valve is so designed that a small current of air is simultaneously drawn over the gearbox. The air is delivered from the volute housing via two independent exits through two jackets surrounding the exhaust manifolds, and thence into two chambers situated on the inside of the tail plate. Pipes with butterfly valves conduct the air from these chambers through the side plates to the down-stream side of the radiators. Two further pipes with butterfly valves also communicate from the engine compartment to the radiator compartments and thus the cooling fans draw air from the top of the engine compartment as well as through the radiator matrices.

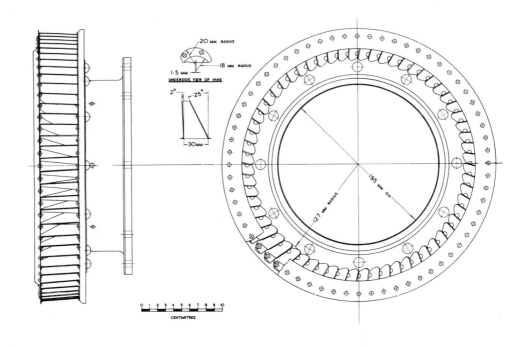

Sirocco Fan

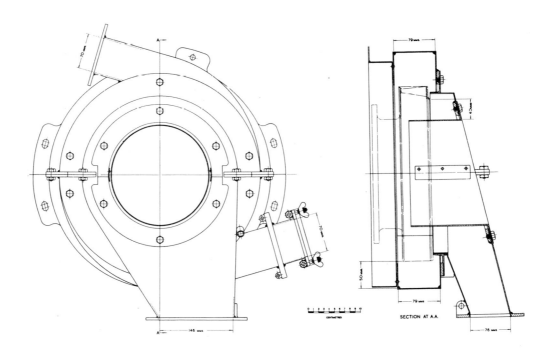

Volute Housing

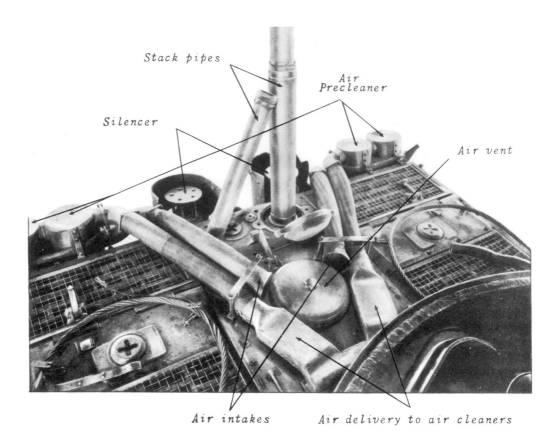

Stack pipes

Air
Precleaner

Silencer

Air vent

Air intakes   Air delivery to air cleaners

The fact that the Pz. Kpfw. VI has been designed for complete submersion to a depth of approx. 15 feet has necessitated very special arrangements for ventilation and the supply of air to the engine under these conditions.

To prepare the system for under water running, all the butterfly valves referred to above are closed by remote controls mounted on each side of the rear bulkhead of the fighting compartment. The sliding valve in the induction trunk of the air circulating fan is moved to the rear and thus air is taken entirely from the front of the vehicle through the gearbox cowling, and delivered as before through the exhaust jackets to the air chambers at the rear. As the butterfly valves are now closed it cannot pass into the radiator compartments as before. The two chambers are interconnected by a trunk fitted with a pipe incorporating a butterfly valve, now open, and thus the air is discharged into the top of the engine compartment. Air replacement for the crew and engine is effected through a stack pipe which is erected at the rear of the tank. The pipe is in telescopic sections and, when not in use, the three upper sections are stowed in the lower, which is permanently fixed to the inside of the tail plate in the engine compartment. Spigotted loosely into the lower section is a pipe connecting to a rectangular section trunk on the floor of the vehicle. This trunk has an open end terminating beneath the turret floor.

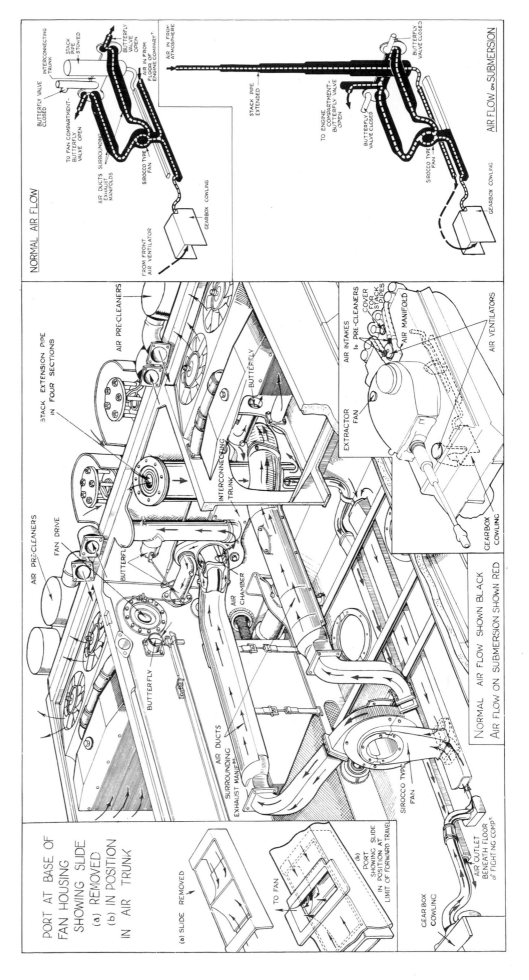

NORMAL AIR FLOW

AIR FLOW ON SUBMERSION

INTERCONNECTING TRUNK

STACK PIPE STOWED

BUTTERFLY VALVE CLOSED

BUTTERFLY VALVE OPEN

TO FAN COMPARTMENT— BUTTERFLY VALVE OPEN

AIR IN FROM FLOOR OF ENGINE COMPART.

AIR DUCTS SURROUNDING EXHAUST MANIFOLDS

SIROCCO TYPE FAN

FROM FRONT AIR VENTILATOR

GEARBOX COWLING

AIR IN FROM ATMOSPHERE

STACK PIPE EXTENDED

BUTTERFLY VALVE CLOSED

TO ENGINE COMPARTMENT— BUTTERFLY VALVE OPEN

BUTTERFLY VALVE CLOSED

SIROCCO TYPE FAN

GEARBOX COWLING

AIR PRE-CLEANERS

STACK EXTENSION PIPE IN FOUR SECTIONS

AIR INTAKES TO PRE-CLEANERS

COVER FOR STACK PIPES

AIR MANIFOLD

AIR VENTILATORS

EXTRACTOR FAN

GEARBOX COWLING

BUTTERFLY

INTERCONNECTING TRUNK

AIR PRE-CLEANERS

FAN DRIVE

BUTTERFLY

BUTTERFLY

AIR CHAMBER

AIR DUCTS SURROUNDING EXHAUST MANIFOLDS

SIROCCO TYPE FAN

GEAR BOX COWLING

AIR OUTLET BENEATH FLOOR of FIGHTING COMPT.

NORMAL AIR FLOW SHOWN BLACK
AIR FLOW ON SUBMERSION SHOWN RED

PORT AT BASE OF FAN HOUSING SHOWING SLIDE
(a) REMOVED
(b) IN POSITION IN AIR TRUNK

(a) SLIDE REMOVED

TO FAN

(b) PORT SHOWING SLIDE IN POSITION AT LIMIT OF FORWARD TRAVEL

After a day on the ranges, the Tiger rumbles back into the compound at the School of Tank Technology, Chertsey. During this period it was used for comparative evaluation with British and American tanks.

The captured Tiger at Chertsey, drawn up alongside a tiny French Chennilette carrier which is also undergoing evaluation. Both machines now reside in the Tank Museum.

Part Three

Despite the fact that it had been laid bare in body and soul by the School of Tank Technology the Tiger continued to evolve and to present its foes with new aspects of its personality so Allied interest continued unabated. In any case the legend was now well established and the tank was still living up to its reputation.

T.I. Summary No. 121 of 19 January 1944 passed on a rumour of a minor variation.

Pz Kw TIGER FITTED WITH S-MINE 35 DISCHARGER

According to a captured document, the Pz Kw Tiger may be fitted with S-mine dischargers designated 'S-Minenwerfer'. An electric igniter (Verkurzte Glühzündstück) is provided. No further information is available.

Then again in February →

Pz Kw TIGER WITH DISCHARGERS FOR S-MINE 35

Reference Summary 121 para. 18, examination of a captured Pz Kw Tiger Model E has disclosed the presence on the superstructure roof of three mounting bases apparently intended for S-mine dischargers. Two of these bases are in the near and offside front corners respectively and the third is close to the nearside edge and approximately level with the rear of the turret. At each of these positions an electric cable conduit emerges through the superstructure roof, and all three cables apparently run to a switch on the engine bulkhead labelled 'Minenabwurfschwalter', i.e. mine discharger switch.

In April 1944 there was news of a more substantial modification.

Pz Kpfw TIGER

Captured German documents show that the new 23 litre 690 B.H.P. engine HL230 is now replacing the original 21 litre 642 B.H.P. engine HL210. The HL 230 may be merely a bored out version of the HL 210; it has the same stroke, 145 mm (5.71 in) but a bore of 130 mm (5.12 in) instead of 125 mm (4.92 in).

The matter of nomenclature would hardly seem to be of much importance but, since it could lead to confusion, M.I.10 released the following in May 1944 →

ABBREVIATIONS IN GERMAN NOMENCLATURE

The following changes should be noted.

(a) *Panzerkampfwagen*
It is proposed in future issues of this summary to adopt the current German abbreviation Pz. Kpfw instead of the shortened form Pz Kw. The latter is now seldom used in German documents, no doubt because of the risk of confusion with Pkw (Personenkraftwagen meaning personnel carrier).

And while we are on the subject.

Nomenclature
'Kraut' (American) = 'Jerry' (English)

What was M.I.10, or indeed what were the Germans, to make of the following?

Extract from A.F.H.Q. Intelligence Notes dated 21.3.44. From a captured enemy document:—

'Consider whether it is worth while to employ heavy tanks or whether you couldn't do the job just as well and more cheaply with other weapons! Every Tiger costs the German people 300,000 work hours.'

The appearance in the field of Tigers with a new pattern, resilient road wheel, prompted the following ➜

Description of new type Bogie Wheel found on
German Pz Kpfw VI Tiger   *23 June 44*

Of two Tiger tanks examined recently by AFV(T) one was found to have the normal type bogie wheels with rubber tyres but the other had what is thought to be a new type of wheel, details of which are as follows:—

The wheels are of the same diameter as the older type but run on a steel rim which is insulated from the hub by two rubber rings clamped between two disc-shaped pressings. To ensure that the rubber rings are evenly and correctly compressed, spacing collars are inserted between the two clamping discs. To assist in assembling the wheels the twelve spacing collars are spot welded to a light circular metal strip.

The central portion of the discs are shaped to form a double cone and the wheel is attached to the hub by three-piece wedges, one outer and one inner set. The inner set is located axially on the hub by a circumferential tongue on the wedges and groove in the hub. The wedges are drawn together by nine special bolts which are a close fit in the inner wedges and are reduced in diameter to give a definite clearance in the outer wedges. A lip machined on the inner wedges prevents the bolt heads from turning and Simmonds type nuts are used on the outside.

When fitting a wheel to one of the hubs the inner set of wedges, with the bolts already in position, is fitted into the groove in the hub and then a piece of iron or copper wire is drawn tightly round the shanks of the bolts and the ends twisted together. This holds the wedges in position while the wheel is mounted on them and also prevents the bolts from being pushed in when the outer set of wedges is assembled.

To facilitate removal of the wheels the outer set of wedges has two drilled and tapped holes in each section so that a bolt can be inserted to force the inner and outer wedges apart. These holes are normally closed by short hexagon headed screws locked by shakeproof washers.

The leading dimensions are as follows:—

Rim, overall dia.	31.75 in	
Rim, width	2.8 in	
Thickness of pressings	0.4 in (approx)	
Rubber rings (uncompressed)	outside dia.	26 in
	inside dia.	23.25 in
	thickness	1.25 in
Wedge cone	34 degrees approx.	

A close-up view of one of the new steel-tyred road wheels.

PANTHERS AND TIGERS (a German view)

A lot has been written in recent months in praise of these two heavyweight German beasts.

The following extracts from German official documents throw another light on the subject, and may excite interest, if not encouragement:—

TIGER

(a) 'When Tigers first appeared on the battlefield, they were in every respect proof against enemy weapons. They quickly won for themselves the title of 'unbeatable' and 'undamageable'.

'But in the meantime, the enemy had not been asleep. A/tk guns, tanks and mines have been developed, which can hit the Tiger hard, and even knock it out. Now the Tiger, for a long time regarded as a 'Life Insurance Policy', is relegated to the ranks of simply a 'heavy tank'... No longer can the Tiger prance around oblivious of the laws of tank tactics. They must obey these laws, just as every other tank must.

'So remember, you men who fight in Tiger tanks — DON'T demand the impossible from your Tiger. DO just what your commanding officer orders. He knows the limitations of his vehicle and guns, and he knows the best use to which they should be put ....'

(b) Report on the effect of Russian anti-tank mines on the Tiger:—

'In certain cases the tracks were broken and in most cases parts of the track were broken, bogie wheels fell out and springs were damaged. Russian mines were most unpleasant.'

BOTH

'The track of a Panther or Tiger sometimes slips or becomes disengaged from the teeth of the driving sprocket and jams, owing to the assemblage of undesirable matter. The consequent tensioning of the track is so great that it is generally not possible to free the track by knocking out the track pin.'

The German report adds that a certain Tiger Battalion solved this problem when the overtensioned track was cut by exploding hand grenades under it, but adds that the practice should not be resorted to unless the tank would otherwise have to be written off.

D.T.D (Major Holmes)   *CONFIDENTIAL*

Herewith as requested a translation of the passages relating to the Tiger suspension in the vehicle documents of tank No 250727.

It appears that, in recent Tigers, we must expect only two bogie wheels per axle instead of three when the operational tracks are fitted. We have had some indications (in captured documents etc.) that the outside detachable wheels were a source of trouble. It will be interesting to see whether the later tanks will have a new symmetrical design of track link.

M.I.10
22 Jun 44

Evidence that German attitudes to their biggest and best tanks were changing is revealed in this translation of a captured document released by 21 Army Group in June 1944, just as the Allies set foot in Normandy.

The Department of Tank Design issued translations of two more German documents dealing with the new pattern wheels towards the end of June with this covering note.

The commander, loader and wireless operator of this Tiger epitomize the confidence that Panzer troops had in these heavy tanks. One of the cylindrical S-mine dischargers is visible on the front, nearside corner of the hull.

Translation from vehicle documents of Pz Kpfw Tiger
Model E No 250727

Suspension (as from tank No. 825)
The interleaved suspension consists of 8 inner bogie wheels and 8 outer bogie wheels. Each bogie wheel consists of two sheet steel discs with steel rims: the discs are secured to the wheel hubs by conical rings. Each hub is mounted on a suspension arm which is connected with the hull wall on the opposite side of the tank by a torsion bar. The suspension arms are each carried on two fabric bearings. All bearings are lubricated with grease from a grease pump (grouped lubrication). The bogie wheels are each carried on the suspension arms by means of two roller bearings and are lubricated through lubricator nipples from the outside.

The torsion bars are made in two different constructions. The stronger bars are always provided for the front and rear suspension arms which are fitted with shock absorbers. For adjusting the suspension arms, a high degree of accuracy can be obtained owing to the differential splining. The suspension arms are set at equal angles with respect to the hull, so that the torsion bar stressing is as nearly equal as possible at all stations. The setting should be checked using the special gauges provided for the purpose. The spacing between the suspension arms and the lower edge of the belly plate is as follows:—

Intermediate suspension arms   134.5mm
Suspension arms fitted with shock absorbers   121.5mm

Up to tank 825, the suspension was an earlier design. Each bogie wheel comprised two sheet steel discs welded on to a hub and fitted with rubber tyred rims. Outside the outer wheel in each case, an additional disc wheel used to be fitted. This was attached by means of a suitable flange. The additional disc wheel had to be removed before the loading tracks could be fitted, because they exceeded the railway loading gauge. The bolts nuts and retaining members which had to be removed when this was done were kept in a small box (021 D2799 U18) until required again.

Pz Kpfw Tiger Model E—Suspension with rubber sprung steel bogie wheels

As from Chassis No. 250822, Pz Kpfw Tiger, Model E will be provided with a suspension comprising *rubber sprung steel bogie wheels*.

This new suspension compares with the former suspension as follows:—

1. Tracks, suspension arms, ball bearings with spacer bushes (shims?) and labyrinth packing (oil seals?) are identical in both types of suspension.
2. The bogie wheel *hubs* of the two types are not interchangeable.
3. Instead of the 3 bogie wheel discs per axle there are now only 2. The outer disc is not removed for railway loading purposes.
   The wheel discs of the two types of suspension are not interchangeable.
4. The steel tyres (used on the new bogie wheels) are not interchangeable with the rubber tyres (used on the old type of bogie wheel).
5. To change a complete bogie wheel assembly. Loosen the securing nuts and draw off the bogie wheel assembly together with the conical securing ring. The bogie wheel assemblies of the two types should only be interchanged with one another in cases of absolute necessity.
6. To change tyres. Loosen the nuts and dismantle the bogie wheel discs.

Pz Kpfw Tiger tanks with the original type of suspension may be fitted with rubber-economizing (*gummisparenden*) bogie wheels instead under unit arrangements. If this is done, however, all the bogie wheels must be changed.

Technical Intelligence Summary No. 135, dated 19 July 1944, carried details of yet another special version of the Tiger.

Pz Kpfw TIGER RECOVERY VEHICLE

Photographs of a captured specimen of the above equipment have been received from Italy. It appears to consist of a normal Pz Kpfw Tiger modified by the removal of the 88 mm gun and the mounting of a winch and derrick on the turret. The winch is arranged high up at the rear of the turret, and what appears to be a socket for the derrick is provided in the centre of the turret roof near the front and facing forwards. The derrick itself is not shown in the photographs. Although the gun and barrel sleeve have been removed, the mantlet is retained, the opening in its centre being covered by a roughly circular plate with a central aperture for the muzzle of an M.G.

But later, on 1 August 1944 ➔

Pz Kpfw TIGER RECOVERY VEHICLE

Reference Summary 135 para. 8, it is now learned that the Pz Kpfw Tiger Recovery Vehicle recently examined in Italy was not a standard German equipment, but a local improvisation.

Three views of the
captured Bergepanzer
or Tiger recovery
vehicle that was found
abandoned in Italy.
This field
modification was
probably unique.

Details of the ammunition stowage was given in T.I. Summary No 139 on 16 August 1944. Since it is not explained elsewhere it should be pointed out that A.P.C.B.C. was Armour Piercing Cap Ballistic Cap, designed for effective penetration at maximum range. A.P.40 was a lightweight Armour Piercing round with a tungsten carbide core that gave best results at shorter ranges while H.E. was High Explosive for use against unarmoured targets.

The performance of the A.P.C.B.C. round was also given.

Pz Kpfw Tiger (8.8 cm Kw.K 36)— AMMUNITION CARRIED

Ammunition stowage in the Pz Kpfw Tiger mounting the original 8.8 cm Kw K 36 (L56) is stated in a captured notebook to be as follows:—

A.P.C.B.C. shell (Pzgr 39)	42 rds
A.P. 40 shot (Pzgr Patr 40)	4 rds
H.E. (Sprgr Patr L4.5)	46 rds
Total	92 rds

No doubt when existing stocks of the A.P. 40 ammunition have been used up, the 4 rounds of this type will be replaced by A.P.C.B.C.

8.8 cm A.A./A.Tk GUN FLAK 36 and 8.8 cm TANK GUN Kw. K 36

Revised Ordnance Board estimates of the penetration performance of the 8.8 cm Flak 36 firing A.P.C.B.C. shell (21 lb large capacity monobloc) against homogeneous armour plate are reproduced below. These estimates are also applicable to the 8.8 cm tank gun Kw K 36 which has a similar piece.

Range Yds	Striking velocity f.s.	Thickness of homo. plate penetrated	
		At normal	At 30 degrees
		mm	
0	2600	141	118
500	2449	130	110
1000	2302	119	102
1500	2160	109	94
2000	2022	99	87
2500	1890	90	80

There is a newer design small capacity 8.8cm shell, so far only found in use with 8.8 cm Flak 41, but which may come in for Flak 36 also. Trials of similar shell in 7.5 cm calibre indicate that its performance will be superior to that of the large capacity monobloc shell, but estimates cannot yet be issued.

214

As Allied troops advanced through Italy, they noted the relatively large numbers of abandoned Tigers in their path and came to the reasonable conclusion that they had been knocked out in action. It seems to be a conclusion that the Allied Command might well have publicized since it was bound to promote confidence, but the Technical Branch preferred to deal with the facts and their imaginitive report was issued in August 1944 under the title 'Who Killed Tiger?'.

As a fairly large number of Tiger tanks were reported to have been knocked out in the breakout from the Anzio bridgehead and the advance on Rome we thought it might be educational to try and find out what weapon or what tactics had been responsible, so that the dose might be repeated on other occasions.

Hearing that there was somewhat of a concentration of bodies in a certain area we made a reconnaissance on the 5th August in an area between Velletri and Cori some 30 miles S.E. of Rome.

In all during this reconnaissance 12 Tigers were found either on the road, by the roadside or within easy sight of the road.

The following is what we found:—

No. 1   On the Via Tuscolana. Pulled up at the side of the road near a bridge diversion. No sign of battle damage but both tracks were off and each had been cut with a gas torch. Blown up and burnt out so the cause of the casualty could not be determined.

No. 2   On the village green of Giulianello. No sign of battle damage other than a penetration of the hull back plate by Bazooka. This is thought to have been done by following troops after the tank had been abandoned, because the engine cooling fan had been penetrated by the shot but was obviously not rotating at the time and, furthermore, several unused rounds of U.S. Bazooka ammunition were found lying near the machine. This tank had not been demolished by the crew and there was no indication of the cause of stoppage.

No. 3   By the side of the road one mile from Giulianello. Signs of two H.E. strikes on the turret and one on the cupola. A further H.E. had struck the upper side plate about track level and may have broken the track which was off on this side.

On the opposite side the three rear bogie spindles were bent upwards and the bogies were riding the track guides. A tow-rope was found in place and the tank had been demolished. If the right hand track had in fact been cut by H.E. it is possible that a recovery crew had been caught while extricating the tank which had become a casualty due to the suspension trouble on the other side.

No. 4   Halfway down a steep bank on the Guilianello-Cori road. No sign of any battle damage or suspension trouble. Tank had been demolished. In this case it is possible that the machine had either become ditched down the bank or had some internal mechanical trouble which could not be rectified.

An interesting point is that this tank had rubber bogie wheels on one side and steel on the other.

No. 5   Found in a small copse about 100 yards off the road. No sign of battle damage but tank appeared to have become ditched in a sunken lane where it had been trying to turn. Broken tow-ropes found in place. No important suspension defects so that the casualty must have been due to internal mechanical trouble possibly caused by trying to extricate itself from the lane. Blown up.

No. 6   Found off the road down a bank where it had been pushed to clear the road. Deep A.P. scoops on front of mantlet and side of turret. Penetration by unknown weapon through 3rd bogie from rear on left hand side. Tracks off, blown up and burnt out.

▶

Not enough evidence to deduce the cause of the casualty except that it was certainly *not* due to the A.P. strikes which were probably sustained in an earlier engagement.

No. 7 Off the road at the edge of an olive grove. Definite evidence of track trouble. Several track guide lugs broken. R.H. sprocket ring cracked in one place and L.H. ring in two places.

Attempts to tow had been made. Demolished.

Possibly on tow because of mechanical trouble and abandoned when tracks rode the sprockets and damaged them.

No. 8 On the level in an olive grove. There were signs of the area having been used by a workshop detachment.

No apparent battle damage other than penetrations of bogie wheels by H.E. splinters.

Casualty probably due to internal mechanical trouble. One demolition charge had been blown.

No. 9 Found up against a house in Cori where it would appear to have been left by a recovery team.

Two H.E. scoops on front plate. Tracks off and obvious signs of suspension trouble. R.H. front bogie bent and out of line. Tracks found near. These showed fractures of several links. Demolished.

No. 10 Off the road in Cori within 10 yards of No. 9 above. One bogie wheel missing and others damaged.

Sprockets cracked in three places.

Tracks off and lying nearby showed evidence of trouble—cracked link and broken guide lug. Demolished.

No. 11 On the bridge at Cori. Within 50 yards of Nos 9 & 10. Tank had fallen through damaged arch of bridge. Both tracks off and laid out on the road behind.

No battle damage to be seen. Demolished.

The presence of Nos. 9, 10 & 11 tanks so close together suggests that Cori may have been a recovery point for tanks with mechanical trouble which were blown up when it was found impossible to repair them.

No. 12 Found on the road from Giulianello to Valmontone in a field by a stream some 300 yards off the road. No battle damage but two bogie wheels on one side were bent and out of line. Tracks were still on. There was evidence in the shrubs nearby that the crew of a recovery section had camped by the tank and had been attempting some mechanical repairs which could not be completed in time so that the tank had to be left and demolished.

Notes Since the above examination was made some information has been received from a P.O.W. which suggests that these 12 tanks were the remnant of 3 Sqn, 506 Heavy Tank Battalion, which was given the job of resisting the Allied break-out from Anzio with 16 tanks.

Some were lost in the engagement while others suffered gearbox trouble and had to be towed out of action. The squadron was ordered to retreat on Cori and during this retreat so much trouble was experienced with the gearboxes and suspensions of towing tanks that attempts at extrication beyond Cori had to be abandoned.

Conclusion Tiger is not yet sufficiently developed to be considered a reliable vehicle for long marches.

TIGER KILLED HIMSELF
AFV(T)
G—H/JB

He suffers from frequent suspension defects and probably also gearbox trouble.

When pushed, as in a retreat, these troubles are too frequent and serious for the German maintenance and recovery organisation to deal with.

216

Abandoned Tigers
were thick on the
ground in Italy but
most were lost
through mechanical
breakdown. Very few
were knocked out by
Allied guns.

Prisoners of war taken in the Italian campaign appear to have been a useful source of information to judge from this comprehensive report which was printed in an R.A.C. Liaison letter in August 1944.

Extracts from report on interrogation

PW stated that the normal stowage in a TIGER is 92 rounds but that the battalion had been increasing stowage in ITALY to 106 rounds (and even on rare occasions to 120 rounds) by the addition of brackets for seven rounds each above the chambers already provided. It is not known whether this modification had been suggested within the Bn or whether it was carried out on instructions from GERMANY.

The maximum stowage carried out by PW was 60 each of AP and HE rounds.

Communications

PW's Tiger was equipped with the Fu 2 intercommunication set and the Fu 5 for communication between AFVs. The CO's tank is believed to have had Fu 7 or Fu 8 as well as ground/air communication.

Routine calls were usually put through hourly in daytime and two-hourly at night.

The frequency used on 30/31 July 1944 was 32 kcs and the call-sign in force for the OC 1 trp, 3 sqn (2 Lt KUENKELE) between 27 and 31 July 1944 was LOEWENZAHN. Previously KUPEERBERG had been his codename.

Tank commanders wishing to contact the OC troop usually announced their name only, i.e. 'NAGEL fuer LOEWENZAHN' would mean that Sgt NAGEL had a message for 2/Lt KUENKELE.

PW maintains that all TIGER tank serial numbers have the prefix 250,000. The first number noted by one PW was 250605 in Dec 43. More recently 251098, 251186 (that of the AFV captured on 31 Jul 44) and 251196 have been encountered.

ENEMY EQUIPMENT

TIGER I

PW mentioned the following three modifications in the Model 'E' over its predecessors:—

Turret top armour

In early March 44 on the beachhead, a number of TIGER tanks were spotted from the air by an artillery recce aircraft and shortly afterwards a concentration of artillery fire was put down, during which the turret top of one TIGER was pierced by a direct hit from what appears to be an American 'Long Tom'.

This incident, which cost two dead of the crew, was duly reported and is considered to have been the reason for the thickening of the turret top armour back and front from *25mm* to *45mm* on the Model 'E' TIGERS which came down from PADERBORN in late May 44.

Tyres on bogie wheels

Earlier models had two-piece bogie wheels and a tyre shaped rather like a 'Vee' fan belt. The tyre was pressed on to the inner half-rim and the other half-rim bolted on, the tyre protruding all round. The defect in this design was that the tyre took all the wear and tended to fly off the rim, especially at speed and in hot weather.

218

The thinner top plates of the Tiger were vulnerable to plunging fire but the mantlet of this tank has withstood considerable punishment.

The latest design was to bed the tyre well down into the rim and to have a subsidiary steel tyre which had contact with the track on its broad outer face and with the rubber tyre on its narrow inner face (the cross section of the steel tyre was approx. T-shaped).

Since the inner diameter of the subsidiary steel tyre was greater than the outer diameter of the rubber tyre bedded in the actual rim, contact between the two tyres was made principally at the bottom.

PW considered the latest design to be excellent: wear and overheating were kept to a minimum and there was no danger of a tyre flying off. The only disadvantage was that bogie wheels had to be returned to the factory in GERMANY for re-tyring.

Sighting equipment
The binocular tank sight TZF 9b, fitted to former models has been replaced by the later monocular sight type TZF 9c. Performance is stated to be the same and the only advantage gained— according to the unit armourer— was cheaper production (RM20,000 — instead of RM 35,000).

The following points still require improvement, according to the same PW:—

Tracks riding on sprocket teeth
One of the most feared situations is when a TIGER tank's tracks ride up over the sprocket teeth when reversing or turning on boggy ground. The tension on the track is enormous and even full release of the tensioning device at the rear will not free the track. In most cases, track bolts cannot be driven out and LAD men usually put a charge under a link and break the track, replacing the broken links from their spares stores.

A tank thus stranded can be towed away slowly but this not only strains the sprocket bearing but puts an exceedingly heavy load on the towing media.

▶

Gearbox preselection and hydraulic steering system
The preselector mechanism and the hydraulic steering both suffer from the German passion for over-designing. They require far too much maintenance – such as scrupulous attention to oil filters which cannot always be given, either due to a lazy driver or to battle conditions – and are the cause of most of the breakdowns in TIGER tanks.

Danger of fire
There are two possibilities of the engine catching fire. One is as a result of the distinctive double backfire which occurs when the engine is switched off: if the exhaust system packings are defective, a spurt of flame can appear which is sufficient to cause an engine fire. This does not appear actually to have happened but another incident in Feb 44 caused 3 Sqn its initial tank loss: a driver had not paid attention to the tightness of the petrol system unions and fuel had leaked down to the flooring of the tank and was ignited by a cigarette end thrown away. The crew got out unharmed but the tank was a total loss. The incident was glossed over but would have had serious consequences on home service, for crews are strictly warned not to smoke inside an AFV and drivers in particular are told 'Be careful, you've got a million marks and three and a half million working hours under your seat' (unter dem Arsch).

Underpowering of engine
Although there is a general grouse that the V–12 HL 230 21 litre MAYBACH engine is underpowered for the TIGER I tank, there seems to be no real evidence for it, because there are few major engine breakdowns and the AFV is claimed to have a good turn of speed in all gears.

The root cause would appear to be short engine life owing to overloading when used for towing but while it lasts the engine gives all that is asked of it.

TIGER tank in action: First major reverse of 3 Sqn 508 Hy Tk Bn
As an illustration of the difficulties encountered in the employment of TIGER tanks it is interesting to reconstruct one of the two mobile engagements on a Sqn basis which the Bn fought in ITALY, when it won a victory and yet lost almost all its tanks.

The action took place between 23 and 25 May 44 in the general area of CISTERNA. 3 Sqn, which had brought down 14 TIGER tanks from FRANCE, lost two burnt out at the end of Feb 44 – one through carelessness on the part of the crew and another by Allied A/tk action. It had received four of the latest pattern AFVs during May 44 and was two tanks over war establishment strength on 23 May 44, i.e. 16 instead of 14.

The Sqn formed up behind a railway embankment between the MUSSOLINI Canal and the level crossing at G 063299 and engaged troop concentrations with HE. It then crossed the embankment and put three AFVs out of action in the attempt (one with gearbox trouble and two with tracks riding over the sprocket teeth). The remaining thirteen crews had all to stop on open ground because the guns had dug into the earth as the tanks came down the embankment and needed pulling through.

The Allied troops were driven back about three kms and a number of SHERMAN tanks surprised and knocked out.

The first loss sustained in action was a TIGER which had one radiator destroyed by an artillery round and had to limp back towards CORI in stages.

Twelve TIGERS were thus left in action during the night 23/24 May 44. On the morning of 24 May 44 a retreat was ordered to everyone's surprise ▶

220

and A/Tk fire accounted for one TIGER (hit on the right reduction gear and subsequently blown up by its crew).

Eleven TIGERs withdrew to the embankment and the OC Sqn ordered five to continue to hold the enemy whilst the six were to tow away the three tanks which had failed to cross.

Four of the six towing tanks experienced gearbox trouble and the OC then ordered the three towed tanks to be destroyed and two out of the five fighting tanks to assist in towing away the breakdowns.

These eight AFVs were got back to an assembly point near CORI, leaving four TIGERs only in fighting order. Of these four, one was hit by A/Tk gun fire and two more experienced gearbox trouble (all three were blown up), so that only one runner was left.

Two converted SHERMAN tanks came down from ROME during the night 24/25 May 44 and extricated the one runner which had also become u/s meanwhile, by towing it in tandem along the railway tracks.

By 25 May 44, the situation had so deteriorated that it was manifestly impossible to get towing vehicles through and the OC ordered the blowing up of the nine TIGERs which had reached the assembly area.

Although a good many of the crews had gone back to ROME with the one runner, the OC and about 45 men were left near CORI. They had to march back to ROME and came under fire several times in the process, arriving in an exhausted condition.

PW states categorically that this action had a profound effect upon the Sqn's morale and also decided against the mass use of TIGER tanks. Of sixteen AFVs put into action, not one would have been lost, had adequate recovery facilities been provided.

Although the OC Sqn's personal courage was not in doubt, it was generally thought that he had not appreciated the situation and had created the disaster by attempting to salvage the three AFVs that jibbed at the embankment. Had he not done so, he might have saved about ten out of the original sixteen.

'Penny wise pound foolish' was the criticism made of him. 3 Sqn also took a poor view of the fact that almost at once a new troop was formed from tanks drawn from 1 and 2 Sqn crews put in, the former crews going back to their Sqn pools.

Railway movement of TIGER tanks

A PW states that the narrow loading tracks for TIGER tanks belong permanently on the special platform truck and are put back on it when the truck returns to its home station.

TIGER tanks only just fit on the width of the truck and are secured by laying wooden beams against the inner sides of the trucks and securing them to the flooring by means of heavy bolts passing through prepared holes.

Loading

One PW described the loading of TIGER tanks at MAILLE-LE-CAMP (France) early in Feb 44 and the unloading a few days later at FICULIE (Italy).

Conditions at both ends were very bad. Deep mud, rain or snow, and biting winds hindered operations and made the job very trying.

The 80 ton platform truck was shunted up to an end loading ramp and secured in position.

By means of an 18 ton half-tracked towing vehicle, the narrow loading tracks were towed off the platform truck and manoeuvred into position on the ground in echelon and at the correct width apart. One broad track ▶

was then undone and the tank driven forward on one track so that the bogie wheels on the opposite side ran off the broad track onto the narrow track.

The intended joining point of the narrow track was between the driving sprocket and the ground. To bring the upper run of the track round the rear idler and over the tops of the bogie wheels, the sprocket hub was used as a capstan by passing a wire rope round it. With the broad track locked and the sprocket on the opposite side rotating slowly, the crew pulled on the end of the wire rope and so brought the track up and over.

Having joined the first narrow track, the broad track on the opposite side was undone and the tank driven forward on the narrow track until the bogie wheels ran over the second narrow track.

Once the tank was fitted with the narrow tracks, the crew had to remove the four outside bogie wheels on both sides.

When this had been done, the half tracked towing vehicle had to tow the broad tracks side by side in front of the loading ramp.

The TIGER was then driven forward so that it straddled the tracks on the ground. Wire ropes were attached to the two lifting eyes at the front of the turret, passed over the front armour and secured at their other ends to the tracks.

The TIGER was finally driven up the ramp, towing its own broad tracks underneath it between the narrow tracks. Once it was in position on the platform truck, the ultimate operation was to bring up the overhanging ends of the broad tracks over the rear armour of the tank, a feat accomplished by wire ropes and pulleys, with the attendant towing vehicle providing the motive power.

Before the tank was ready to travel, the turret had to be traversed to approx 5 o'clock to allow for the right-handed tunnels which are mostly encountered on the route from FRANCE to ITALY.

Train make-up
PW was told by Reichsbahn workers that not more than four TIGER tanks could be incorporated in one train and that the interposition of two normal platform trucks between each special platform truck was necessary in order to obtain adequate braking power on down gradients over the ALPS. In PW's train these dividing trucks carried lorries and cars.

Suspension problems
On this occasion the crews experienced a setback which rendered suspension repairs necessary in ROME. When they replaced the outside bogie wheels, the nuts and bolts securing them were tightened up on the one side with a long cranked ring spanner whilst (to save time) the nuts and bolts on the other side were tightened by a GEDORA ratchet box spanner. It was not realized that the box spanner would not give the leverage obtained with the special tool. During the journey towards ROME, the outer bogie wheels on the one side all became loose and finally one came adrift. Other damage was caused by the floating of the bogie wheels.

Had the crew been zealous enough to do the job properly, they would have had to take off the track and outer bogie wheels but, as weather conditions were against it, they merely reached inside and tightened up the inner nuts and bolts as best they could at the expense of major repairs later on.

Other tank crews experienced the same trouble but learned to err in

Invulnerable they may have been when confronted with a Sherman but the roll-call of abandoned Tigers goes on, a testament to mechanical vulnerability.

future on the side of over tightness by using a pipe on the special spanner for increased leverage.

TIGER tanks as towing vehicles
If a TIGER tank has gearbox trouble, it is customary to dismantle the flexible couplings in the half-shaft drives and to tow it out of the immediate battle area by another TIGER, using two tow ropes secured in 'X' formation to correct the tendency of the towed tank to sway.

Should, however, the track on a TIGER have ridden up over the sprocket teeth, the tractive effort required to move it is so great that two TIGERs pull in tandem, each towing with crossed tow ropes.

Opinions of TIGER and SHERMAN tanks
The gun layer – an experienced tank man – was inclined to be very boastful where German tanks were concerned. He had landed in AFRICA in May 41 and stayed in the desert for nearly two years (no home leave and only the rarest visits to towns). His memories of the campaign are chiefly a record of the numbers of British AFVs knocked out by the invincible Mk IIIs and IVs, tinged with a reluctant admission that the same tanks were matched in Oct 43 at ALAMEIN by General Grants and General Shermans. He was critical of the fact that the employment of these AFVs had not been appreciated by the Germans and that the launching of the British push came as a surprise to the Armoured Divs.

His confidence has been fully restored since he transferred to TIGER tanks. On every occasion he stresses the great feeling of security which a crew has inside an AFV with such armour. Crews feel very certain of their ability to engage and destroy any target. He claims that he once ran into fire from the flank from seven 17 pdr A/Tk guns at close range and, having turned the hull of his tank so that a three quarter view was presented to the fire; proceeded to destroy five out of seven A/Tk guns with HE rounds. Several hits were registered on the frontal armour of the TIGER but penetration was not achieved. Deep dents only resulted, with flaking from shell spliners.

The only situation in which he felt uncomfortable was to receive A/Tk gun fire from the flank and, having engaged the gun after having turned his AFV into the optimum position, to receive fire at right angles from an undetected A/Tk position in his rear. His reaction would then be to swing his turret as fast as possible and engage the more dangerous of the two targets.

The only time when a General SHERMAN stands a chance of knocking out a TIGER (in his opinion) is when it can close to less than 800 metres. He has observed that, even granted great superiority in numbers, SHERMAN tank crews do not venture willingly to close in, even on sides away from the principal pre-occupation of the TIGER's fire. He claims that 3 Sqn has accounted for 63 SHERMANS since arrival in this theatre, 17 of which fall to his account.

The general opinion of the SHERMAN for its class was high. PW was instrumental in capturing two on the beachhead (one with a radial engine and one with twin Diesel engines) and the Bn had ample time to acquaint itself with these AFVs before removing the turrets and passing them back to 4 (workshops) Sqn for use as recovery vehicles less turrets.

His biggest criticism of the SHERMAN is of the visibility afforded to the commander when his hatch is closed down. He regards the periscope as extremely poor.

The Tiger I was the only type of German heavy tank to see action in the four principal theatres of war; North Africa, Italy, Russia and North West Europe. Yet for all that only relatively few of them were built. German archives indicate that 1354 were completed as tanks while three more hulls were expended in firing trials. In August 1944 the Allies attempted to establish production figures by collating chassis numbers with surprisingly accurate results.

Production

Production of the Mark VI tank, Model E, was started in the third quarter of 1942. The number of tanks assembled from that time to June 1944 is estimated at 1,225 with 650 produced in 1943. An accurate estimate is possible since Mark VI chassis and gearboxes were manufactured by the same firm and each runs in a single serial number band from the start of production to the present time. The only manufacturer of Mark VI chassis and gearboxes in 1942 and 1943 was Henschel und Sohn, Kassel, identified by the code dkr.

In 1944 there is evidence that two new models of Mark VI came into production. The chassis serial number band alloted to Model E is from 250000 to 255000. Captured German documents refer to Mark VI tanks with serial numbers 256689 and 256697 before June 1944, but do not indicate the maker, model or number produced. Another captured German document indicates that the chassis serial number band from 280000 to 290000 has been allotted to Mark VI model B. Only one case, undated, occurs in the sample, chassis number 280637 manufactured by Henschel.

The 1,225 production in the chassis serial number band from 250001 to 251225 is based on 73 cases ranging from 250012 to 251202. The following table lists Mark VI E production from the third quarter of 1942 to June 1944, based on chassis serial numbers:

Table 3
Mark VI E Production Estimate based on
Chassis Serial Numbers

Dates	Chassis serial number band	Output	Average Monthly Production
September thru December 1942	250001–250100	100	25
1943	250101–250750	650	54
January to June 1944	250751–251225	475	95
	Total	1,225	

The production of gearboxes for Mark VI tanks totalled 1,400 by June 1944, as listed in table 9. Allowing approximately 15 of the total number produced for use as replacements, this checks closely with the chassis production figures of 1,225 Mark VI tanks.

A few Tiger hulls were diverted from production to serve as experimental targets during evaluation of their armour qualities.

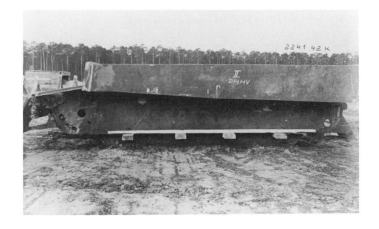

Table 9
Production of Gearboxes for Mark VI E

Dates	Gearbox Serial Number Band	Estimated Gearbox Production
September thru December 1942	1–120	120
1943	121–850	730
January to June 1944	850–1400	550
	Total	1400

There are not sufficient engine numbers in the sample to permit an estimate of engine production. Engine HL 210 P45 was manufactured by Maybach, who produced 75% of the engines represented by the sample, and aam (unidentified) who manufactured 25%.

Meanwhile eagle-eyed investigators had noticed something else.

EXTRACT FROM WAR OFFICE TECHNICAL INTELLIGENCE SUMMARY NO. 142, DATED 6th SEPTEMBER 1944

14. NEW TYPE OF GERMAN TANK TRACK
It is reported from France that recent Panthers and both types of Tiger are now being fitted with tracks having chevron-patterned half-inch raised strips on the sole bars, presumably in order to obtain better track adhesion.

The tracks on the Panther and first type of Tiger have six raised strips on each sole bar whereas the tracks on the latest Tiger have only five.

On some vehicles examined, the strips had been almost completely worn off.

Like some vision of impending death, the Tiger 'concentrated the mind wonderfully'. This interesting memorandum, issued in September 1944 has a pencilled note in the margin alongside the passage (e) (1)*which reads; 'Not to be passed on to troops, C.O.'; it is not difficult to see why.

Experiences with Tiger Tanks by 2nd N.Z. Division

In the battle for Florence contact was made by the 2nd New Zealand Division for the first time with Tiger Tanks in any number. The following are some preliminary points which emerged during these encounters, regarding the characteristics and use of this enemy A.F.V. Several of them confirm views previously expressed in official papers.

(a) *Employment* Tiger Tanks were employed, usually well sited and well camouflaged with foliage so as to be difficult to pick up as follows:
(1) In hull-down positions to delay infantry and pick off our tanks.
(2) From pre-selected positions which were reached via covered routes. From these positions the enemy would fire a few harassing rounds, withdraw and occupy an alternative position.
(3) As close support to enemy infantry, to thicken up artillery concentrations and to engage buildings occupied by our troops.
(4) With, almost invariably, the support of at least one other tank or SP gun, which remained silent until or unless needed.
(5) Sometimes with infantry accompanying it. These troops, who might only be six to twelve in number, deployed on the flanks up to fifty yards from the tank.

226

Effective choice of ground and careful use of foliage for cover were characteristic of the way the Tiger was used in a defensive position.

(b) *Vulnerability*

(1) The heavy front and rear armour of the tank make the likelihood of it being knocked out by hits on these parts remote. Frontal attack and flank attack together are therefore desirable. The side armour is definitely vulnerable to 17-pdr fire. The back of the tank over the engines is also a weak spot and a large exhaust hole just over the left centre of the back provides another weak point. HE is considered by some to be the most effective ammo. to use against these parts.

(2) The Tiger was usually well enough sited to make the deployment of a sniping anti-tank gun, M10 or towed gun for stalking purposes, difficult. Unless very careful recce is carried out to site the gun to the best advantage and to locate supporting tanks or SP guns, the effort may be useless. The maximum time for recce and the maximum information appear, therefore, essential for a troop commander who is called upon to engage a Tiger.

(3) The gun and tank seem to be slow to manoeuvre and fire. It can also be effectively blinded by 75mm American smoke ammunition. On one occasion two smoke rounds, followed by A.P., were enough to force a Tiger to withdraw. This is a method of attack recommended by our own tank commanders.

(c) Tigers were sometimes used almost recklessly, their crews taking risks to a degree which indicated that they have the utmost confidence in the vehicle. This can render them vulnerable to tank hunting squads armed with PIAT or other close range anti-tank weapons. The Tiger when closed down and attacking on its own at some distance from its supporting gun is definitely vulnerable to such weapons.

(d) The concentration of field artillery to counter Tigers is effective.

(1) Even if a brew-up does not result, the tank has invariably withdrawn. It appears obvious that tank crews do not like the shellfire, as the possibility of damage to vital parts (tracks, suspension, bogies, wireless aerials, outside fixtures, electrical equipment etc.) is always present.

(2) Medium artillery has been incorporated in several of our concentrations. Medium artillery is ideal if sufficiently large concentration is brought to bear, but owing to dispersion of rounds, it is prefereable to include a good concentration of field guns to thicken up.

(3) We have had no experience of heavy artillery engaging Tigers although it is known that they have done so. It is hard for our tanks to locate a well camouflaged Tiger sited in a defensive role and stationary. Artillery OPs, if given a suspected area, can be used to advantage. A case did occur when a suspected object was located in an area reported to contain a Tiger and the OP commenced to range. A round falling in the vicinity of the suspect completely blasted away all camouflage and the Tiger beat a hasty retreat.

(e) The following are some experiences of anti-tank gunners in contact with Tigers:—

(1)* A Tiger observed 3,000 yards away was engaging three Shermans. It brewed up one Sherman while the other two withdrew over a crest. A 17-pr was brought up to within 2,000 yards and engaged the Tiger side on. When the Tiger realized that it was being engaged by a high velocity gun it swung round to 90 degrees so that its frontal armour was towards the gun. In the ensuing duel one shot hit the turret,

▶

another the suspension, while two near misses probably richocheted into the tank. The tank was not put out of action. The range was too great to expect skill but our tactics were to make the Tiger expose its flank to the Shermans at a range of about 500 yards by swinging round to the anti-tank gun. This he did, and on being engaged by the Shermans it withdrew. The infantry protection of some 6—12 men was engaged by our MGs.

(2) One Tiger was just off the road at a road and track junction engaging our forward troops in buildings, another Tiger about 50 yards up the side road supporting the firing tank. A field artillery concentration which appeared to be from one battery was called for and, although no hits were observed, both tanks withdrew.

(3) A Tiger on a ridge was engaged by what appeared to be a battery of mediums. After the first few rounds had fallen the crew baled out (it is not known why) and shortly afterwards while still being shelled one man returned to the tank and drove it off. The remainder of the crew made off in the direction of their tank some ten minutes later.

(4) A tank was located in the garage of a two-storey house from which it was driven 20 yards, fired a few harassing rounds, and returned to its hideout. Many hits were recorded on the building by our 4.2 inch mortars, firing cap-on, but little damage was visible. The tank was withdrawn from the area each night even though it was in an excellent concealed position and protected by infantry. The house was examined later and although it was considerably damaged and there were several dead Germans about, there was nothing to indicate that damage had been done to the tank.

S-MINE DISCHARGERS ON TANKS

Nine months after they were first reported it seems that the anti-personnel mine dischargers were no longer fitted to Tigers. This is how it was reported in T.I. Summary No. 144 of 20 September 1944.

From examination of a number of Pz Kpfw Tigers, Model E, in Normandy it appears that S-mine dischargers are no longer being fitted on these tanks. This is to some extent confirmed by an official German Handbook on this tank in which passages referring to the positions of S-mine dischargers on the hull roof have been deleted.

Pz Kpfw TIGER MODEL E COMMANDER'S TANK

There seems to have been little of any import to say about the Tiger for the next three months. In T.I. Summary No.157 of 20 December 1944 contained one item of interest.

A semi-official German document states that the Commander's version of the original Tiger tank has a crew of 5 consisting of commander, signal officer (who also acts as gunner), No. 1 signal operator, No. 2 signal operator (who also acts as loader) and driver.

The vehicle is either equipped with two wireless equipments 'Fu 5' and 'Fu 8', in which case it is allotted the vehicle type number Sd Kfz 267, or it has an 'Fu 5' and an 'Fu 7' equipment, in which case it is referred to as Sd Kfz 268.

'Fu 7' is the standard ground-air co-operation wireless equipment and 'Fu 8' is a standard equipment for intercommunication between formations and has a range of about 6 miles using R/T on the move.

The vehicle type numbers Sd Kfz 267 and 268 were originally allotted to two of the three Pz Kpfw III commander's tanks with dummy armament. These are now obsolete and it has no doubt been found convenient to reallot their type numbers to the corresponding current equipments. The difference between the Sd Kfz 267 and 268 are probably confined to the wireless equipments.

The fighting in France, from June 1944 onwards, saw a new element gaining prominence in anti-tank warfare. It involved low level attacks by rocket firing aircraft, notably Typhoons and Tempests. The former are credited with the amazing total of 135 enemy tanks destroyed in one day – 7th August 1944 – alone, although opinion on their overall effectiveness is now often questioned. To the Allied tank man this heaven-sent assistance was something of an unknown quantity so a report published in January 1945 went into some detail.

Tiger— Attacks by Rocket Firing Aircraft

It was reported at one stage of the battle of the Ardennes Salient that rocket firing aircraft were destroying or disabling large numbers of German Tiger tanks. It was further rumoured that the method of achieving these results was by aiming at the turret top. In view of these reports, steps were taken to obtain information concerning this problem, and it is thought that this will be of interest.

The rocket at present in use is of pure HE type, the head containing 14 lbs of explosive. MAP do not claim that this will pierce more than 50mm of plate. HC and AP rockets have been developed, but on account of the present inaccuracy of this weapon and the fact that these are virtually one purpose projectiles, they are not used at the present time.

The following plates only of the Tiger II are thus vulnerable. (Since the projectile is pure HE, angle of attack is of little consequence).

Turret roof	40mm nearly horizontal
Hull roof	40mm nearly horizontal
Belly	40mm at front 25mm at rear
	(There is a vague hope that a rocket could be bounced so as to detonate beneath the vehicle)

It is learned that the present method of attack is to dive at approximately 30 degrees to the ground. This, in fact, is a steep dive. If steeper angles are used ranges of engagement become longer, in order to give the aircraft time to pull out. The side of the vehicle is invariably attacked since it presents the largest target area. This is, of course, because the present rocket is not highly accurate. Sketches have been prepared to show Tiger Is as they appear to the pilot of an aircraft attacking at 30 degrees to the horizontal.

The large area presented by the turret and hull tops may appear surprising. These, however, are, of course, due to the great width of these tanks. It is also interesting to note that if the area presented by the suspension is also regarded as being vulnerable the odds are probably more than even that any hit on these vehicles will either immobilize or destroy them.

Trials against Churchill showed that the 14 lb rocket head was capable of removing its turret. If this is the case with Tigers the area presented by the turret side also becomes vulnerable. MAP are doubtful, however, if this object would be achieved and state that a practical trial is the only method of verification.

230

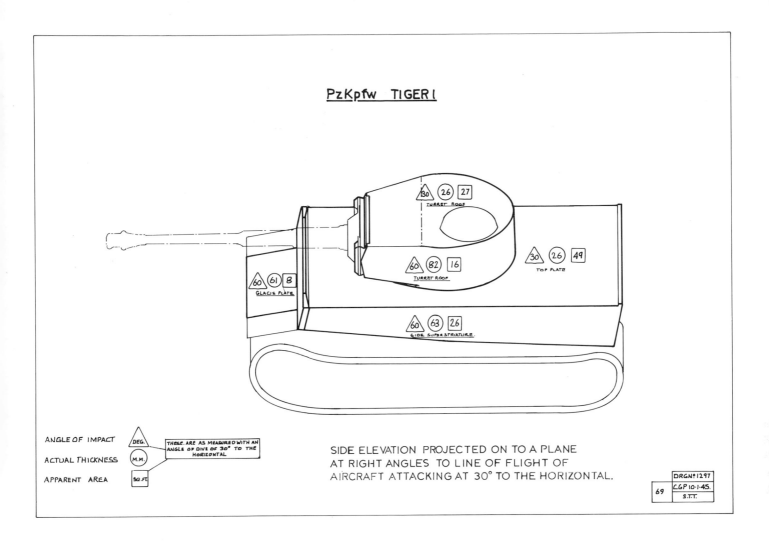

PzKpfw TIGER I

30 | 26 | 27
TURRET ROOF

60 | 82 | 16
TURRET ROOF

30 | 26 | 49
TOP PLATE

60 | 61 | 8
GLACIS PLATE

60 | 63 | 26
SIDE SUPERSTRUCTURE.

ANGLE OF IMPACT — DEG.
ACTUAL THICKNESS — M.M.
APPARENT AREA — SQ.FT

THESE ARE AS MEASURED WITH AN ANGLE OF DIVE OF 30° TO THE HORIZONTAL

SIDE ELEVATION PROJECTED ON TO A PLANE
AT RIGHT ANGLES TO LINE OF FLIGHT OF
AIRCRAFT ATTACKING AT 30° TO THE HORIZONTAL.

DRGN.º1297
69 | CGP 10·1·45.
S.T.T.

Events move fast in wartime and, already, the Tiger I was being replaced on the production line, if not in the field, by newer, more powerful models. This raised some questions about an apparent attempt by the Department of Tank Design to obtain heavy enemy tanks in wholesale quantities.

M.I.10 A/M 2992

CONFIDENTIAL

D.T.D. (Major Steane)

Ref. your enquiry as to when the original Tiger tank (Pz Kpfw Tiger Model E) went out of production, there seems to be very little doubt that the date was June or July 1944. This is supported by evidence from date markings on tank components. A fairly large number of these were recorded for the first six months of 1944, but none later than June 1944. Production of Royal Tiger with the original turret appears to have started in 1943 (the exact starting date is uncertain, but the new turret was introduced not later than April 1944). In other words the original Tiger is definitely out of production now, though it was being produced after the introduction of the Royal Tiger.

In the circumstances, how is your recent request for five Panthers and five Tigers for firing trials to be interpreted? Are the Tigers to be old Tiger (Model E) or Royal Tigers (Model B)?

M.I.10
22 Jan 45

Two views of a Tiger knocked out in north-west Europe. An anti-tank gun had penetrated the hull side of this tank, which also displays an interesting combination of early-pattern commander's cupola with the new-style steel rimmed wheels.

Another abandoned Tiger, this time showing the new type of cupola and the old rubber-tyred wheels.

This Tiger, photographed near Rouen, is coated in *Zimmerit*, a non-magnetic layer of hardened putty that protected it from magnetic anti-tank charges.

Pending the arrival in Europe of the American M26 Pershing heavy tank it is clear that the Tiger would only meet its match by mass producing inferior types; if it took four Shermans, on average, to despatch one Tiger then the Allies could do it. Things were different on the Russian front. The Soviet Union had always favoured heavy tanks to support their medium T34s and, by 1944 they had machines in the field that were more than a match for the Tiger. Thus German tank crews were on the receiving end of a form of retribution that they had been dishing out to their opponents for two years. In an attempt to redress the balance, at least on the mental plane, propaganda was directed at the Tiger crews which, it was hoped, would steady morale and restore confidence. A translation of one such injunction was translated and released by the School of Tank Technology on 30 January 1945 under the title '"Tiger" versus "Stalin" '.

The new Soviet heavy tank, 'Josef Stalin', has caused the German tank experts no little worry. It is, therefore, of interest that the following unconvincing description of a 'Tiger' versus 'Stalin' engagement is printed in the official 'Notes for Panzer Troops' of September 1944, presumably as an encouragement to the German tank arm.

A 'Tiger' squadron reports one of a number of engagements in which it knocked out 'Stalin' tanks:

The squadron had been given the task of counter-attacking an enemy penetration into a wood and exploiting success.

At 1215 hrs the squadron moved off together with a rifle battalion. The squadron was formed to move in file by reason of the thick forest, bad visibility (50 yds) and narrow path. The Soviet infantry withdrew as soon as the 'Tigers' appeared. The A/tk guns which the enemy had brought up only three-quarters of an hour after initial penetration were quickly knocked out, partly by fire, partly by crushing.

The point troop having penetrated a further 2,000 yds into the forest, the troop commander suddenly heard the sound of falling trees and observed, right ahead, the large muzzle brake of the 'Stalin'. He immediately ordered: 'AP-fixed sights-fire' but was hit at the same time by two rounds from a 4.7cm A/tk gun which obscured his vision completely. Meanwhile the second tank in the troop had come up level with the troop commander's tank. The latter, firing blind, was continuing the fire fight at a range of 35 yards and the 'Stalin' withdrew behind a hillock. The second 'Tiger' had in the meantime taken the lead and fired three rounds at the enemy tank. It was hit by a round from the enemy's 122mm tank gun on the hull below the wireless operator's seat but no penetration was effected, probably because the 'Tiger' was oblique to the enemy. The 'Stalin', however, had been hit in the gun by the 'Tiger's' last round and put out of action. A second 'Stalin' attempted to cover the first tank's withdrawal but was also hit by one of the leading 'Tigers' just below the gun and brewed up.

The rate of fire of the 'Stalin' was comparatively slow. The squadron commander has drawn the following conclusions from all the engagements his squadron has had with 'Stalin' tanks:

(1) Most 'Stalin' tanks will withdraw on encountering 'Tigers' without attempting to engage in a fire-fight.
(2) 'Stalin' tanks generally only open fire at ranges over 2,200 yards and then only if standing oblique to the target.
(3) Enemy crews tend to abandon tanks as soon as hit.
(4) The Russians make great efforts to prevent 'Stalin' tanks falling into our hands and particularly strive to recover or blow up such of them as have been immobilized.
(5) 'Stalin' tanks *can* be brewed up although penetration is by no means easy against the frontal armour at long ranges (another 'Tiger' battalion reports that 'Stalin' tanks can only be penetrated by 'Tigers' frontally under 550 yds).
(6) 'Stalin' tanks should, wherever possible, be engaged in flanks or rear and destroyed by concentrated fire.
(7) 'Stalin' tanks should not be engaged under any circumstances by 'Tigers' in less than troop strength. To use single 'Tigers' is to invite their destruction.
(8) It is a useful practice to follow up the first hit with AP on the 'Stalin' tank with HE, to continue blinding the occupants.

▶

The Inspector-General of Panzer Troops (who is responsible for this official publication) commented as follows on the above remarks:

(1) These experiences agree with those of other 'Tiger' units and are correct.

(2) Reference para. (4), it would be desirable for the enemy to observe the same keenness in all our 'Tiger' crews. No 'Tiger' should ever be allowed to fall into the enemy's hands intact.

(3) Reference paras 5 and 6, faced as we are now with the 122mm tank gun and 57mm A/tk gun in Russia and the 92 mm AA/Atk gun in western Europe and Italy. 'Tigers' can no longer afford to ignore the principles practised by normal tank formations.

This means, inter alia, that 'Tigers' can no longer show themselves on crests 'to have a look round' but must behave like other tanks — behaviour of this kind caused the destruction by 'Stalin' tanks of three 'Tigers' recently, all crews being killed with the exception of two men.

This battalion was surely not unacquainted with the basic principle of tank tactics that tanks should only cross crests in a body and by rapid bounds, covered by fire — or else detour round the crest. The legend of the 'thick hide', the 'invulnerability' and the 'safety' of the 'Tiger', which has sprung up in other arms of the service, as well as within the tank arm, must now be destroyed and dissipated.

Hence, instruction in the usual principles of tank versus tank action becomes of specific importance to 'Tiger' units.

(4) Reference para. 7, though this train of thought is correct, 3 'Tigers' do not form a proper troop. Particularly with conditions as they are at the moment, circumstances may well arise where full troops will not be readily available. And it is precisely the tank versus tank action which is decided more by superior tactics than superior numbers. However it is still true to say that single tanks invite destruction.

(5) It may be added that the 'Stalin' tank will not only be penetrated in flanks and rear by 'Tigers' and 'Panthers' but also by Pz Kpfw IV and assault guns.

Conditions in Russia were tough on men and machines, with sustained fighting in sub-zero temperatures.

This Tiger has been running without the leading external road wheel on each side. This was done deliberately to prevent a build up of ice or mud, which could force the tracks to ride over the teeth of the drive sprocket and disable the tank as effectively as the most powerful anti-tank gun.

Technical Intelligence Summary No. 183 was the last one to be issued that contained a reference to the Tiger I. By the time it appeared it cannot have been of more than academic interest since the date was 9 August 1945, five days before the unconditional surrender of Japan. By that time the war in Europe had been over for three months.

TIGER MODEL E COMMANDER'S TANK (Pz. Bef. Wg. Tiger Ausf E) Sd Kfz 267 and 268

The handbook for the turrets of these equipments gives the following details:
1. *Crew*: 5 consisting of: Commander
                          Wireless Officer (Gunner)
                          W/T Operator I (Loader)
                          W/T Operator II (hull gunner)
                          Driver
2. *Armament*: As for the Pz Kpfw Tiger Model E, except that the co-axial M.G. together with its ammunition, spares and tools is dispensed with.
3. *Ammunition stowage*: 26 fewer 88mm rounds and 1500 fewer 7.92 mm rounds are carried in the Commander's vehicle, giving the following totals:
          88mm   — 66 rds.
          7.92cm — 22 bags, each containing 150 rds.
4. *Intercommunications*: The following intercomm. equipments are provided:
   (a) Bordsprechanlage B (Internal communication equipment B)
   (b) Fu 5   (consisting of 10w transmitter 'c' and ultra-short wave
               receiver 'e' in turret)
               and *either*
       FFu7 (consisting of 20 w transmitter 'd' and ultra-short-wave
             receiver 'd 1' in hull of Sd Kfz 268)
             or
       Fu8   (consisting of 30 w transmitter 'a' and medium-wave
              receiver 'c' in hull of Sd Kfz 267)

The end of the war did not signal an end to Allied interest in the Tiger, the only difference was that the emphasis had changed. Now it was no longer a question of divining the beast's innermost secrets in order to destroy it before it got you but, rather, to evaluate it with a view to incorporating any suitable design features in future British and American tank designs. One subject that was considered to be of special interest was the submersion capability of the early Tigers and, in order to examine this more closely a team of British officers from FVDD at Chertsey visited the German testing station at Haustenbeck to interview the chief designer, examine the equipment and salvage any useful documents.

RESTRICTED
F.V.D.D COVER SHEET TO GERMAN REPORTS
ON
SUBMERSION TRIALS AT HAUSTENBECK

ORIGIN

A number of reports covering the development of submersion for the Tiger tank has been received at S.T.T. Most of these have been translated. Some have been chosen as the most useful and reproduced for circulation.

OBSERVATIONS

1. Haustenbeck was the Test Establishment for Henschel. The engineer in charge was Arnoldt who specialized in submersion problems and later gas proofing. The establishment was also used by the Army and the Armament Ministry and Arnoldt reported directly to them.
2. The Tiger was designed before 1942 with submersion in view as a means of crossing rivers. Development work was done at Haustenbeck where a wading pit 20 ft deep and suitable for 100 ton vehicles was completed in March 1943. Trials began in April 1943.

   Trials continued on a less urgent basis up to the summer of 1944 when, according to Arnoldt, complete success in wading to depths up to 3.5 m (11.5 ft) had been achieved.

   Due to the urgency of the military situation and production difficulties, the scheme was not fitted to production vehicles.
3. At about this time, gas proofing was considered and coupled with sealing for immersion. A gas chamber was built and gas sealing had been developed at the time the U.S. Army overran the Establishment.
4. Herr Arnoldt gave a demonstration of submersion on a Tiger tank to British representatives in October 1945.
6. The submersion problems solved by Arnoldt were:—
   (a) The cooling of the engine by flooding the radiators.
   (b) Provision of air for the engine and crew by a vertical pipe from the vehicle.
   (c) Prevention of CO_2 in the Fighting Compartment by keeping it at a pressure higher than that in the Engine Compartment.
   (d) The sealing of hatches etc., by built-in rubber seals.
   The submersion problems left unsolved by Arnoldt are:—
   (a) Submersion with the engine stopped.
   (b) Vision for the Commander.
   (c) Sudden changes in air pressure in the crew compartment with changes in engine loading or speed.
   (d) The waterproofing of all electrical equipment.

CONCLUSION

The value of these reports lies in the indication of the problems still to be solved in any submersion project.

FUTURE ACTION

Copies of these reports are being sent to all interested Departments for information.

Assistant Director (Flotation & Wading)
F.V.D.D.
Chobham Lane, Chertsey
8.12.45

Underwater Trials with Tiger V 3
Haustenbeck, 27th April 1943

The concrete basin specially constructed for submersion trials (Tiger) allows tests to be carried out to a depth of 6.6m (21.8 ft). The total volume of water is approximately 4400 cu. metres (972,000 gals). The exit and entrance to the basin is on a slope of about 150 deg. (1 in 4). The test tracks leading into the basin are undulating. In the deepest parts of the basin there are two heavy sluices for emptying the basin and this can be done in 9—11 minutes. The water flows away into a wide ditch next to the basin. The water is pumped in from a specially constructed reservoir by means of electrically driven centrifugal pumps. One pump supplies 260 cu. m (80,000 g.p.h.) per hour and the other 80 cu.m (17,700 g.p.h.). About 12,000 cu. m (2,650,000 gals) of water is stored in the reservoir.

The basin is close beside the experimental workshops and dismantling sheds so that experiments can be carried out without complications and formalities.

There is a control bridge over the basin and behind it, on the concrete bank, there is an observation post in which there is a telephone, a wireless transmitting and receiving set, as well as other instruments and supply lines.

The experiments are controlled from the observation post by means of telephone, radio, wireless and flashing gear.

The experiments are planned as fundamentally as possible in order to turn out a vehicle that is absolutely ready for use. Experiments in 6.5 m (21.3 ft) of water without a crew are also contemplated. Research is being carried out on remote control, temperature measurements, water conditions, C.O. gases, petrol fumes and special modifications relative to the danger from explosion, without endangering human life. The essential instruments, controls etc. will be manufactured at the proving station and are already in preparation. Special instruments have been developed and constructed for carrying out the submersion trials so that a great number of different tests and observations can be made. The main measurements are taken thermo-electrically. All the life-saving and protective equipment is already here, and more equipment, instruments and indicators are on order and are continually being delivered. An installation is now being developed here which will indicate the ground characteristics on the bottom of unknown stretches of water. Accurate checks on the direction and strength of the wind and eddy formations are provided. There are two supply lines to bring fresh air from a distance, which are used in accordance with the direction of the wind. When it is calm, the exhaust gases, which have a large C.O. content, remain in the basin and are sucked back into the vehicle through the intake pipe. In addition there is an installation in preparation for ruffling the surface of the water by means of an aircraft propellor with a rating of 3000 PS (296 hp). It acts on an area 60 x 80 m (66 x 88 yds) in the direction required. This provides the actual conditions which troops will encounter when crossing wide stretches of water.

The trials carried out here and the resulting effects never arise in actual practice, especially as a vehicle never remains shut off in very deep water during complete calm as it does in the test basin. If the test results with regard to C.O. are satisfactory in the test basin, they can be guaranteed good in practice, when crossing the bed of a wide river.

There is a bridge 7.5 m (24.5 ft) in height across the centre of the present basin. From there various measurements can be taken above the

The experimental wading tank at Haustenbeck. British officers watch a wading demonstration after the war. All that shows of the Tiger is the breathing tube.

The Tiger emerges, dripping, after a succesful run through the test tank.

238

Unlike the version seen in Tunisia, this Tiger has the wading tube mounted on the commander's cupola. Also visible is the rubber cap that sealed the hull machine gun position.

The same tank, with a spare set of tracks, loaded on to a Gotha 80-ton transporter trailer.

vehicle as regards calm, direction of wind, motion of the waves, the amount exhaust gas being sucked in through the collapsible air intake, the C.O. content and the spray entering the vehicle.

For special measurements there is a float with a crew of one man for carrying out investigations on the surface of the water and at the opening of the collapsible air intake.

UNDERWATER TRIALS WITH A TIGER

HAUSTENBECK   *20 JUNE 1943*   *VK 4501/V3*

The following trials were carried out with the Tiger VK 4501/V3.

(1) The vehicle was required to be watertight and have complete freedom from C.O. in the fighting compartment, in conjunction with the temperatures to be observed so that it should be capable of underwater travel.

(2) In all, a total of 355 C.O. measurements have so far been carried out on land. Freedom from C.O. in the fighting compartment has been completely achieved. Up till now, 300 C.O. measurements have been carried out under water to a depth of 5m. The presence of C.O. in the fighting compartment was never established, although C.O. gases were present in the engine compartment owing to the fact that the exhaust did not always seal, no C.O. gases were ever recorded in the fighting compartment.

(3) With the collapsible air intake pipe projecting about ½m above the surface of the water the Tiger can submerge to a maximum depth of 4.5m.

(4) A concrete basin was constructed for the tests. Instead of being 4 m in depth it was a bare 7 m to allow of tests and research being carried out to this depth. The basin was ready on 6.4.43. On 7.4.43 the first underwater trial was carried out in 4 m of water. After this, until 16.4.43, thirty submersions were carried out in 4 m of water, at different engine speeds, several of them being continuous submersions lasting 1–3 hours. Temperature measurements were carried out with thermo-electric instruments specially arranged for the purpose. More than 40 measuring points were continuously observed and recorded.

(5) When absolute freedom from C.O. under water had been achieved, and the water which had penetrated owing to bad sealing was under control, preparations were made for journeys into open water. These were begun in June. Tests in the Baltic and North Sea were not at first undertaken because of the salt water. On this matter I am awaiting further instructions from the Heereswaffenamt, Herr Dipl. Eng. Jaeger.

(6) All the modifications etc. shown by the trials to be necessary, have immediately been reported step by step to the Heereswaffenamt, and the design departments and the workshops. Work is being carried out on all the modifications. No time is being lost in making the vehicles submersible as quickly as possible.

(7) Work is going forward during the trials on an installation which will allow the engines of armoured fighting vehicles to be stopped under water, and the vehicles to remain stationary in the deepest parts for hours without their engines running. Steps are also being taken so that when the engine is stationary the water running into the vehicle can be

▶

disposed of and the explosive fuel gases which may possibly form in the engine compartment can be let off. This suggestion which I have made affords the crew the greatest security under water. These tests are shortly due to begin.

Probably the last official word on the Tiger was penned by the Motion Study Wing of the Military Operational Research Unit in 1947. It included the results of a very thorough study of the three German heavy tanks of the war, the Tiger I, Panther and Tiger II. Captured tanks operated by experienced British tank crewmen were thoroughly examined for operational efficiency and comfort. The report is naturally lengthy and very detailed, even when it is singled out from the others the section dealing with the Tiger I runs to fifteen pages, some of which deal in minute detail with the stowage arrangements and availability of ammunition for the loader, much of which has been edited out of the following extract.

MILITARY OPERATIONAL RESEARCH REPORT
No. 61
STUDY No. 11
MOTION STUDIES OF GERMAN TANKS

Prepared by: Captain G. Tunnicliffe, Gen. List
ABSTRACT

This report describes the Motion Study undertaken on the German Tiger, Royal Tiger and Panther Tanks. The objects of the studies were first to examine the main armament loading arrangements and assess the loading times, and secondly to examine the crew's controls and accommodation.
(The report is *not* intended to give a technical assessment of the vehicle. Tehnical data is only given where it is necessary for simplification or clarification of description.)
Our detailed conclusions are made in Section 5 of this report. Mainly they are as follows:—
(a) Little consideration has been given, in the design of these vehicles, for the comfort of the gunner, and most of the crew's controls are so positioned as to be operated only with discomfort and fatigue. A short study of each vehicle's mock-up by a physiologist would have revealed most of these undesirable qualities.
(b) The gunner and bow-gunner should have adequate vision facilities; in all three tanks this is not possible with the equipment provided.
(c) The ammunition bin fittings are badly designed in all three tanks; hence, loading times are high and the loaders are more prone to injury than they would be when loading from well-planned bins.

Section 1
INTRODUCTION AND METHODS OF STUDY

This series of studies was undertaken at the F.V. Wing M.C.S. and at F.V.D.D., with the objects of firstly, inspecting the main armament loading arrangements and comparing them with those of British tanks, and secondly, examining the crew's position and seating from a physiological viewpoint and to assess how they would affect operation of the various controls and devices of each crew member.

The report is divided into four main parts. The first three of these deal with the detailed description of each of the three tanks. The last part is in the form of a summary of the first three and compares the features of each tank with the others', and with those of British tanks. It is hoped that this part of the report will give a clear picture of the good and bad features of the three German tanks to British designers.

The study of each vehicle was set out as follows:—
(a) The controls and seating were tested for 'usability'.
(b) The main armament ammunition stowage was inspected, and it was determined from which racks/bins rounds would be loaded in action.

241

(c) The loaders were instructed in the best method of loading from these racks/bins, and were then practised in the drills before the trials began.

(d) A series of loading trials was then carried out and the loading times timed with a stopwatch.

(e) A further series of loading trials was conducted, and the loading was filmed with cine-cameras, which recorded the loading movements for subsequent detailed analysis.

(f) Any details of exceptional interest in the vehicles were filmed, using both cine and still cameras, for record purposes.

SECTION 2
MOTION STUDY OF
PZ. KPFW. VI. FÜR 8.8 cm KW.K 36 (L/56) – SD. KFZ. 182
(THE 'TIGER' MODEL 'H')

1. INTRODUCTION

Ammunition stowage and loading have been the major interest in the study of this vehicle, since the crew's positions and controls are described in detail in the omnibus report of the Tiger issued by the School of Tank Technology.

We recommend that the S.T.T. Report be read in conjunction with this report.

2. DESCRIPTION OF THE VEHICLE

The Tiger is a heavy tank weighing 56 tons in battle order. Its armament comprises an 8.8 cm KW K 36 gun mounted co-axially with a 7.92 mm MG 34 in the turret. Another MG 34 is mounted as a bow gun in the hull front vertical plate.

The vehicle is 20ft 8½in long (excluding the gun). 12ft 3in wide and 9ft 5in high. The five members of the crew are the commander, gunner and loader in the turret and the driver and bow-gunner in the hull front.

3. THE COMMANDER

(a) *Seat and Position.* The commander has three alternative positions – sitting on the upper seat, sitting on the lower seat, or standing on the turntable. He would use the first position when the vehicle was not in action and he could keep his roof hatch open: he would use the other two positions when the vehicle was in action and 'closed down'.

Although the upper seat is comfortable in itself, the upper position is cramped because the shield, which protects the commander from the movement of the gun, presses against his right side and presses him against the turret wall.

No backrest is provided. The commander's back presses uncomfortably hard against his steel respirator case which is usually stowed behind him. His discomfort would increase when the vehicle was moving.

When sitting in the lower seat, the commander is again pressed in by the gun shield and his left leg chafes against the traverse gearbox. The upper seat drops to form a backrest and the position is more comfortable than the upper one.

When standing on the turntable and the vehicle is moving, the commander could be thrown against the seats to his rear and the traverse gearbox to his left front. He is also hemmed in between the gearbox and the gun.

(b) *Controls and Vision.* The commander can traverse the turret by means of a small handwheel mounted on the left. (it can be operated only in conjunction with the gunner's handwheel, since a latch on the latter

242

locks both controls until released by the gunner). The commander's handwheel is badly positioned and awkward to operate, since the left wrist must be twisted to grasp the handle which cannot be gripped by the whole hand. In addition, the wrist chafes against the cupola locking control rod when the wheel is operated from the upper position.

The commander's vision equipment is described in detail in the S.T.T. Report. It comprises five glass-covered vision slits in the cupola and a scissors telescope on an adjustable mounting on the inside of the turret roof. The vision slits do not cover the entire 360 deg. field round the tank and the two rearmost slits are awkward to look through when seated.

No scissors telescope was fitted in the vehicle inspected. The telescope would be used primarily for observation of fire and the commander would be able to observe without exposing his head outside the turret.

(c) *Conclusion.* The commander's traverse handwheel is basically sound but badly positioned; the vision equipment is reasonable but not fully adequate; and, principally, his positions are cramped and uncomfortable.

4. *THE GUNNER*

(a) *Seat and Position.* The gunner sits in front of the commander on the left side of the main armament. His seat is elliptically shaped and padded. It is mounted on a horizontal arm and is not adjustable. The back rest is also padded and curved to fit the gunner's back.

Although the seat and backrest are comfortable, the position is very cramped. The gunner's feet rest, with toes pointing downwards, on the power traverse footplate, which is centred only 8in in front of, and 12in below the seat. The gunner's knees are consequently sharply bent, forced half-right by the legshield on his left and confined between the shield and the elevating handwheel.

In addition, when the gunner leans forward, his body is further twisted; operation of the elevating wheel also increases his discomfort, because he must move his legs further over to the left to reach and operate the controls.

(b) *Gun Controls.* The elevating handwheel is mounted on a horizontal shaft passing transversely under the gun. It is 9in in diameter and situated on the right of the gunner, who would normally operate it with his right hand. The handle on the wheel is too short to be gripped by the whole hand and the resultant lack of purchase impedes its operation.

The traversing handwheel is $10\frac{1}{2}$in in diameter and is situated in front of, and above the level of, the gunner's seat. The wheel is mounted horizontally with the handle on the underside. A plunger-type latch is pivoted to the handle and must be released before either the gunner or the commander can use their respective handwheels.

The gunner's handwheel was remarkably easy to operate, but the reduction of two turns per degree of traverse is so high that traversing through and arc of about 30 degrees or more is slow and tedious.

The gunner's wheel is geared to the commander's and rotates more quickly than it. If the commander traverses rapidly, the gunner's handwheel rotates so rapidly that the gunner is liable to lose control and take his hand from the handle.

The normal drill when using hand traverse would be for the gunner to elevate the gun with his right hand and traverse it with his left hand. In doing so, his left wrist is liable to chafe against the turret ring casing. If he uses his right hand for traversing, he is liable to scrape the back of it on the sharp edge of the clinometer.

▶

The hydraulic power traverse system is controlled by a rocking footplate on the floor in front of the gunner's seat. The footplate is pivoted along its transverse axis. In the neutral position, the plate is tilted lower at the front than at the back. On left traverse, the heel end of the plate is depressed until the plate is horizontal. On the right traverse the toe end of the plate is depressed to an angle of 24 deg. from the horizontal.

Since the transverse pivot of the plate is only 8in forward of the front of the gunner's seat, its operation is both awkward and fatiguing. The investigator's boots allowed him barely sufficient ankle flexibility to operate the pedal, and quick yet accurate control of the turret's traverse was almost impossible. In addition, when the operator removed his boot from the pedal, the latter did not usually return to neutral and the turret continued to traverse independently. Another weak feature was that, when the gun was elevated, the gunner's movements inadvertently tilted the footplate and traversed the turret. The design and position of the footplate are poor, accurate control of the turret on traverse is almost impossible, and the strain of operating the plate is very fatiguing.

The main armament is electrically fired by a curved steel bar pivoted on to the shaft of the elevating wheel. The bar can be operated by one finger but the gunner must first of all release the wheel handles, unless the latter is at top centre of its arc of operation.

The MG firing pedal is operated by the gunner's right foot. The gunner can easily reach it, but in doing so, and in actually operating the pedal, he is liable inadvertently to tilt the power traverse footplate.

(c) *Sighting and Vision.* The gun sight is a binocular telescope, type TZF 9(b). The browpad is well-shaped but the rubber is too hard for comfort. It interferes with the gunner's headset when he is sighting.

The clinometer is mounted on the right of the sight and is positive in action. It is convenient to use, but the lower end is sharp and projecting and is liable to catch the gunner's right hand.

The only other vision device for the gunner is a glass-covered vision slit, 5in wide and $\frac{3}{8}$in high, let into the turret wall at 11 o'clock and facing half-left. A block facing forward would have been more useful, since the gunner might have used it when looking for targets over a wider angle than that afforded by the sighting telescope.

(d) *Conclusion.* In general, the gunner's position is very bad. It is very cramped, the gun controls are badly designed and positioned, and the vision facilities are inadequate.

5. *THE LOADER*

(a) *Seat and Position.* The loaders station is on the right side of the main armament. A padded seat and backrest are provided and the loader sits facing rear in relative comfort. The seat is not adjustable, but can be lifted and swung sideways under the gun when not required.

The loader's station is roomy and there are few obstructions to the loading. Both factors are important when handling the large ammunition used in the tank.

(b) *Coaxial MG 34.* The loader has great difficulty in loading the coaxial MG because it is mounted so near to the main armament. This position is a very bad feature, since, as the MG cannot be reloaded quickly, belts can only be fired intermittently and targets appearing for only a few seconds are likely to be missed during reloading.

(c) *Vision.* The loader's sole vision device is a glass-covered vision slit similar to the gunner's. It is situated in the turret wall at 2 o'clock and faces half right. This is desirable since it covers a field of view not covered by the commander's set of slits in the cupola.

(d) *Conclusion.* Apart from the difficulty of loading the MG, the loader's position is satisfactory.

6. *THE DRIVER*

(a) *Seat and Position.* The driver sits in the front left corner of the hull. The seat is padded and is adjustable for forward-backward movement. The backrest is padded and hinged to the seat. Its angle of tilt is adjustable and the backrest can be dropped back flat to allow the driver easy access to the turret. The driver's legs are hemmed in uncomfortably between the steering band casings.

Since the height of the seat is non-adjustable, the driver has no 'opened up' position.

(b) *Driving Controls.* No detailed study was made of the driving controls, but their design and position are similar to the *lower* set of controls in the Royal Tiger.

(c) *Vision.* The driver's main vision device is a visor, protected by a laminated glass block about 10in wide and 3in high and mounted in the hull front plate. The block can be partly or wholly obscured by an exterior sliding shutter which is adjusted by a handwheel on the mounting. The angle of view is satisfactory only when the shutter is fully open.

In addition to the glass block, an episcope 5in wide is mounted in the driver's roof hatch door and faces half-left.

(d) *Conclusion.* Although the driver's position is otherwise reasonably comfortable, his leg-space is inadequate and the absence of an 'opened-up' position is a further disadvantage. Driving is simplified by the automatic gearbox.

THE BOW GUNNER

(a) *Seat and position.* The bow gunner's position is in the front right corner of the hull. His seat is similar to the driver's, but the backrest is smaller and less comfortable. The bow-gunner's knees are cramped in the confined space between the steering band casings, but the position is otherwise spacious and comfortable.

(b) *The Bow Gun.* The MG34 bow gun is housed in a ball-mounting in the front vertical plate. It is controlled by a pistol grip and a headpan on the mounting. Since the gun is breech-heavy, a compensating spring is fitted to balance it. However, in the vehicle inspected, the gun and mounting are still unbalanced and the headpan pressed down heavily on the bow gunner's head, causing *acute* discomfort.

The bow gunner also operates the wireless set in the vehicle; this is conveniently situated on the gearbox to his left, where it is easily accessible.

(c) *Sighting and Vision.* The MG is sighted by a standard episcope telescope (type KZF 2) fitted with a soft, shaped browpad. This is satisfactory. The only other vision device is a 5in wide episcope mounted in the roof hatch and facing half-right. If it had been mounted facing forward, it would have given the bow gunner a much wider angle of vision. In addition he could have looked for targets without moving the unwieldy gun.

(d) *Conclusion.* Although his seat is comfortable and his position otherwise spacious, the bow-gunner must sit with his knees in a cramped

▶

position and, when he uses the bow gun, the headpan presses heavily on his head and causes acute discomfort.

LIGHTING
Festoon lamps are fitted.
(a) on the turret roof in front of the commander's cupola,
(b) on the turret roof above the gunner's position,
(c) on the turret roof above the loader's seat,
(d) on the driver's instrument panel,
(e) on the wireless set.

This lighting arrangement is reasonable, but when the vehicle is operating in semi-darkness or in overcast weather, the loader will not be able to see the ammunition in the pannier racks. A festoon lamp in the two panniers on the right side of the hull would have provided reasonable illumination.

CREW ACCESS

(a) *Hatches.* The driver's and bow gunner's hatches are identical. Both are circular and open sideways with spring assistance. The hatches allow good access to each position but the doors cannot be closed from inside the vehicle without exposing the crew member's arms.

The commander's fixed cupola is circular and the door is hinged on the right side and opens with spring assistance. The open door does not fall back flat but stays almost perpendicular and therefore increases the overall height of the tank. The fitting of the set of vision slits for the commander necessitates a deep cupola which restricts his access to and from the turret. The cupola is also used by the gunner, who has no roof hatch of his own.

The loader's hatch is rectangular and the door is hinged at the front. The system for providing spring-assisted opening comprises a spring piston and an arm, mounted on the inside of the turret roof. This occupies valuable headroom, and an orthodox coil spring (as fitted to the cupola door) would have been more satisfactory. The door falls flat on the turret roof when opened and does not increase the height of the tank. The loader must expose himself when closing it from inside the turret.

An escape hatch is provided in the right rear quarter of the turret wall. It is circular and the door is hinged at the bottom and drops outwards. Neither opening nor closing is spring-assisted, and once the door is opened, it is too heavy to be closed from inside the turret. In addition, when the door is open, it fouls the hull as the turret is being traversed. Since the loader would not leave the turret when the tank was in action, it appears that the hatch is used solely for escape in emergency, and that empty cases would be flung through the loader's roof hatch.

(b) *Conclusion.* None of the access hatches is completely satisfactory.

(c) *'Baling Out'.* The loaders who took part in the trial were timed leaving various crew stations, opening their hatches and getting outside the vehicle as quickly as possible. They took the following times:—
Commander 9 secs., gunner 12 secs., loader 7.2 secs., driver 7 secs., bow gunner 7 secs.
The gunner 'baled-out' through the commander's cupola.

MAIN ARMAMENT LOADING TRIALS
(a) *Details of the Stowage.* A total of 92 rounds of fixed ammunition is stowed in the Tiger, in ten bins arranged as shown in [*Diagram reproduced*].

A close-up view of one of the hull escape hatches. This one serves the wireless operator's position.

Bin A in right rear pannier holds	16 rds AP or HE
Bin B in right forward pannier holds	16 rds AP or HE
Bin C in left forward pannier holds	16 rds AP or HE
Bin D in left rear pannier holds	16 rds AP or HE
Bin E under right rear hull floor holds	4 rds AP
Bin F under right forward hull floor holds	4 rds AP
Bin G under left forward hull floor holds	4 rds AP
Bin H under left rear hull floor holds	4 rds AP
Bin J under turntable holds	6 rds AP
Bin K in driver's pannier holds	6 rds AP

No ammunition is carried in the turret. All rounds are stowed horizontally in sheet metal bins with folding doors.

Except for bins J and K, the bins are arranged symmetrically on each side of the hull centre line. It was therefore necessary to study only one side of the vehicle, and the results obtained apply equally to the other side with the turret traversed through 180 deg. For example, comments and loading times for Bin B at 11 o'clock apply equally to Bin D at 5 o'clock. *There are never less than 20 rounds available to the loader in any turret position.*

Two fully-experienced loaders took part in the trial:—
Loader A – Gunner Cumpston, height 5ft 11in and
Loader B – Trooper Egan, height 5ft 4in.

(b) *Bins A, B, C and D.* These bins are situated in the panniers on each side of the hull. The door of each bin is closed at the top by two toggle clips, and is hinged at the centre and bottom. When open, the doors fold down on to the floor and do not foul the turret when it is being traversed.

Each bin holds 16 rounds of AP or HE ammunition, stowed in four layers of 4 rounds each. The layers are each supported by three fixed horizontal steel arms connected by transverse strips. Each arm is shaped ▶

A typical ammunition locker in a damaged tank.

to fit the underside of the rounds. The first round of each layer is prevented from rolling by two spring retainer bars fitted to the two arms supporting the case of the round. The remaining three rounds in each layer are held in position by similar retainer bars which are linked together and all three of which unlock as a single unit.

There is a danger of the loader jamming his fingers between the transverse strip and the round which he is removing from the rack; both of the loaders in the trials injured their hands several times in this way. The strips also impede removal of the rounds from the bin. Considering these disadvantages, the inclusion of the strips in the design of the bin seems of doubtful value.

The method of loading differs according to the position of the rounds in relation to the gun. Rounds in Bins A and C have their bases to the front and those in Bins B and D bases to the rear.

The nearest round in each layer is comparatively easy to load; however, as the loader empties the bin, it becomes increasingly difficult for him to remove the remaining rounds, first because they are so far back in the rack, secondly because the supporting arms are fixed and impede the sliding of the rounds towards the loader, and thirdly because the transverse strips obstruct his hands as he draws the rounds to the front of the bin. A considerable amount of time is therefore wasted because the arms on top of the layer do not spring upwards when not required, to allow greater access to the rounds in the lower layer.

(c) *Bins E, F, G and H.* These bins are situated under the hull floor and immediately in front of Bins A, B, C and D respectively. When the doors of any of the latter are open, they lie on the hull floor and prevent removal of the rounds from any of the corresponding floor bins in front of them. It is therefore unlikely that Bins E, F, G and H would be used while ammunition was still obtainable from any of the pannier bins.

Each of the floor bins holds four rounds of AP ammunition stowed horizontally on top of each other. The rounds in Bins E and H are stowed base forward and those in Bins F and G base to the rear. The rounds are carried in wooden end supports, as shown in [*diagram reproduced*]. The projectile supports pivot forward against the bin side and the base supports can be lifted up in a metal grove and dropped in the rear of the bin. This movement of the projectile supports allows the loader greater access to the lower rounds.

As the bins are arranged symmetrically on each side of the centre line of the hull, loading from Bin D at 11 o'clock is identical to loading from Bin G at 5 o'clock. It is therefore necessary only to study the two bins on the right side of the hull, i.e. Bins E and F.

Rounds in Bin E can be loaded when the turret is at 12, 1 and 2 o'clock. Between 1 and 2 o'clock, the bins are most accessible and the top round can be loaded in an average of 5.5 secs. After removal of the first round, the end supports must be removed and the rounds are lower down and more awkward to handle. The average loading times for second third and bottom rounds are 7.7, 10.6 and 18.8 secs. respectively.

(d) *Bin J.*
This bin is under the floor on the right side of the hull and is not available until a trapdoor in the turret floor is lifted. Rounds can be removed from the bin only when the turret is at 12 o'clock, and the bin would be used solely for replenishment.

The bin contains two layers each of 3 rounds, all stowed horizontally.

The innermost round in each layer is stowed base to the rear and the other two in each layer base forward.

Although the bin is for replenishment only, the rounds can be loaded direct to the gun when it is exactly at 12 o'clock. The average loading time per round is 6.4 secs., which includes the time taken to remove the wooden chocks seperating each layer.

(e) *Bin K.* This bin is in the pannier on the left of the driver. It contains six rounds stowed horizontally base to the rear in three layers of 2 rounds each; the bin fittings are similar to those in the other pannier bins.

The rounds cannot be reached from the turret and are for replenishment only.

CONCLUSION

This vehicle has already proved its fighting qualities in action, and many reports have been written on its good and bad features.

From the motion study of the items studied the main features are as follows:—

The loader's position is the only really comfortable one; all the others are restricted and would cause discomfort.

The gunner's position and the layout and design of some of his controls are bad.

▶

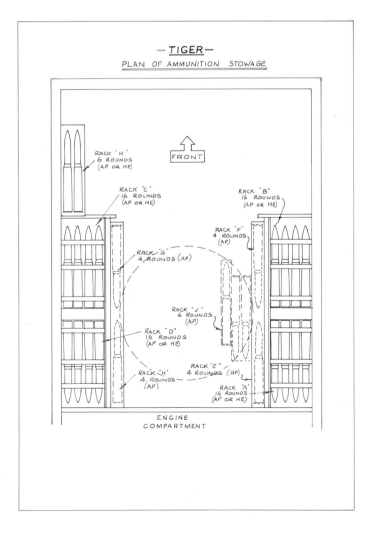

—TIGER—
PLAN OF AMMUNITION STOWAGE

RACK "K"
6 ROUNDS
(AP OR HE)

FRONT

RACK "C"
16 ROUNDS
(AP OR HE)

RACK "B"
16 ROUNDS
(AP OR HE)

RACK "F"
4 ROUNDS
(AP)

RACK "G"
4 ROUNDS (AP)

RACK "J"
6 ROUNDS
(AP)

RACK "D"
16 ROUNDS
(AP OR HE)

RACK "H"
4 ROUNDS
(AP)

RACK "E"
4 ROUNDS (AP)

RACK "A"
16 ROUNDS
(AP OR HE)

ENGINE
COMPARTMENT

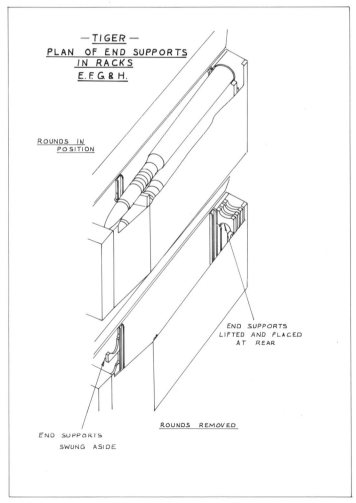

—TIGER—
PLAN OF END SUPPORTS
IN RACKS
E. F. G. & H.

ROUNDS IN
POSITION

END SUPPORTS
LIFTED AND PLACED
AT REAR

ROUNDS REMOVED

END SUPPORTS
SWUNG ASIDE

Loading times for the main armament are unnecessarily high by reason of the bad stowage design.

Listed below are the good and bad features of the vehicle's ammunition stowage, loading arrangements and crew positions and controls:—

GOOD FEATURES	BAD FEATURES
Availability of ammunition	Gunner's cramped position
Loader's seat and spacious position	Commander's cramped position
	Design of gun controls
Sprung roof hatch doors	Design of ammunition bins
Position of wireless set	High loading times
	Difficulty of loading coaxial MG
	Driver's and bow-gunner's feet are cramped
	Design of bow gun mounting
	Escape hatch cannot be closed from inside the turret

We have followed the Tiger tank from the day it first became known to British military intelligence to the end of the war and beyond and, in doing so, we have noted one or two special-purpose variations on the way. However there was one other unusual version of the tank which has not been covered although it first appeared in the summer of 1944. This is the Sturm Tiger, which was so far removed in both purpose and appearance from the conventional tank that it is probably best dealt with separately.

It was left to the *Daily Mirror*, in the issue of 9 March 1945, to reveal the new weapon to the public.

Extract from War Office Technical Intelligence Summary No. 156, Dated 13th December 1944

HEAVY HOWITZER ON TIGER TANK CHASSIS
An official German document mentions the existence of a Pz. Stu. Mrs. Kp. Tiger, i.e. an armoured assault company equipped with heavy howitzers on Tiger chassis. The heavy howitzer (Morser) may be assumed to be a large calibre, low velocity weapon capable of firing at elevations of over 45 degrees.

Since this is an armoured assault weapon, it is probably designed mainly for short range use, i.e. up to about 3000 yards.

There is no indication whether the chassis is that of the original Tiger Tank (Pz. Kpfw. Tiger, Model E) or that of the Royal Tiger (Pz. Kpfw. Tiger, Model B).

'TIGER' GUN – AND SHELL

A captured German Tiger tank with the blunt muzzle of a great 15 in howitzer protruding. This calibre is as great as that of a battleship's big guns.

This same vehicle was examined by the United States Army but, evidently, they were not yet clear whether this was the same equipment referred to in the Intelligence Summary or not.

ETO ORDNANCE TECHNICAL INTELLIGENCE REPORT NO. 184
SUBJECT: 38 cm Rocket Projector on Tiger I Chassis
Observations by: Capt. R.E. Howell and Sgt. B. C. Washer, Ord. Tech. Intell. Team No. 9.

GENERAL

A 38cm (15 inches) rocket projector mounted on a modified Tiger I chassis has been examined in the Ninth U.S. Army area. Although the German nomenclature for this equipment is not known, it may be the vehicle referred to in German documents as the 'Panzer Sturm Mörser Tiger'.

The vehicle on which the rocket projector is mounted is a modified version of the Tiger I Chassis, with a rectangular superstructure replacing the turret.

The rocket projector is radically different in design and construction from any weapon previously examined. The propellant gases are deflected between the tube and liner by an unusual obturator, and escape through a perforated ring at the muzzle. The splined projectile fired by the projector is approximately five feet long and weighs 726 pounds. An uncomfirmed report states that the range of the rocket is 6000 metres (6552 yards). The same source reports that the vehicle has a crew of seven, including a tank commander, a forward observer and five men to operate the vehicle and rocket projector.

CHASSIS

a. The suspension, power train, engine and hull are those of the Pz Kpfw Tiger, Model E (Tiger I). The normal superstructure and turret of the tank have been replaced by a heavy rectangular superstructure of the type used on the 'Panzerjager' self-propelled guns. The superstructure is made of rolled armour plates and is of welded construction with the side plates interlocked with the front and rear plates. A heavy strip of armour is used to reinforce the joint between the front plate and glacis plate on the outside.

A ball-mounted machine gun, MG34, is set into the front plate on the right side.

b. Armour thickness and angles of the superstructure:

	Thickness	Angle to vertical
Front plate	150mm (5.9 in)	45 deg.
Projector Mantlet (average)	69mm (2.4 in)	Rounded
Projector shield (average)	150mm (5.9 in)	Rounded
Side plates	80mm (3.2 in)	20 deg.
Rear plates	80mm (3.2 in)	10 deg.
Top plate	40mm (1.6 in)	Horizontal

c. Dimensions of the superstructure:

Front plate
width at base 126 inches
width at top 101 inches
height (base to top) 73 inches
Side plates
length at base 126 inches
length at top $86\frac{1}{2}$ inches
height (base to top) $38-\frac{5}{8}$ ins
Overall height from ground 9 ft 3 ins

252

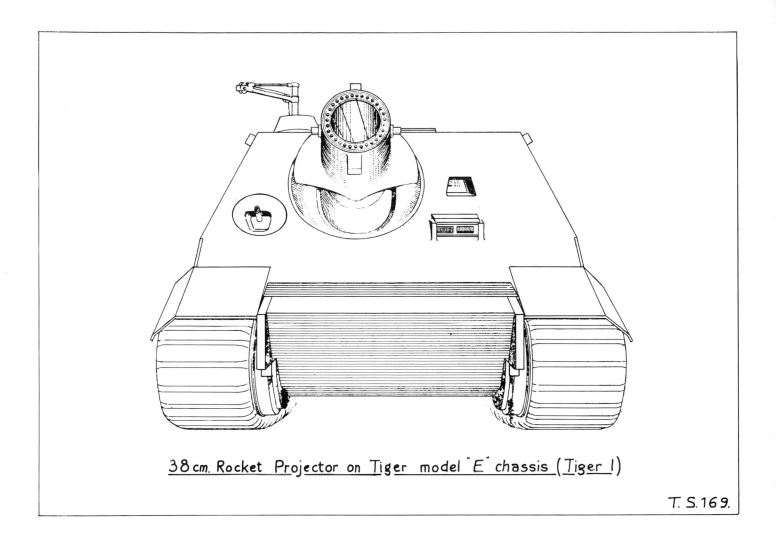

38 cm. Rocket Projector on Tiger model ‘E’ chassis (Tiger I)

T. S. 169.

The evaluation of the Sturm Tiger carried out by the US Army was so thorough that there was no need for British Military Intelligence to repeat the exercise so they contented themselves with a summary based on the American findings.

Appendix D to War Office
Technical Intelligence Summary
No. 169 dated 21st March 1945

38 cm (15 in) ROCKET PROJECTOR ON Pz. Kpfw TIGER MODEL E CHASSIS (STURM MÖRSER)

INTRODUCTION

A completely new German SP equipment consisting of a 38 cm rocket projector mounted on a modified Tiger Model E (Tiger I) chassis has been captured in the Ninth US Army sector in GERMANY and a sketch appears at the end of this Appendix.

The projector fires a 726 lb rocket to an estimated range of about 6000 yards and is mounted in the 6 inch thick front sloping plate of a 'Jagdpanther' type of roofed superstructure affording considerable armour protection, which has been superimposed on a standard Tiger E hull. It is estimated that the equipment weighs about 61 tons in action.

This weapon is believed to be designed to give close support to infantry in the assault on strongly defended localities. Its exact German nomenclature is unknown though it may be the vehicle recently referred to in a German official document as a 'Sturmmörser' on a Tiger chassis.

The rocket projector is manufactured by the DUSSELDORF plant of RHEINMETAL BOERSIG and the work of imposing the 'Jagdpanther' type

253

of superstructure on the Tiger Hull is carried out by the Berlin firm ALKETT, as is shown by the vehicle name plate with chassis number, which bears their impress. The vehicle examined had been allotted the chassis number 0327. This number does not fall within the range of normal Tiger E chassis numbers and it would therefore appear that a new band of numbers had been allotted to Tiger E hulls converted to mount rocket projectors.

According to a PW statement of undetermined reliability, ammunition for the SP projector is carried in a tracked vehicle (with a Tiger E chassis?) equipped with an electric crane, each carrier having a stowage capacity of about 40 rockets.

The following details are based on examination of one equipment in fair condition and include information supplied by Ordnance personnel of Ninth US Army.

ARMOUR

The projector mantlet, supporting bracket and the spherical cradle are castings. Otherwise the superstructure armour appears to consist of rolled plate. The superstructure sides are interlocked in addition to being welded to the front and rear plates. There is a thick strip of armour plate extending between the inner edges of the track guards at the joint of the hull glacis plate and the superstructure front plate.

The hull armour was not examined in details, but appears to be identical with that of a Tiger E, and the upper nose plate and glacis plate are retained.

The hull armour plates of the vehicle were coated with 'Zimmerit' plaster, but the superstructure plates were not.

THE PROJECTOR

The projector is of a completely new type, embodying many interesting features made necessary by the fact that a pure rocket of large calibre is breech loaded and launched from within the fighting compartment of an AFV. Apart from loading the heavy projectiles, the main difficulties to be overcome are:—

(i) The exclusion from the fighting compartment of the rearward flow of propellant gases normally associated with a rocket projector.

(ii) Ensuring that the propellant gases have an outlet on firing, in order to reduce recoil stresses to a minimum in the absence of a recoil mechanism.

(i) is overcome by using the initial propelling gases to actuate a flat steel obturator band fitted to the front face of the breech block, while (ii) is catered for by forming an expansion chamber of 1½ inches in depth all the way round between the rifled liner and the jacket, and giving an outlet at the muzzle.

(a) *Construction of the projector tube*

This consists of a ½ inch thick rifled steel liner and a full length jacket.

The liner is rifled with 9 grooves having a RH twist with a pitch of approximately one turn in 17.6 calibres. To facilitate engagement of the driving segments of the projectile a considerable lead is provided on the non-driving edge of the groove.

In order to provide a space between the liner and the jacket, the liner is supported at the rear on four equally spaced steel blocks and at the front on a bearing ring bored with 31 holes and inserted between liner and jacket.

The jacket appears to be constructed of two parts secured together and locked by a key at the top. At the muzzle end are four projections integral with the jacket. Two lie one above and one below the piece and are square shaped with dimensions 9½ cm deep, 11 cm wide and 7 cm thick. The other two are cylindrical, 8 cm in length and are placed one on each side.

The purpose of these projections is not known at present, but a PW declares that similar equipments with a much longer projector exist. It is quite possible that if an extension tube is fitted these projections are machined up to serve as anchorages.

A large mantlet curving rearwards is formed on the front portion of the jacket.

The rear portion of the jacket extends into the fighting compartment, where it forms the breech end.

(b) Breech mechanism
This is a horizontal sliding block, rack and pinion operated, and is fitted with a trip action percussion firing mechanism.

The block, which is really a large steel plate, slides to the right on opening in grooves machined in the rear of the jacket.

The operating mechanism consists of a simple rack and pinion, the rack being screwed to the lower edge of the sliding block while the crank handle operated pinion is carried in a bearing on the lower side of the breech end.

The firing mechanism consists mainly of a striker, mainspring and lanyard-operated firing lever contained in a block which slides vertically in a slideway built up by screwing undercut bars to the rear face of the breech block. This 'sliding block' firing mechanism is provided to enable the block to be lifted while the breech is open for the insertion of a percussion tube into a chamber bored in the rear of the firing hole bush. The rocket is fired by a flash directed at its igniter situated centrally in the base plate.

The obturator deserves special mention. It fits into a circular recess in the front face of the breech block and consists of a flat ring accurately machined to bear against a corresponding surface in the breech end, an inner ring and an adjusting ring.

The obturator ring is 'L' shaped in cross section and is fitted with an inner ring bored with 80 half-inch holes communicating with the inside face of the obturator ring in order that the gases may force the ring against its seating to give a seal. The obturator ring is a very close fit on a flange of the inner ring.

An examination of the breech spare parts box reveals that six adjusting rings are provided varying slightly in thickness. One of these is fitted behind the obturator ring, adjustment being necessary to compensate for wear of ring or seating, sliding surfaces of breech block or jacket or slight irregularities in manufacture.

(c) Safety arrangements
The firing lever cannot be operated until the breech is fully closed, when a projection on the lever may enter a recess in the breech face.

Applied safety is present in the form of a thumb catch which locks the firing lever when turned.

(d) Round Retaining Plunger
A plunger, bevelled on its front edge, is fitted into the top of the bore at the breech end. Its function is to drop behind the round to prevent slip back at angles of elevation and maintain the rocket at the correct distance for firing (approximately 5 inches from face of breech block).

▶

A bracket cut with a cam groove and bolted to the top of the breech block forces a locking plunger over the retaining plunger as the breech closes.

(e) *Elevation*

This is carried out by means of an arc bolted to the left of the rear bracket driven by a pinion through worm and worm wheel gearing. The handwheel is on the left. Elevation is from 0 deg. to approximately 85 deg.

(f) *Traverse*

Traverse is 10 deg. to left and right and is carried out by a similar gearing with the pinion, worm and worm wheel bolted above the breech opening to the top of the jacket. A short arc is fixed to the top of the rear bracket. A pointer and scale plate graduated 0—200 mils (10 deg.) each side are provided.

The centre of gravity is apparently unaffected by the loading of the rocket, as elevation and traverse are just as easy. The handwheel is above the breech opening.

(g) *Sighting Arrangements*

The optical portions of the sight were missing.

The sight bracket is bolted to the inside of the superstructure front plate and is operated by an adjustable motion link from the left trunnion. It is presumed that a rocking mechanism and range scale have been removed or that they were incorporated in the optical portions. The sight bracket at the top is provided with a deflection mechanism consisting of a worm and segment which gives a deflection of 10 degrees on either side. It is operated by a milled handscrew on the worm spindle and the deflection is recorded on a drum in front of the handscrew, graduated from 0—100 mils and used in conjunction with another scale engraved from 0—2 (on both sides of a zero line in hundreds of mils).

(h) *Projector supporting arrangements*

The projector is mounted in a large cast bracket secured to the inside of the front superstructure plate by six wedges welded in position. The supporting bracket is hollowed out to receive a spherical casting, which forms the cradle, and is provided with trunnions which ride in bearings placed each side of the supporting bracket to give elevation. For traverse the projector is given two vertical bearings in its spherical cradle.

Another, rearward directed bracket is bolted to the rear of the spherical cradle. This carries various fittings including elevating and traversing arcs, travelling, traverse and elevation locks and appears to be enlarged to give balance.

(i) *Dimensions* (approximate)

Calibre	38 cm
Thickness of liner	13 mm
Length of liner	188 cm
Length of projector	206 cm
Distance from liner to inside of breech face	47.5 mm
Thickness of breech block	59 mm
Depth of rifled groove	5 mm
Width of rifled groove	10 mm
Width of lead to rifling	27 mm

AMMUNITION

This consists of a large rotated rocket, unstreamlined and having a general shape similar to that of early design shells of large calibre.

256

Construction

It is in the form of a 3 piece steel body consisting of the *nose*, which contains the explosive charge, the *rear portion* which contains the propellant charge, and the base plate.

The sections are screwed together and locked by securing screws diametrically opposed.

The nose

This is 95.7 cm long and contains at the front a fuze well, 4.0 cm deep and 6.2 cm in diameter. It accounts for about 60% of the total weight of 726 lbs.

The rear portion

This is 46.9 cm and is slotted at the rear to receive the rotating segments of the base plate which is held to the rear portion by two locking screws.

The base plate

The thickness of the plate is about 2.4 cm and it contains 32 inclined venturis arranged in a circle around the periphery of the base. There are nine rotating segments on the base plate to correspond with the rifling. At the centre, the plate is bored to form a well for the igniter.

The fuse

A nose percussion fuse with optional delay is contained in a two piece steel collar in the fuse well. It is armed by rotation and constructed of aluminium.

Markings

The projectile is dark green in colour with a 2.0 cm wide white band about its centre of gravity.

The following warning was found stencilled in white on the nose: 'Achtung! Feuchtigkeitsempfinalich. Ver Regen und Wasser Zu schutzen' — Warning! Sensitive to damp. Protect from rain and water.

Each section of the projectile is stamped with a number and each projectile has a number stencilled in black. The projectile examined was marked 569 in black.

LOADING ARRANGEMENTS

The rocket is loaded by hand with the projector at 0 deg. elevation from a loading tray mounted on tubular supports from the floor, fitted with six steel rollers and arranged to fold into the floor of the fighting compartment when not in use.

The roof of the fighting compartment is fitted with a set of overhead rails to carry a hand operated winch which may be run from side to side to place rockets on the loading tray and assist in stowage.

AMMUNITION STOWAGE

There are stowage arrangements for 12 rockets in the vehicle, six on either side of the fighting compartment. It is possible that in action a thirteenth rocket is carried in the projector. The rockets are stowed horizontally and held in position by collapsible cradles.

A hand operated ammunition 'stowage' crane is supported in brackets welded to the offside of the superstructure rear plate. It enables rockets to be lifted from a supply vehicle and lowered through the roof ammunition hatch into the fighting compartment.

CONSTRUCTION AND LAYOUT

The hull is similar to a normal Tiger Model E tank. A fixed turret is superimposed on the hull with a single front plate extending upwards

257

from the rear edge of the standard Tiger E glacis plate and sloped at 45 degrees to the vertical. The sides extend upwards at 20 degrees to the vertical from the top edges of the normal Tiger E superstructure sides, which they overlap slightly. The rear plate starts at the forward edge of the engine compartment top and is sloped at about 10 degrees. The fighting compartment is roofed in by a 40 mm thick plate.

The fighting compartment itself gives an impression of roominess when no rockets are stowed in it, but with 12 rockets stowed in position there is little room available to the crew. The MG/Wireless operator, in particular, has a most awkward position in the front offside of the hull.

It is not known for certain how many men constitute the crew of the vehicle, but there is certainly a commander, driver, MG/Wireless operator, projector layer and one loader. It is possible that there are two loaders, but this does not seem likely in view of the limited space in the fighting compartment, when the vehicle is fully stowed and the fact that it is quite possible for one man to load a rocket with the assistance of the mechanical crane provided in the fighting compartment.

SMOKE

One of the new German AFV smoke bomb projectors with 360 deg. traverse is mounted in the square-shaped rear portion of the loading hatch in the offside of the roof. There is a circular opening towards the rear of the roof plate on the nearside which has been closed by a plate welded in position. It is possible that the smoke bomb projector was originally mounted here, but that the opening was permanently welded up when it was decided to place the projector on the offside of the vehicle.

VISION ARRANGEMENTS

For the commander there is a circular opening at the rear of the roof plate slightly to the nearside, closed by a plate, which can be traversed through 360 degrees.

There is an opening in this plate for receiving an episcope and another opening through which a periscope could be raised or lowered.

There is a slit in the nearside of the superstructure front plate, just above the driver's episcope slit, for the projector layer's sighting instrument. This aperture can be closed by a strip of thick armour plate moving vertically on a rack and pinion and operated by a handwheel. A further mechanism operated in a similar manner enables a slit in this cover plate to be adjusted according to requirements.

The ball mounted MG in the offside of the superstructure front plate is sighted by means of a KZF 2 in the normal way.

PORTS AND HATCHES

There are two 'wedge and chain' type pistol ports, one on either side of the front portion of the superstructure side plates.

There is a large rectangular loading hatch in the roof plate slightly towards the offside measuring about 5 ft 2 in by 1 ft 7¼ ins. It is closed by two plates, the front portion by a rectangular plate and the rear portion by a square shaped plate (about 1 ft 7¼ in by 1 ft 5¾ ins.) which can be opened independently of the rectangular plate and is provided with a spring balancing mechanism. It opens upwards and to the rear.

In the superstructure rear plate there is a large circular hatch (diameter about 1 ft 7¼ ins) closed by a cover plate on a single hinge opening outwards and to the nearside.

WIRELESS

The vehicle examined was equipped with the normal AFV wireless equipment (Fu 5) stowed in the front of the hull to the offside. 'Intercom' stations were found for the commander and driver, but it is possible that there were further stations for the projector layer and loader, though they were no longer present in the vehicle examined. A rotary transformer is stowed under the W/T operator's seat. An aerial is mounted on the offside top of the superstructure rear plate beside the stowage crane.

VENTILATION

There is an electric extractor fan on the offside front of the roof.

So now they knew everything about the Sturm Tiger except what it could do as a weapon. Short of carrying out a full-scale firing trial on a captured machine, the only answer was to wait until a set of range tables turned up. This did not take long and the resulting translation was summarized in two reports dated 28 March 1945 and 4 April 1945, respectively.

38 cm (15 in) ROCKET PROJECTOR ON Pz Kpfw TIGER MODEL E CHASSIS (STURM MÖRSER)

Ref. Summary 169 Appendix D further details of the 38 cm rocket projector and its ammunition have been obtained from a captured German Range-Table for this equipment, dated August 1944.

The official nomenclature of the projector is 'Raketenwerfer 61'N (R.W.61) and it is fired in both the upper and lower register. Two projectiles are provided:—

(a) H.E. (38 cm. R. Sprenggranat 4581)
(b) Hollow charge (38 cm. R. Hohladungsgranat 4592)

The range-tables provide for a range of propellant temperatures from −40 deg. C to +50 deg. C, a seperate table being given for each 5 deg. C step within these limits.

The maximum ranges for the H.E. projectile at temperatures −40 deg. C, 0 deg. C, +15 deg. C and +50 deg. C are as follows:—

−40 deg. C	4200 metres	(4593 yards)
0 deg. C	5150 metres	(5532 yards)
+15 deg. C	5560 metres	(6180 yards)
+50 deg. C	5900 metres	(6452 yards)

The range-table weight of projectile is 761 lbs with variations in steps of 12 lbs to be expected.

T.I. SUMMARY NO. 171, DATED 4th APRIL 1945

38 cm (15 in) Rocket Projector on Pz Kpfw Tiger, Model E Chassis (Sturm Mörser)

Additional information to that contained in Summary No 170 para 7, has been obtained from a captured German range-table.

(a) *Projectiles*:
Both types of rocket (HE and Hollow Charge) use the same rocket motor unit – Treibsatz 4581. They are fused differently – see (b).

Weights of individual rockets vary considerably about the mean 345 kg (761 lbs) and each rocket is stencilled with its weight to the nearest 5 kg (12 lb). A special weight correction table is used in conjunction with the range-tables.

The effect of the temperature on the burning rate of the propellant, and therefore on range and accuracy, necessitates the division of the range-table into 5 deg. C stages as already reported. It also involves the use of a thermometer to measure the temperature of the propellant. If the thermometer is not available, the average day temperature is used, or, if the rockets have been stored in a warm vehicle, then the mean between the average day temperature and the temperature inside the vehicle.

(b) *Fuses*:

The H.E. rocket uses the nose fuse — A.Z.KM.8.— a nose percussion fuse with optional delay of 0.12 secs.

Hollow Charge rocket uses the nose fuse — A.Z.KM.10 — a nose percussion fuse with no delay.

For transport, fuses are set to position marked +, those fuses which have a red ring are 'travel safe' in the bore, indicating the practice to travel with one round already located in the projector.

When using the delay fuse, richochets may occur if the angle of impact is less than 250 mils (14 degrees) and when the angle of projection is less than 150 mils (8 degrees 26 seconds) and the fuse may not function until the second or third strike.

The projectile may break up in such instances when the ground is hard. For the same reason, the delay fuse is not used when firing against buildings.

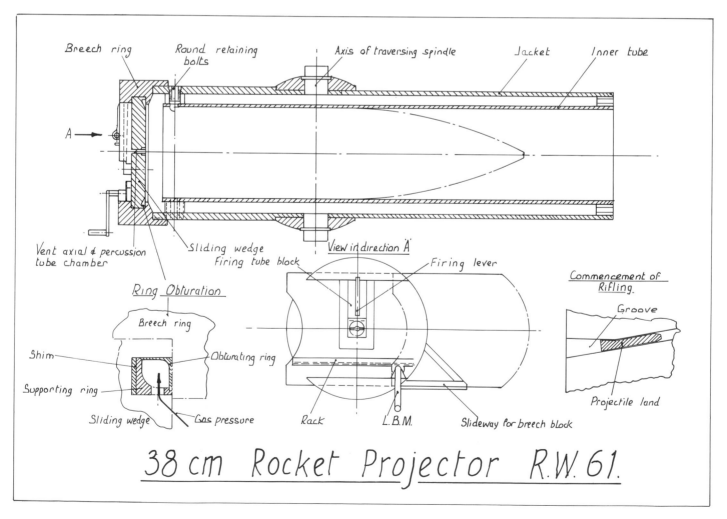

38 cm Rocket Projector R.W. 61.

260

The final word on the Sturm Tiger came to light in September from sources within Germany.

BAOR TECHNICAL INTELLIGENCE REPORT
NO. 35
21 September 1945

38 cm Rocket Projector RW 61 on Tiger E chassis — Sturm Mörser 38
Some historical information on this equipment, first reported in 21 AG Technical Intelligence Summary No. 30 has been supplied by Ing Kleinschmidt of Rheinmetall-Borsig AG, Werk Unterlüss. It is not known how reliable Kleinschmidt's information is but it is believed that he was not concerned with the development of the projector. His information is given from memory.

The development of the projector was begun and completed in 1943, being based on a former Naval project for engaging submarines from land, according to Kleinschmidt. The rocket used was the 38 cm R Tg, originally designed for being fired from a barrel on a swivelling carriage in an emplacement. To attain mobility the German Navy planned to mount the projector on an S.P. carriage but the project was not pursued.

The project was then taken over by the Army and the G.S. specification for the equipment was altered. The range was to be increased from 3,000 to 5,000 metres and the anti-submarine naval round was to be fitted with a percusssion fuse and was also to be capable of ricocheting. The rocket therefore was to be completely redesigned. The complete equipment was envisaged as a mobile 'Assault' weapon for attacking strongly defended emplacements and must therefore have good armour protection and be capable of carrying a large number of rounds. For these reasons the Tiger Model E chassis was chosen for the S.P. carriage.

Fourteen rockets can be stowed in the vehicle, six on either side in the fighting compartment, one in the projector and one in the loading tray directly behind the projector. Stowed rockets are placed on the loading tray with the aid of a winch running on rails stretching across the underside of the roof of the fighting compartment.

The projector was developed by Rheinmettal-Borsig and the mounting of the projector and conversion work on the Tiger chassis was done by Alkett of Berlin.

An American soldier peers down the muzzle of a Sturmtiger. A round is in the tube and the holes around the circumference show how the blast from the rocket was expelled.

261

Loading up a
Sturmtiger; the
round, in its wooden
jacket, is rolled
alongside the tank.

A hand operated crane
is used to hoist the
round aboard.

Spare rounds stowed
inside the tank.

The automatic loader
pushing a round into
the breech.

262

CARBURIZING (also known as CEMENTING or CASE-HARDENING)

The process of increasing the carbon content of steel by heating the metal in contact with carbonaceous material, and thereby enabling the surface to develop a much greater hardness than the interior when the carburized steel is heat treated. In 'gas carburizing' a gas rich in carbon is used instead of solid material.

FACE-HARDENED ARMOUR

Armour with a hard face but tough back. This armour is usually made by carburizing one surface of the plate so that the surface becomes much harder than the body of the plate when the plate is heat treated. Face-hardened armour may also be produced by flame hardening.

FLAKING OR DISCING

Terms used to describe the type of plate failure which is accompanied by an approximately circular piece of much greater diameter than the projectile coming off the back of the plate. It occurs when the plate has insufficient shearing strength in a direction parallel to its surface. Flaking or discing is dangerous in single-skin armour.

FLAME HARDENING

A face-hardening process which consists in using an oxyacetylene flame to heat the surface layer of metal to above the critical temperature and then quenching it rapidly by a spray of water falling behind the flame.

HOMOGENEOUS ARMOUR

Armour which has approximately the same composition and hardness throughout its thickness.

HOMOGENEOUS HARD ARMOUR

A homogeneous armour of a hardness too great to be conveniently machined by ordinary commercial methods, i.e. of a Brinell hardness greater than 400, usually 440–480.

MACHINEABLE QUALITY ARMOUR

A homogeneous armour sufficiently soft to be machined by ordinary commercial methods, i.e. of a Brinell hardness less than 400.

PETALLING

This is said to occur when metal displaced on perforation forms a ring of petals round the hole in the plate. With thin plates petals are formed on the back only. With thick plates they may form on the front as well. Petalling is the most desirable type of back damage on a penetrated plate, since with perfect petalling, none of the armour is projected into the vehicle as is the case when the defeat of the plate is accompanied by flaking or plugging. There are, however, intermediate conditions under which the petals formed on the back during penetration do not remain attached to the plate.

PLUGGING

A plug is said to be formed when the pressure of the head of the projectile causes the separation by pure shear of an approximately cylindrical plug of the plate metal. After petalling, it is the least undesirable form of failure, since less metal is projected into the tank than with flaking.

Printed for Her Majesty's Stationery Office by Acolortone Ltd Dd. 737392 C40 1/86